WARRIOR

ELITE

31 HEROIC SPECIAL-OPS MISSIONS FROM THE RAID ON SON TAY TO THE KILLING OF OSAMA BIN LADEN

NIGEL CAWTHORNE

Ulysses Press

Published in the United States by
ULYSSES PRESS
P.O. Box 3440
Berkeley, CA 94703
www.ulyssespress.com

ISBN13: 978-1-56975-930-1
Library of Congress Catalog Number: 2011925190

Printed in the United States by Bang Printing

10 9 8 7 6 5 4 3 2 1

Acquisitions: Kelly Reed
Managing Editor: Claire Chun
Editor: Richard Harris
Copyeditor: Lauren Harrison
Proofreader: Barbara Schultz
Production: Judith Metzener
Front cover design: Double R Design
Back cover design: what!design @ whatweb.com
Cover photos: Front cover courtesy of Department of Defense and Sgt. Rob Summitt, US Army. Back cover courtesy of Department of Defense and Cpl. Dick Kotecki, USMC. Use of Department of Defense imagery does not imply or constitute endorsement.

Distributed by Publishers Group West

CONTENTS

INTRODUCTION

WE ARE IN AN AGE of asymmetrical war. No longer do vast armies of ill-trained conscripts confront each other in huge and, hopefully, decisive battles. These days the threat does not come from large-scale invasion force, but rather from small and dedicated—indeed, fanatical—terrorists who care nothing for their own lives or anyone else's. They cannot be fought with massed ranks of unwilling draftees. What is required are small forces of highly trained fighters. What is needed is a warrior elite.

Fortunately, even in seemingly soft Western democracies, such troops are available. In America, they can trace their roots back to Rogers' Rangers, who fought in the woods of New England during the French and Indian War of 1754–1763. Although the Rangers' leader, Major Robert Rogers, later backed the British during the American Revolution, the tradition was taken over by the "Swamp Fox," Francis Marion, who led daring raids on British forces in South Carolina and Georgia.

During the Civil War, Colonel John Singleton Mosby of Virginia raised a band of well-disciplined Confederate raiders.

Because of his stealth and almost uncanny ability to elude capture, Mosby came to be known as the "Gray Ghost."

In World War II, special-operations units began to multiply. The public found themselves regaled with the daring exploits of the Devil's Brigade, Darby's Rangers, Merrill's Marauders, and the Alamo Scouts.

The Devil's Brigade was known formally as the 1st Special Service Force, so it is the direct predecessor of the Green Berets. It was in fact a joint U.S.–Canadian outfit created on July 9, 1942, at Fort William Henry Harrison, Montana. Its forte was close-quarter combat against numerically superior forces, and it saw action in Italy and France.

Darby's Rangers were the 1st Ranger Battalion under the command of Major William O. Darby. They achieved their greatest fame when they scaled the cliffs of Pointe du Hoc as part of the D-day landings in Normandy to take out the gun batteries there that overlooked both Omaha and Utah beaches when US troops were landing.

Merrill's Marauders was the name given to Colonel Frank D. Merrill's 5307th Composite Unit (Provisional), which fought the Japanese in the jungles of Burma, beating them in 5 major battles and 17 smaller skirmishes. The Alamo Scouts were a force of volunteers who fought in the Philippines. Never numbering more than 70 men, they earned 44 Silver Stars, 33 Bronze Stars, and 4 Soldier's Medals. In just under 80 dangerous missions, they never lost a man in action.

One of the most dangerous tactics employed in World War II was the amphibious assault. Special Underwater Demolition Teams, Scouts and Raiders, and Naval Combat Demolition Units went in ahead of the main force to clear the beaches and reconnoiter landing sites. These units were the forerunners of today's US Navy SEALs.

Introduction

During the war in North Africa, the British started a group of elite fighters they called the Special Air Services—the SAS. This was the inspiration for America's Special Forces, which drew its first recruits from veterans of the Office of Strategic Services, which had been inspired by Britain's Special Operations Executive. In 1961, President John F. Kennedy gave official sanction to Special Forces to wear their now famous green beret.

The 1st Special Forces Operational Detachment–Delta, also known as Delta Force, was started in 1971 by Colonel Charles Beckwith after he had spent a year as an exchange officer with the SAS. Israel's Sayeret Matkal borrows its motto—"Who Dares Wins"—from the SAS. Australia and New Zealand also have SAS regiments, while the Canadians have their own Special Forces. Germany has its GSG-9; France its GIGN; Poland its GROM. The British also have their SBS, the Special Boat Service, an elite corps of Marine commandos. These groups train together and sometimes see action together, notably in Iraq and Afghanistan.

There and elsewhere, these elite forces are on the front line in the war on terror. Their missions are largely top secret. Details of their operations only leak years later. While their personnel are the bravest of the brave, their heroism is rarely recognized. The honors they earn are usually awarded privately. In the media, false names are used and their faces are blacked out in photographs.

It is important, however, that all of us acknowledge their valor. They are the guardians of our freedoms and they are out there now, risking their lives so that we can sleep comfortably in our beds.

Nigel Cawthorne
Bloomsbury, UK, May 2011

CHAPTER 1

RAID ON SON TAY

AT 2317 ON NOVEMBER 20, 1970, 56 Green Berets took off from Udon Air Force Base in Thailand to make the most daring raid of the Vietnam War. They were going to penetrate deep into Communist North Vietnam to rescue US prisoners of war being held there. The maneuver was fraught with danger, and a raid by ground forces into enemy territory risked escalating the war still further. But American prisoners had been paraded by the Communists on TV, and it was known that they had been beaten, tortured, and maltreated. To free them was worth any risk.

US Special Forces had been involved in the Vietnam War since the beginning, first as advisors, then as specialist combat troops. In 1962, President John F. Kennedy authorized the formation of the 5th Special Force Group, which established its headquarters in Nha Trang, capital of the coastal province of Khánh Hòa, two years later. In March 1965, 3,500 US Marines landed at Da Nang, followed by large numbers of other ground troops. Almost from the beginning, the Communists took prisoners, often downed airmen, and imprisoned them in the North.

Aerial photography revealed a compound at Son Tay, a military town some 23 miles from the North Vietnamese capital of Hanoi and more than 300 miles behind enemy lines. It was suspected of being a prisoner-of-war camp. A large *K* was seen drawn in the dirt. This was code for "come and get us." By early May 1970, US intelligence had discovered that the camp contained 55 US prisoners of war, six of whom were ill and in urgent need of rescue. Throughout the Vietnam War, the North Vietnamese refused to abide by the Geneva Conventions, so there was no way to get aid to American captives via diplomatic channels. Many had died in captivity, and talks in Paris about an exchange of prisoners had been stalled for two years. It seemed to many that there was no alternative but to go and get them.

A feasibility study team called Polar Circle was set up. One of its members was Lieutenant Colonel Warner A. Britton, a World War II search-and-rescue pilot who would fly one of the helicopters on the raid. It would be no easy task. There were more than 236,000 enemy soldiers in the Son Tay area, along with the most concentrated surface-to-air missile defenses seen so far in the history of warfare. Nevertheless, Polar Circle decided that Special Forces could pull off a rescue mission, and a planning-and-training group was set up at Eglin Air Force Base in Florida, where a replica of the prison compound was built, along with a scale model that cost $60,000.

The commander of the mission, Colonel Arthur D. Simons, then went to Fort Bragg, North Carolina, home of the Green Berets, to ask for volunteers. He needed a hundred men, preferably with recent combat experience in Southeast Asia. There would be no additional payment, and the men were not told what the mission was about. Five hundred volunteered; 103 were accepted. Another 116 Air Force personnel would provide support.

It was decided that the mission would take place at night, if possible in a cloudless sky, as in-flight refueling would be necessary on the return trip. It should take place when there was a quarter moon low in the sky to provide optimal illumination for low-level flight. This made the first possible window for the mission October 18–25. But the president was not available to authorize it, so it was put off until November 18–25. This gave Special Operations more time to rehearse and to prepare their equipment. The first full-scale dress rehearsal, including a 687-mile round-trip flight, took place on October 6, and there were a total of 31 practice assaults on the replica compound.

Between November 10 and 18, the assault force moved to Takhli Royal Thai Air Force Base in central Thailand. From the moment they got on the C-141 transport plane in Florida, the rescue mission became a covert operation, which meant those involved had to be "sterile." They were not allowed to wear military uniforms or insignia and were stripped of all personal effects.

It was only after several days of confinement at Takhli that the men were given details of their mission. They were ushered into a briefing room where the commander of the ground force, Lieutenant Colonel Elliot P. "Bud" Sydnor, unfurled a map of the Hanoi area with a big circle around Son Tay and said, "Gentlemen, we're going in." Everyone burst out laughing. No one had expected an operation that would take them to the enemy heartland. But any trepidation they felt faded when they were told that their mission was to rescue American POWs.

Colonel Sydnor did not play down the dangers. The men were told that they had a 50-50 chance of not coming back. They were told that if anything went wrong and they could not be extracted, they should pull back to the Red River and make a last stand there, taking out as many of the enemy as they could. The men were then given the opportunity to withdraw from the mission. No one did.

Weather forecasts showed a typhoon was heading toward the South China Sea. This would prevent a diversionary attack being launched from the US aircraft carriers in the Gulf of Tonkin on November 21, so the date for the assault was set for November 20.

President Richard M. Nixon authorized the mission, now known as Operation Kingpin, on November 18. On the evening of November 20, the 56 Green Berets were moved up to Udon, where their helicopters—one Sikorsky HH-3E Jolly Green and five Sikorsky HH-53C Super Jollys—were waiting for them. The men were organized in three platoons. A 14-man assault group, code-named "Blueboy," would crash-land inside the prison compound. A 22-man command group, code-named "Greenleaf," would land outside, blow a hole in the prison wall, and provide immediate ground support for the assault group. Finally, a 20-man support group, code-named "Redwine," would provide backup support for the other two groups and defend the prison area against any counterattack made by the North Vietnamese Army.

The Special Forces raiders would be heavily armed. Between them they would carry 51 sidearms, 48 CAR-15 carbines, four M60 machine guns, two M16 rifles, two shotguns, and four M79 grenade launchers. They also carried 213 hand grenades, 15 Claymore mines, and 11 demolition charges, and they were weighed down with wire cutters, bolt cutters, chain saws, crowbars, axes, ropes, and bullhorns. Some of the equipment was store-bought for the mission. There would be 116 aircraft—47 Air Force and 59 Navy—supporting the operation, with 29 aircraft crewed by 92 airmen in direct combat roles.

Navigation was done by two C-130 Combat Talons that had been developed specifically to support Special Forces missions. They were fitted with forward-looking infrared (FLIR) so that they could "see" at night. One would lead the helicopters, carrying the three platoons of Green Berets who were going to make the attack on the compound. The other would lead an aerial strike formation that followed.

Cherry 1, the lead C-130 of the assault force, had problems starting its engines and took off from Udon AFB at 2318, 23 minutes late. A minute before, the helicopters with the cargo of Green Berets had left the ground. Two HC-130 aerial refuelers were already in the air, heading for a rendezvous point over Laos. The strike formation had begun taking off earlier, as elements were coming from a base in South Vietnam and other bases deeper in Thailand. The strike force's lead C-130, code-named *Cherry 2*, had taken off from Takhli at 2225. It was after midnight when the last of the strike force, five A-1 Skyraider attack aircraft, followed.

There were clouds over Laos, so the helicopters had to climb to 7,000 feet to refuel. They then formed up behind *Cherry 1* for the run into North Vietnam. To stay in formation, *Cherry 1* had to slow to just above its stall speed to allow the helicopters to keep up. In fact, they had to travel above their usual top speeds by "drafting," and they were swept along by flying in the slipstream of the C-130 in front.

At the time, there was no satellite Global Positioning System (GPS), so the C-130s had to navigate by using their FLIR to identify geographical features on the ground. They flew at 500 feet and made their approach from the southwest in the hope that the attack formations would be masked by the radar "clutter" thrown up by the mountains there. Meanwhile, aircraft from the carriers in the Gulf of Tonkin began staging mock attacks on Haiphong Harbor and other strategic targets in North Vietnam to swamp the Communists' air-defense system and turn its attention away from the approaching rescue.

Twelve miles from the target, the assault force broke formation. Four of the helicopters dropped to 200 feet to make their assault. The other two headed for an island in a lake near the target where they waited as backup. *Cherry 2* then climbed to 1,500 feet with *Cherry 1*, which headed for Son Tay to drop flares to illuminate the target, along with firefight simulators and napalm.

Moments later, the first of the assault helicopters flew low over the prison, strafing the guard towers with its Gatling guns. Then the assault force went in, guns blazing. At 0219, *Banana*, the HH-3E carrying Blueboy, made a hard landing inside the small prison compound. The impact threw the door gunner from the aircraft and dislodged a fire extinguisher, which broke the ankle of flight engineer Sergeant LeRoy Wright. The helicopter's rotors also fouled on some trees. But this did not matter. *Banana* had been expendable from the outset. There was an explosive charge on board that would be rigged to detonate when the assault team cleared the compound.

Blueboy's leader, Captain Dick Meadows, used a bullhorn to announce that they had come to rescue the POWs.

They were answered by North Vietnamese soldiers, woken from their slumber and in various states of undress, who opened fire. The defenders were quickly overcome, and Blueboy began searching the buildings for prisoners, killing more guards as they went.

Meanwhile, *Apple 1*, carrying Greenleaf, mistakenly landed outside a different compound, an old school being used as a barracks. A firefight erupted. At least 16 enemy soldiers were killed. Seeing *Apple 1*'s mistake, the pilot of *Apple 2* landed the Redwine team outside the prison compound. The strike formation arrived and A-1s began dropping napalm, white phosphorous bombs, and more firefight simulators.

Realizing his mistake, the pilot of *Apple 1* re-embarked Greenleaf and flew them the 450 meters to the prison compound. This was a dangerous maneuver. For a moment, Redwine thought the incomers were enemies, until the commander figured out what was going on. Greenleaf then took up position on the eastern side of the prison compound.

A convoy of trucks carrying North Vietnamese reinforcements approached from the south. Redwine stopped it in its tracks by taking out the lead vehicles with M72 light antitank weapons. An A-1 was called in to take out a bridge, preventing more Vietnamese troops being brought up. A disappointing radio message came from Meadows: "Negative items." Blueboy had found no prisoners. There was nothing left to do but get out of the place.

Pathfinders cleared a landing zone for exfiltration by blowing up an electricity pylon and blacking out half the town. Redwine blew a hole in the wall of the compound so that Blueboy could get out. The helicopters were called back, and the raiding party got back on board. They had spent less than 30 minutes on the ground.

By this time, the North Vietnamese air defenses were active. The radars of SAM missile sites were searching for airborne targets. F-105 Wild Weasels detected the targeting radars and fired on the missile sites. Nevertheless, the North Vietnamese managed to fire off at least 36 SAM missiles. But the C-130 Combat Talons dropped MK6 log flares to confuse heat-seeking missiles. However, one F-105 was enveloped in burning rock fuel by a near miss and had to break off. A second was hit, and its gas tanks were damaged. Losing fuel, it failed to make it back to the KC-135 airborne tankers that were in position over Laos. Its engine flamed out, and the two-man crew ejected over the mountains. They landed uninjured in hostile territory. *Apple 4* and *5*, the backup helicopters that had sat out the raid, went after them. After refueling, they began searching the area where the men had ejected. Soon after daybreak, the two men were successfully rescued and delivered back to Udon. They had spent three hours on the ground.

By 0315, the assault formation had left North Vietnamese airspace. After refueling, they headed back to Udon, landing safely. The entire operation had taken just five hours. Sergeant Wright had a badly fractured ankle, while Sergeant Joseph M. Murray had a minor gunshot wound to the inside of the thigh—the only injury due to enemy action. It was estimated that, in total, 50 enemy were killed.

Back at Udon, the men were disappointed that they had not returned with any prisoners. They wanted to go back the next night and try again. But intelligence revealed that the POWs at Son Tay had been moved sometime before the raid, possibly due to the danger of flooding in the area. They were now at what had been dubbed Camp Faith, which was 15 miles closer to Hanoi and consequently a more risky target. By then, the enemy were alerted and the typhoon was on its way.

However, the operation was considered a tactical success—the raiding party had gone into North Vietnam, secured the target, and gotten out again with minimal casualties. Six of the ground force were awarded the Distinguished Service Cross. The other 50 got Silver Stars. Fifteen more were awarded, along with five Air Force Crosses. The Air Force commander, Brigadier General LeRoy J. Manor, received the Distinguished Service Medal.

There is an intriguing tale that one of the Operation Kingpin helicopters was used to transport a stolen water buffalo calf found at the landing zone back to the search-and-rescue base in Thailand, where it became the company mascot.

Although the raid was an intelligence failure, it proved that special-operations raids behind enemy lines were possible. But the Vietnam War was already becoming unpopular. The raid was criticized in the media. It was said that the raid would result in worse treatment for the other American prisoners held in the North Vietnamese prison system. In fact, when news of the raid spread, it boosted the POWs' morale. They knew that America had not forgotten them. Instead of being spread out in small compounds, they were gathered together in larger camps, making communications and organization easier. They were also given better treatment, but most would have to wait two more years before they returned home.

After the war, businessman Ross Perot held a big party in San Francisco for the former prisoners held at Son Tay and the men who risked their lives trying to rescue them. Some

16 years after the raid, its tactical success is thought to have contributed to the formation of a unified US Special Operations Command, whose sole mission is special operations.

CHAPTER 2

SPECIAL OPERATIONS AT SEA

ON MAY 18, 1972, the Cunard Cruise Line's New York office received a phone call demanding a ransom of $350,000. Otherwise, the call said, the British cruise liner *Queen Elizabeth 2*, which was sailing from New York to Southampton, England, with 1,438 passengers and 900 crew on board, would be blown up and sunk in the mid-Atlantic. British Special Forces immediately went on the alert. The *QE2* was some 1,500 miles out of New York and still 1,000 miles from her destination.

The British Ministry of Defence sent two airplanes. A Royal Air Force Nimrod marine reconnaissance plane was to remain on station to maintain radio communication, while a C-130 Hercules carried a Special Forces-led team hastily assembled at RAF Abingdon in Oxfordshire, England. The unit comprised bomb-disposal expert Captain Robert H. Williams, who had been seconded direct from lecturing duties, Special Air Services Staff Sergeant Cliff Oliver, and Lieutenant Richard Clifford and Corporal Tom Jones from the UK's Special Boat Service (SBS), the Marine equivalent of the SAS.

Captain Williams had not been trained in parachute jumping and had to be given instruction during the flight. None of the team was told the exact location of the ship before they were sent off.

Meanwhile, the FBI sent agents to Cunard's New York office and kept Scotland Yard and Interpol informed of developments. The caller who had demanded the ransom said that there were a total of six bombs on board. These would be detonated by two accomplices if the ransom was not handed over; they did not care if they died. One accomplice was a former convict; the other had terminal cancer. The caller said they had thought of asking for $1 million, but they were "reasonable people," so they asked for just $350,000, which was to be paid in $10 and $20 bills. They would call back later with more instructions.

In London, at a meeting of Cunard's parent company, Trafalgar House Investments, it was decided that they would pay the ransom, if necessary, saying that they could not take risks with the lives of their passengers and crew. The ship was insured for $30 million with Lloyd's of London. Royal Navy vessels were sent, and shipping in the area was alerted in case they could help.

Out in the middle of the Atlantic, the *QE2* slowed to a halt as the planes approached. Despite fog and rain, puzzled passengers thronged to the rails as the British planes circled overhead. It was only then that the captain came on the loudspeaker system to tell them that there might be bombs on board and assure them that all necessary precautions were being taken.

"It was cloudy and rainy, with a 20-knot wind on the surface—in fact, rather difficult conditions," said Squadron Leader George Bain, pilot of the C-130 Hercules. "We would not normally drop men in conditions like this. But we knew it was important to carry out the mission."

Despite the weather, the four-man team jumped from the Hercules some 800 feet in a cloud base of 300 to 500 feet over the mid-Atlantic swell of around 10 feet.

"The men had to jump into a cloud," said Flight Lieutenant Keith MacBrayne on board the Nimrod. "There were waves of about 10 feet down there. I would not have jumped myself, even for money."

On board was parachute instructor Sergeant Geoffrey Bald to brief Captain Williams on the jump. Williams had only made two jumps before, from a light aircraft, four years earlier.

"I have not jumped since," said Captain Williams.

He had done no military parachuting. Now he would make a jump into the ocean in conditions likely to tax a veteran parachutist.

"I gave him half an hour's ground training at Abingdon before he came to Lyneham to board the aircraft," said Sergeant Bald. "And on the way over the Atlantic, I gave him further instruction and assurance."

The four men, dressed in frogman suits, jumped in two sticks of two, on two separate runs.

"They had to jump blind into cloud, so it was a little tricky," said Sergeant Bald. "As we passed over the QE2, we saw that they had landed 200 yards off the ship's beam and were being picked up by a launch within a very few minutes of landing in the sea."

Bald's verdict on Captain Williams's debut jump? "He made a good and controlled exit—a first-class performance for an inexperienced jumper."

Williams himself later said he was scared stiff and airsick and was relieved to find that the parachute opened above him after he jumped.

"I was once interested in doing free-fall parachuting," he said. "But when I found I did not like it, I stopped."

Some equipment, including a 12-gauge shotgun, was lost in the jump. With the men safely in the water, the passengers began taking photographs. A launch was sent out from the ship to collect the four men. Once on board the *QE2*, they were then taken to the bridge, where they were briefed by Captain William Law. The crew had searched the ship and identified two suspect suitcases on the boat deck and four large containers on the car deck. Captain Williams, the bomb-disposal expert, examined these while the equipment was being mustered.

Cunard had raised the ransom, and the FBI delivered it to a phone booth as instructed, but no one arrived to collect it. Meanwhile, an examination of the suspect packages and a thorough search of the ship, to everyone's relief, found no bombs. When the ship arrived in Southampton, the passengers and the Special Forces team were greeted with champagne. The four men were awarded the Queen's Commendation for Brave Conduct, and Lieutenant Clifford was named the Royal Navy's "man of the year." In the future, the SBS would keep a parachute-trained team on standby for future operations of this type.

Later that year, the SBS were on board the *QE2* again, following the terrorist attacks by the Black September wing of the Palestine Liberation Organization at the Munich Olympics. The liner was carrying a sizable Jewish contingent on a cruise to Israel, and it was thought advisable to give them an SBS guard. Another *QE2* cruise to Israel in 1976 again required the protection of the SBS. This time, members of the unit posed at tourists aboard the liner with their Browning 9-mm pistols concealed under their T-shirts. Some SBS men brought their wives to add to the mission's cover. As before, the cruise was completed without incident.

The SBS team set up after the *QE2* incident saw action again after 9/11. This time, Special Forces had made an attack on a ship at sea at night. Following al-Qaeda's unprovoked attack on the US, the UK joined the US in the invasion of Afghanistan. This seemed to many to invite an attack on Britain.

On December 22, 2001, just three months after 9/11, the British Secret Service spotted a cargo ship steaming toward the UK that they believed to be primed as a massive chemical weapon. Named the MV *Nisha*, it was thought to have been crewed by 16 terrorists who, it was thought, were planning a massive suicide attack on London. As the ship turned into the English Channel, both the SAS and SBS were alerted.

At 0645, battle-hardened troops who had recently returned to Britain from Afghanistan were awakened and told to assemble at the SBS headquarters in Poole, Dorset. As they had been hoping to spend Christmas with their families, this is not what they wanted to hear.

Earlier that morning, the Company Sergeant Major had received a call from the Cabinet Office Briefing Room in Whitehall, where military officers and government ministers assessed any threat to national security. He put out the word and by 0830 the SBS began to assemble. There were only a handful of them. Two of the regiment's three combat squadrons were in Afghanistan. The third squadron, now back in Britain, was serving as the maritime counterterrorist squad. But to take the *Nisha*, they would need an assault team of about 70, and they had been promised the support of 26 SAS men who were on their way from their base in Herefordshire. As it was a seaborne operation, the SBS would take charge.

Although there was a healthy inter-unit rivalry between the SAS and SBS, they often trained together, as well as alongside the Green Berets, Delta Force, and the US Navy SEALs. Indeed, as part of joint SAS–SBS training, they practiced seaborne assaults on HMS *Rame Head*, a World War II–vintage escort ship moored off Whale Island in Portsmouth. Twice a year, the SBS also carried out a joint exercise with the SAS, attacking a moving vessel—a fast hydrofoil Seacat ferry. One of these exercises usually took place just before Christmas, when conditions are likely to be at their worst. However, this would be the first time that they were to undertake a direct action assault, or DAA, on a vessel at sea for real. The only time they had come close was the jump on the *QE2* nearly 30 years before, and none of the men of the *QE2* operation were still on active service. Back then, they had been boarding a friendly ship that was stationary. This time, they would attack a hostile ship that was making good headway through rough seas.

By 1700 on December 22, 2001, the mixed squadron of SBS and SAS men had assembled at Poole. Normally, the men would have at least 24 hours to plan and prepare for such a mission. But the MV *Nisha* was only 200 miles away from London. She was making 16 knots. At that speed, she would reach her target in 13 hours. But the situation was even more urgent than that. As the ship's cargo was thought to be deadly to anyone downwind if it went off, they would have to get to the *Nisha* before she got close to the Britain's coastline. Consequently, they planned to hit the vessel early the following morning in what they were calling Operation Ocean Strike.

The inflatable rubber assault boats, weapons, ammunition, and specialized assault equipment were loaded into 20 customized Mercedes-Benz vans. With a police escort, the convoy set off at high speed for the Royal Air Force base at Yeovilton in Somerset. Once there, they took over one of the hangars where they would bed down for the night. A makeshift operations room had been set up with naval charts and aerial photographs pinned to the walls. Intelligence agents from MI5 and MI6 had managed to provide plans of the *Nisha* that the Special Forces could use to plan their assault. Meanwhile, the SBS men prepared the explosive charges they were going to need to gain entry to the ship.

At the time, the SBS's regimental headquarters was in Afghanistan, so it fell to the Company Sergeant Major to give the briefing. Their mission was to stop the ship and arrest the terrorists. They would hit the *Nisha* just before first light in international waters off the coast of Sussex. It was vital that the ship was stopped before she reached the Thames estuary.

They would attack simultaneously from above and below—the SAS would rappel down from helicopters while the SBS would come alongside on their rigid inflatables. The aim was to swamp the opposition with firepower. A photograph of the *Nisha* then flashed on a screen. She was about 450 feet long with five cargo holds and a tall white superstructure four stories high at the back. The SAS coming in on Chinooks would land on the roof. Snipers on board two Lynx attack helicopters following would give covering fire to take out any opposition. The SAS would then break into the crews' cabins and neutralize them while they were still in their beds.

Meanwhile, the SBS's rigid inflatables would be launched over the horizon from the frigate HMS *Sutherland*. When they reached the *Nisha*, the SBS would scale the starboard bow using hook-and-pole ladders. Once on board, they would search the cargo holds from bow to stern. Each four-man team would have a man from the Explosive Ordinance Disposal (EOD) unit attached to deal with any bombs they came across. Sixteen men from the Joint Nuclear, Biological, and Chemical Regiment would be standing by with a full NBC— Nuclear, Biological, Chemical—decontamination unit. Holding cells for any prisoners had been set up at the army base on Thorney Island in Chichester Harbor. Following the Lynxes with the snipers on board, there would be four Sea Kings carrying a command and control team along with men from Special Branch to formally arrest the terrorist and HM Customs and Excise to check for other contraband.

The *Nisha* displaced around 17,000 metric tons unladen and stood 80 feet out of the water at the stern. On her way to Britain, she had been seen in the Red Sea and off the coast of Somalia, where she was thought to have picked up members of al-Qaeda who operated in that area. She also stopped off at Mauritius to pick up her cargo: 26,000 tons of raw sugar. The island had been plagued by terrorists allied with the Lebanese terrorist faction Hezbollah, and it had come to the attention of Mauritian police that two Hezbollah operatives had recently bought a large quantity of the pesticide Lannate. The Mauritian authorities had told the local CIA bureau chief that the Lannate had left the island on the *Nisha*, which was headed for the Tate and Lyle sugar refinery in Silvertown, east London, some four miles from the city. The active ingredient in Lannate is a chemical called methomyl, which is highly toxic—not only to insects but also to humans. Fields where Lannate has been used to kill pests have to be sealed off for seven days before it is safe to return. Intelligence agencies had already identified methomyl as a chemical terrorists could use as a crude nerve agent.

Sugar is highly flammable, and it is often used in home-made explosives. If terrorists were to detonate the sugar in the hold of the *Nisha* outside the Tate and Lyle refinery with the wind coming from the east, deadly methomyl would be blown across the city of London, killing tens of thousands of people and paralyzing one of the world's key financial centers. The resulting economic chaos would be felt globally. The loss of many Wall Street traders with offices in the World Trade Center on 9/11 would be a pinprick by comparison. The *Nisha*, it seemed, was one great big improvised chemical nerve bomb.

The CIA bureau chief in the Mauritian capital of Port Louis contacted CIA headquarters in Langley, Virginia. The CIA, in turn, contacted their counterparts in MI5 and MI6, who passed the intelligence on to the British government. As the order to take out the *Nisha* had come from the highest level in Whitehall, Special Forces were given permission to use "any means necessary" to halt the ship.

After the briefing, the men who would rappel down onto the roof of the bridge drew straws to see who would go first. Then at 2300, the regimental doctor came around with NAPS, the "nerve agent pre-treatment set" thought by some to have been responsible for Gulf War syndrome. But there was no reluctance to take it, as the men on this mission genuinely faced the threat of chemical agents. The unit's medics were also given two vials of atrophine, an antidote to nerve gas. After that, the assault force tried to get some rest, but the NAPS tablets had left them restless and irritable.

Despite the dangers of a daylight assault, the British government thought that boarding a merchant vessel in international waters in the middle of the night might appear a little heavy-handed. But the SBS, naturally, wanted the cover of darkness for their attack. They compromised. Daytime starts officially at 0530 hours. But at that time, in December, it is still dark, so the initial assault could benefit from the cloak of the night to retain the element of surprise. The follow-up would take place after dawn broke, so the British government could maintain that it had been a daylight raid.

At 0455, two Chinooks took off from RAF Yeovilton, Somerset, each carrying a squadron of Special Forces. The trip out to the *Nisha* was to take 35 minutes, but it was going to be a rough ride. Even the run up to the attack was hazardous. The weather had closed in. Cloud cover had descended to 150 feet. There was a 30-knot wind and a 15-foot swell. Traveling at 120 miles per hour, the lead Chinook with 30 men on board had to fly low enough to stay under the *Nisha*'s radar sweep and high enough to miss the tops of the waves. This would have been hard enough in daylight, but the pilot was flying on instruments. They had night-vision goggles, but the sea was obscured by the green glow of sea spray. Behind the lead Chinook came the two Lynxes carrying the sniper teams and the four Sea Kings carrying command and control, and backup, spread out in a *V* formation.

At 0527, the lead pilot caught sight of the *Nisha*'s flashing navigation lights. They were still four miles from the target. The Special Forces men braced themselves. A Chinook has no armor plating, so once over the target, it is vulnerable even to small-arms fire. If a helicopter had been downed and sunk in the middle of the Channel, the emergency air bottles the men carried strapped to their chests would have been no good to them. The water there was so deep that they would have run out of air before they reached the surface.

The men put on their respirator masks, as they intended to use CS gas, also known as tear gas. Then they checked that there was a round in the chamber of their main armament. Most carried Heckler & Koch MP-5 9-mm machine pistols, British Special Forces' weapon of choice for close-quarters battle. Others carried pump-action shotguns, which were good for blowing doors off, or H&K G3 sniping rifles, the shortened version with the retractable sock. After flicking the safety off, they put on thick leather gloves to protect their hands from rope burns as they rappelled down to the ship.

With minutes to go, the men got to their feet. They were wearing coal-black counterterrorist gear made from fire-retardant rubberized cotton. This was flexible enough to run in and waterproof enough to go diving. The suits' tight black hoods covered their heads, and their faces were hidden by the respirator masks. Not only was this practical dress for an attack, it had the added advantage of intimidating the enemy. Hanging from their webbing were canisters of CS gas and the stun grenades developed by the SAS known as "flash-bangs." As well as their main armaments, they carried knives strapped to their chests, had Sig Sauer 9-mm pistols on the hip, and toted backpacks full of explosives, should they be needed.

At 0530, the lead Chinook flared out into a hover. The men in the back could feel the icy wind as the side door was flung open. Through the open door they could see the superstructure of the *Nisha* pitching below them. When the Chinook descended to about 50 feet, the helicopter's load-master kicked out the ropes. The descent looked impossible.

The pilot had to hold the helicopter steady without becoming entangled in the rigging. Below, it was only just possible to make out the unlit roof of the bridge the Special Forces men were to aim for. This was such a dangerous descent that under normal circumstances the mission would have been aborted. But the possible threat was so enormous that they knew they had to go ahead.

Gradually the pilot eased the helicopter in close enough to the roof for them to make the drop. The maneuvering took a minute—more than enough time to rouse any terrorist on board. Then came the cry: "Go! Go! Go!"

As the helicopter pitched wildly in the high wind, the men grabbed the ropes and flung themselves out the door. The descent toward the pitching ship was hair-raising, and most men made a heavy landing. The first man on board saw a lighted door below him. A crewman came out and began climbing the stairway up to the roof. The SAS man had not had time to remove his heavy gloves, so his weapon was useless as he would not be able to get his gloved finger into the trigger guard. Direct action was called for. As the crewman reached the top of the steps, the lead man took a swing at him with his fist, knocking him off the ladder. He fell onto the steel deck below with a heavy clank and did not get up.

The SAS man then took of his gloves, unclipped his MP-5, and started down the stairs. The rest of his four-man team was now right behind him. At the bottom of the stairway, they stepped over the unconscious crewman and approached the door that led to the bridge. This was the most dangerous part of the operation. While the rest of the men on board might be asleep in their bunks, the bridge was bound to be manned, and by now they must have known that someone was coming.

Bursting though the door, the lead SAS man shouted, "Get down! Get down!"

Three men at the back of bridge froze in shock at the sight of four men in black waving submachine guns at them. The lead SAS man strode across the bridge, grabbed the first man and threw him face down on the floor. The other two got the idea and were soon face down on the floor, too. They were Asian in appearance, and they looked as if they had been interrupted while sitting at the back of the bridge enjoying a game similar to dominoes.

There was a fourth man on the bridge. He appeared to be the captain. One of the SAS team put a pump-action shotgun to his head and ordered him to maintain the present course. The man was too frightened to do anything, so the SAS man took his hands and put them on the wheel, indicating with his hands that he should continue dead ahead. Then he told him in words and gestures to slow the ship to a halt. By then, 60 seconds had elapsed.

The team on the bridge heard the boom of a shotgun in the crew's quarters below. Quickly they cuffed the men on the bridge with plastic strip. As more gunfire sounded from below, they dragged the man who was unconscious on the deck outside under shelter and cuffed him, too.

With the bridge secure, they called the command and control unit, giving a brief situation report. Leaving two men in charge of the bridge, the SAS team leader and his partner headed back out on deck and down the stairway to the floor below. From the lower decks, they could hear the sounds of grenades going off. A blast blew open a doorway, and the two of them charged in. A second team had already taken the radio room. A third had secured the third floor, and a fourth had hit the crew's quarters. Meanwhile, the Chinooks had pulled away, allowing the Lynx helicopters to take up their positions on either side of the *Nisha,* where their sniper teams could give the assault force cover.

At the bows, the seaborne assault force had arrived in their inflatables. Despite the mountainous seas, they had managed to scale the sides of the ship and climb down into the front hold, where they began their search. From there, they managed to break though the sealed hatch into the next hold, then the one after. Just two minutes into the assault, and the ship was crawling with black-clad figures.

The two men from the bridge had dropped their respirators because the face masks had steamed up in the cold night air. From a stairwell, they saw a wispy white vapor emerging. It was gas. Quickly they pushed their respirators back into position. But it was too late. One of the men vomited into his face mask. Frantically, he searched for a vial of atropine, thinking he had been hit with nerve gas. But then he realized that he recognized the smell. It was one he was familiar with from exercises. The gas was CS, let off by another team on the floor below.

In the crew's quarters, the SAS used a shotgun to blast a door off its hinges, then lobbed in a CS canister. Two crewmen were rudely pulled from their beds in their underwear and cuffed with plastic strip in the corridor. Soon the companionways were full of men in a state of undress with their hands cuffed behind their backs. With the aid of powerful torches, the Special Forces men combed the bowels of the ship. They used explosive charges to blow open storerooms. They found a workshop that could have been used as a bomb-making factory. An EOD team was left there to deal with anything they found.

Deciding any current danger had been neutralized, the troops began to bundle their prisoners outside before they succumbed completely to the effects of CS gas. They were lined up, face down on the open deck. While the prisoners were now away from the CS gas and could breathe freely, they were exposed to the cold, so the troopers went back into the crew's cabins to grab blankets and coats for them.

After 15 minutes, the entire ship was secured. Dawn was now breaking, and the Sea Kings dropped more EOD teams and a Special Branch antiterrorist squad. A Customs and Excise launch pulled alongside, and a replacement crew from the Royal Navy took control of the ship. Thirty minutes after arriving on the *Nisha*, the Special Forces were winched off the ship and flown back to Thorney Island. Then they were taken to RAF Yeovilton and back to Poole for debriefing.

The *Nisha* was sailed to Sandown Bay on the Isle of Wight, where she was searched a second time. Nothing suspicious was found. The crew suffered cuts and bruises in the assault. Two Special Forces men had been injured: One was hit when a fire extinguisher he had hurled at a door bounced back at him; the other was bruised by a CS canister that rebounded.

CHAPTER 3

THE MUNICH OLYMPICS

THE TERRORIST ATTACK on the Munich Olympics in 1972 began with a Special Forces failure but ended in triumph. At 0430 on September 5, five Palestinians from the group Black September climbed the six-foot fence surrounding the Olympic Village in Munich, West Germany. Several people saw them but thought nothing of it. The terrorists were wearing tracksuits. The athletes regularly hopped over the fence, and the terrorists had their weapons hidden in sports bags. Security was lax. The German hosts were deliberately creating a free-and-easy atmosphere to help counter memories of the Nazi presence at the Olympics of 1936.

Inside the Olympic Village, the five armed men were met by three more members of Black September, a terrorist group that took its name from September 1970, when Palestinian guerrillas were expelled from Jordan. Somehow they had obtained credentials to enter the village. They also had some stolen keys to the apartments occupied by the Israeli Olympic team and officials at 31 Connollystrasse. When they tried the first apartment, Israeli wrestling referee Yossef Gutfreund heard the key in the door and went to investigate. As the door slowly opened, he saw masked men carrying guns.

Throwing his 300-pound weight behind the door to block their entry, he shouted to the other Israelis to get out. Weight-lifting coach Tuvia Sokovsky smashed a window and escaped, along with race-walker Dr. Shaul Ladany. Two team doctors, four athletes, and the delegation head Shmuel Lalkin seized the chance to hide.

Wrestling coach and former champion Moshe Weinberg attacked the terrorists, allowing one of his wrestlers, Gad Tsobari, to escape. He ran across the road, weaving in and out, dodging bullets.

"He ran so fast, he would have beaten Borzov, the Russian gold medalist," said one onlooker.

The strapping Weinberg managed to knock one of the terrorists unconscious and stabbed another with a fruit knife before he was shot in the cheek. He was then forced to take the terrorists to find more Israelis. But instead of taking them to the second apartment that housed fencers, shooters, and track athletes, he took them to the third apartment that was occupied by the wrestlers and weight lifters who might be depended on to put up a fight. Weinberg then turned on his captors again. This time he was riddled with machine-gun bullets. Weight lifter Yossef Romano, a veteran of the Six-Day War, also attacked and wounded one of the intruders before being killed. The remaining nine hostages were then tied up.

By this time, the authorities were alerted, and the terrorists demanded the release of 200 Palestinians held in Israeli jails and their own free passage out of West Germany. Although 12,000 men surrounded the building where the hostages were being held, the West German police were neither trained nor equipped to handle the situation. The Israelis refused to release the prisoners and offered to send a unit of the Sayeret Matkal, the Israeli Special Forces, to Germany.

The Sayeret Matkal had proved themselves just four months earlier. On May 8, 1972, four Black September terrorists had hijacked a Boeing 707 en route from Vienna. On the ground at Lod International Airport in Tel Aviv, the hijackers demanded the release of 315 Palestinian terrorists in prison in Israel; otherwise, they threatened to blow up the aircraft and the 92 passengers on it. Negotiations failed. At 1600 on May 9, 16 Sayeret Matkal commandos dressed in white overalls approached the plane, masquerading as service crew. Catching the terrorists off guard, they stormed the aircraft. Within 10 minutes, two of the hijackers were dead and their two female accomplices arrested. They were sentenced to life imprisonment, but were released in a prisoner exchange following the Lebanon War of 1982. Three of the passengers were injured; one woman died from her wounds. The commandos were led by Ehud Barak, who went on to become prime minister. One of his men was Benjamin Netanyahu, another prime minister in the making. During the assault, Netanyahu was accidentally shot by another member of the rescue team but survived.

However, there was a bloody price to pay. On May 30, three Japanese terrorists arrived at Lod airport on an Air France flight. Once in the baggage claim area, they opened their bags and took out grenades and assault rifles and opened fire on other passengers in a kamikaze assault. They killed 26 people, including a dozen Christians from Puerto Rico making a pilgrimage to the Holy Land, before two were shot dead and the third arrested. Members of the Japanese Red Army, they had been trained in Lebanon by the Popular Front for the Liberation of Palestine.

Seeking to avoid such bloodshed, the West German government refused Israel's help. Instead they offered the terrorists money. Their reply was, reportedly, "Money means nothing to us; our lives mean nothing to us."

The terrorists refused to negotiate and threw the bloody corpse of Moshe Weinberg out on the street as a demonstration of their resolve.

Having tried to put their militaristic past behind them, the nearest thing the West Germans had to Special Forces was *Bundesgrenzschutz*, the Federal Border Police. But they were not trained for antiterrorist operations, nor had they come up with any specific plan for an assault. Nevertheless, they went into the Olympic Village wearing sweat suits and carrying submachine guns. The hostage taking was being televised by camera crews who had assembled from around the world to cover the Olympics. So the terrorists could see the Bundesgrenzschutz taking up position. They threatened to kill two of the hostages, and the border police withdrew. By this time, the hostages were being physically abused. One had been shot in the shoulder; another was clubbed with a rifle butt when he appeared at a window.

At 1800 that evening, the terrorists changed tactics and demanded to be flown to Cairo. While the Egyptian authorities refused to get involved in the hostage crisis, the West Germans agreed to give the kidnappers safe conduct out of the country. At 2210, a bus arrived in Connollystrasse. It took the terrorists and their hostages to two military helicopters that would fly them to Fürstenfeldbruck military airfield, where a Boeing 727 was waiting. It was a trap.

Five German marksmen were in position. However, apart from competitive shooting on the weekends, they had no special training. Three were on the terrace of the control tower. A fourth lay by the runway behind a low concrete parapet. The fifth took cover behind a fire truck. When two of the terrorists appeared on the tarmac to inspect the plane, the German marksmen opened fire. Two terrorists were killed, and a third was mortally wounded. But the others shot out the airport lights as the pilots ran for their lives.

At that point, a SWAT team could have taken their position, but a police "special assault unit" had helicoptered in and landed at the other end of the airfield, some two kilometers away, and six armored personnel carriers they ordered up got stuck in traffic.

The terrorists turned on the hostages, killing three. Then the German police engaged the terrorists in a firefight. At the end of it, all nine hostages lay dead, along with four of the seven terrorists and one policeman. A helicopter pilot was also critically wounded. The disaster was compounded when, the following month, more Palestinian terrorists hijacked a Lufthansa jet and forced the German authorities to release the three surviving terrorists.

In April 1973, six months after the Munich massacre, West Germany set up a dedicated antiterrorist squad. Again, due to German sensitivity, it would not be part of the military; rather, it would be manned and controlled by the Federal Border Police. It would be known as *Grenzschutzgruppe 9*, the GSG-9, or Border Guard Group 9. Recruits were volunteers from the Federal Border Police. Soldiers who wanted to join would have to leave the army and sign up to the Bundesgrenzschutz before they were eligible.

GSG-9 specializes in counterterrorism and airborne operations. They train with Delta Force and the US Long Range Reconnaissance Patrol School in Weingarten, Germany. No expense is spared on equipment—the British SAS adopted the Heckler & Koch MP-5 submachine gun after seeing it in action with GSG-9. GSG men go through more than 4,000 rounds apiece during practice each year.

Germany's GSG-9 had its baptism of fire in Operation Feuerzauber ("Magic Fire") in 1977. On October 13, four terrorists hijacked Lufthansa Flight 181 carrying 86 passengers and five crew members en route from Majorca to Frankfurt, diverting it to Rome. The terrorists demanded the release of seven members of the Baader-Meinhof gang held in Germany and two Palestinians held in Turkey. For that, and $15 million, they would release their hostages.

For the next four days, the plane skipped from airport to airport across the Middle East. Finding the runway at Aden blocked, Captain Jürgen Schumann landed the Boeing 737, now short of fuel, on a sand strip nearby. When he returned to the plane after inspecting the landing gear and talking to the authorities, the terrorists shot Captain Schumann in the head, then ordered the copilot, Jürgen Vietor, to fly the plane on to Mogadishu in Somalia.

A GSG-9 team had already been put on alert. Its commander, Ulrich Wegener, loaded his men on a specially outfitted Boeing 707, which landed at Mogadishu on October 17—just hours behind the hijacked plane. By that time, Captain Schumann's body had been flung out on the tarmac and the terrorists were threatening to blow up the plane, having already doused the passengers with duty-free liquor. However, the terrorists were told that the West German government had agreed to their terms and were asked to extend their deadline to the following morning, as it would take time for the freed prisoners to reach East Africa.

Meanwhile Wegener had surrounded the 737 with snipers. Within an hour of landing, he was running through the assault plan with his 20-man GSG-9 force, along with two SAS observers that Wegener had invited to join the rescue. They had brought with them "flash-bang" stun grenades, recently developed by the regiment. When detonated, these created a deafening bang and a blinding flash, causing disorientation for a couple of seconds—long enough for the rescuers to overwhelm the kidnappers.

Around midnight, GSG-9 scouts crawled to within a hundred feet of the 737 and, through infrared goggles, identified the location of two of the terrorists. The order for Operation Feuerzauber to go ahead was given. At 0100, GSG-9 men with blackened faces approached the plane from the rear. Climbing rubber-tipped ladders, they placed magnetic charges on the doors.

Then the GSG-9 and Somali militiamen had started a bonfire in front of the cockpit as a diversion to draw the terrorists forward. At 0208, the rear doors were blown and the SAS men threw the flash-bangs in. GSG-9 men rushed into the plane. One woman terrorist was shot in the head. A second, wounded, hid in the aircraft's bathroom, and the hostages were being hurriedly evacuated from the rear doors.

Terrorists in the cockpit threw grenades into the cabin, but fortunately they exploded under the seats, only slightly injuring a flight attendant and one GSG-9 man. The two male hijackers were then finished off with multiple shots to the head. Within seven minutes, the plane was secure, and by 0500 the 90 surviving hostages and their rescuers were on their way back to Germany.

The surviving terrorist spent a year in jail in Somalia. In 1994, she was found living in Norway and was extradited to Germany, where she was sentenced to 12 years but was released after three due to ill health.

Since then, the GSG-9 have rid Germany of the Baader-Meinhof gang. In 2001, they arrested 9/11 terrorist suspects in Germany. They also saw action Iraq during the Second Gulf War. Two GSG-9 men were killed near Fallujah on April 7, 2004. They are regular winners of the SWAT World Challenge, held in the US since 2004.

CHAPTER 4

THE MAYAGUEZ INCIDENT

In 1975, the 21st Special Operations Squadron was involved in the operation to rescue the crew of the SS *Mayaguez*, an American container ship seized in the Gulf of Thailand by Cambodian Communists, the Khmer Rouge, who had recently taken over the newly renamed Kampuchea. The operation to rescue the crew of the hijacked ship became known as the *Mayaguez* incident and is considered the last official battle of the Vietnam War.

On the afternoon of May 12, the *Mayaguez* had been sailing some 60 miles off the coast of Kampuchea, as Cambodia was then known, in what her crew thought were international waters. However, she passed within eight miles of Kao Wai, an island claimed by Kampuchea. Consequently, the Kampucheans considered the *Mayaguez* to be within their territorial waters. Soon after 1400, the Khmer Rouge closed on her in US-made PCF Swift Boats, left behind when Cambodia had fallen to the Communists the previous month. The *Mayaguez*'s commander, Captain Charles T. Miller of Fountain Valley, California, had not been warned that he was sailing into dangerous waters. But since the Khmer Rouge had taken over Cambodia, they had seized seven South Vietnamese vessels, captured 27 crewmen from seven Thai fishing boats, fired on a South Korean freighter, and held a Panamanian ship for 35 hours.

As the Swift Boats approached, the Khmer Rouge fired a 76-mm shell across the *Mayaguez*'s bow. While Captain Miller told the engine room to slow, he sent off an SOS. A rocket-propelled grenade (RPG) then persuaded him to stop altogether. Seven members of the Khmer Rouge boarded the *Mayaguez*. Their leader, Battalion Commander Sa Mean ordered Captain Miller to sail to the port of Ream on the mainland. Captain Miller showed Sa Mean that the radar was not working and mimed that, without it, the ship risked hitting rocks and sinking. Mean then radioed his superiors and was told to stay where he was. And at 0455, the *Mayaguez* dropped anchor off Kao Wai.

The ship's distress calls had been picked up and reported to the US Embassy in Jakarata, Indonesia. At 0512 EST, the message had reached Washington, D.C., and President Gerald Ford was informed. While a meeting of the National Security Council was being convened, US Navy reconnaissance planes were already out looking for the hijacked ship.

The taking of the *Mayaguez* presented a problem for the president. The US had no diplomatic representation in Cambodia since the US Air Force Special Operations Force had helped evacuate the embassy in Operation Eagle Pull just 30 days before. That had been followed by the fall of Saigon to the Communists and by the evacuation of the embassy there, assisted by the 21st Special Operations Squadro, in Operation Frequent Wind on April 29–30. There were also echoes of the *Pueblo* incident back in 1968, when a US intelligence ship had been seized by the North Koreans, and lack of decisive military action left the crew as hostages in enemy hands for 11 months. This time swift action was called for.

The aircraft carrier USS *Coral Sea* was diverted to the Gulf of Thailand with a destroyer escort. The 1st Battalion of the 4th Marines was airlifted from the Philippines to Thailand, followed by the 2nd Battalion of the 9th Marines.

Early the next morning, Navy reconnaissance planes located the *Mayaguez*, drawing Khmer Rouge fire as they flew over. Captain Miller was ordered to get his ship under way and follow one of the Swift Boats that made off to the northeast. The reconnaissance planes followed and soon realized that the *Mayaguez* was heading toward the mainland. Determined to stop this, US commanders sent attack aircraft from Nakhon Phanom Royal Thai Air Force Base in Thailand to buzz the ship. Captain Miller was ordered to drop anchor off the island of Kaoh Tang, 30 miles from the coast. More US attack aircraft arrived and fired in front of the bows and behind the stern to indicate that the ship should not move again. The 39-man crew was then taken off the ship.

Seven CH-53 Sea Stallions of the 21st Special Operation Squadron and five HH-53 Jolly Greens of the 40th Aerospace Rescue and Recovery Squadron moved up to U-Tapao Royal Thai Navy Airfield on the coast, carrying 75 volunteers from the 656th Air Force Security Squadron (AFSS). One of the CH-53s crashed on the way, killing the five-man crew and 18 men from the AFSS. It was not a good start. The operation to retake the *Mayaguez* was then postponed until the Navy task forced had arrived and the Marines were assembled. Meanwhile, US attack aircraft were deployed to prevent any shipping between Kaoh Tang and the mainland.

On the morning of May 14, the crew of the *Mayaguez* was loaded onto a fishing boat, which left Kaoh Tang following two Swift Boats toward the mainland port of Kampong Som. The attack aircraft were joined by an AC-130H Spectre gunship, which fired on the Swift Boats. One boat turned back; the other was sunk. The fishing boat was then attacked and nearly sunk before the airmen realized that crew from the *Mayaguez* were on board. It continued forward, and nothing could be done to stop it without risking the lives of the American sailors.

When the Marines arrived in Thailand, they made an aerial reconnaissance of Kaoh Tang Island, where it was estimated that there were 20 to 30 Khmer Rouge guerrillas. A compound was spotted where it was thought that some of the crew of the *Mayaguez* might still be held. Otherwise, the island was covered in jungle and the only viable landing zones were the beaches on either side of a northerly promontory. The Marines would be carried there by 21 SOS CH-53s and the HH-53s. An hour later, more Marines would board the *Mayaguez* from the frigate USS *Harold E. Holt*.

The rescue operation began at 0600 on May 15, when three HH-53s dropped D Company of 1/4 Marines on the *Holt*. At the same time, three more HH-53s and five CH-53s approached the landing zones on Kaoh Tang. They were met with fire from automatic weapons and RPGs. It seems that there were more like 300 Khmer Rouge guerrillas on the island, rather than the 20 or 30 they had expected. One of the CH-53s crash-landed, but disembarked 20 Marines and its crew of five unhurt. They set up a perimeter but could be neither rescued nor reinforced for 12 hours.

A second CH-53 was hit by two RPGs. It exploded and crashed into the sea 50 meters from shore. Five Marines, two Navy corpsmen, and one of the pilots were killed. Another Marine died of his wounds as he clung to the burning wreckage. Three Marines made it to shore, where they were killed. Another drowned on the way. The forward air controller managed to direct air strikes on the island using his survival radio. Then he, nine other Marines, and three crewmen had to swim for four hours until they were picked up by the guided-missile destroyer USS *Henry B. Wilson.*

Things went little better on the other beach. The first CH-53 landed safely. As the Marines were disembarking, one of the helicopter's engines was put out of action by automatic fire. It managed to take off but ditched in the sea. All but one of its crew were picked up. A second helicopter that lay down suppressing fire while the first was getting away was so badly damaged that it had to turn back without dropping its Marines. It eventually crash-landed on the Thai coast, and its occupants were rescued.

At 0720 the *Mayaguez* was bombarded with tear gas. The *Holt* came alongside, and 48 Marines wearing gas masks scrambled aboard—to find the ship empty. At 0800, six sailors from the Military Sealift Command went on board. Within five minutes, they got an emergency generator running. A quarter of an hour later, the Marines raised the flag. The anchor chain was cut and, at 1035, the *Holt* took her under tow while MSC engineers tried to get her engines going.

The Marines on the beach were still having trouble. An AC-130 Spectre gunship had to be brought in while four more helicopters dropped another 110 men. Out of the eight SOS helicopters used in the first wave of the assault on Kaoh Tang, three had been destroyed and another four had been too badly damaged to continue. One of the three HH-53s used to drop the Marines on the *Holt* had also been put out of action, so search-and-rescue helicopters had to be used to help deliver the second wave. Even then, one CH-53s was so badly damaged it could not land.

While the landing had been going on, the crew of the *Mayaguez* had been released. All of them had been in Kampong Som. Fortunately, a raid by B-52s from Guam on the port there had been canceled at the last minute. They were found alive and in good shape on board a fishing boat and transferred to the *Wilson*. By noon, they were back on their own ship.

Once it had been confirmed that no crewmen had been left on the island, the SOS began extraction of the Marines. The first attempt was made at 1415, only to be repelled by heavy gunfire. Another HH-53 was damaged and had to make an emergency landing on the USS *Coral Sea*. It was only at 1600 that an OV-10 Bronco forward air control plane arrived to take command of the air support. At 1730 another HH-53 went in with fire support from two other helicopters and the gig from the USS *Wilson* with four M60 machine guns mounted on it. Even then the Jolly Green could not set down because of the wreckage of a CH-53 on the beach. It was hit repeatedly and rocked dangerously as the men jumped on board. Nevertheless, five airmen and 20 Marines managed to clamber on board and were delivered safely to the *Coral Sea*. Another HH-53 was badly damaged while searching for the Marine reported to be clinging to the wreckage of the downed CH-53. Finding no one, it managed to make it back to the *Coral Sea*.

More helicopters had to be brought in from Nakhon Phanom Air Force Base to complete the evacuation. As night fell, another 94 men were extracted. The Khmer Rouge then launched a ferocious attack, and the remaining 72 found themselves in danger of being overrun. As the round trip to the *Coral Sea* was 30 minutes, First Lieutenant Bob Blough, flying *Jolly Green 44*, decided to drop his cargo of Marines on the *Holt*. He achieved this in darkness with only his front wheels touching down. But within five minutes, he was back on the beach to pick up 40 more.

The last 32 were picked up by a CH-53 under heavy fire. After a quick search of the beach for stragglers, they headed for the *Coral Sea*. The Marines that had been killed had to be left where they died. Then a huge BLU-62/B 15,000-pound "daisy cutter" bomb—the largest conventional bomb in the US arsenal at the time—was dropped.

Despite every effort, three Marines—Lance Corporal Joseph N. Hargrove, PFC Gary L. Hall, and Private Danny G. Marshall—were left behind. Because the Marines were dispersed among three ships, their absence was only discovered hours later. A rescue mission was considered too dangerous, and there was no evidence that they were still alive. The *Holt* continued to patrol the coast of Kaoh Tang in case anyone swam out. However, 20 years later, a former Khmer Rouge guerrilla reported that the three men had survived for several weeks. One of them, thought to be Hargrove, put up a fight when he was captured and was summarily executed. The other two were taken when they crept into Khmer Rouge camp to scavenge for food. They were stripped, tortured, then bludgeoned to death. All three were awarded the Purple Heart posthumously. Theirs are the last names on the Vietnam Veterans' Memorial in Washington, D.C.

Technical Sergeant Wayne Fisk, who searched the beach for stragglers, was awarded a Bronze Oak Leaf cluster to his Silver Star. Lieutenant Blough was also awarded a Silver Star. Four SOS airmen were awarded the Air Force Cross.

Two Special Forces airmen were killed, along with 14 Marines and two Navy corpsmen. Six airmen and 35 Marines were wounded. An estimated 60 Khmer Rouge guerrillas were also killed. The SS *Mayaguez* continued in service until she was scrapped in 1979.

CHAPTER 5

RAID ON ENTEBBE

ISRAELI SPECIAL FORCES, the Sayeret Matkal or "General Staff Reconnaissance Unit," had to stand by helplessly when their athletes were massacred at the Munich Olympics in 1972. The unit was formed in 1957 by Avraham Aman, an officer who had formerly been part of the Palmach guerrilla force that pushed the British out of Palestine. Initially a secret organization, Sayeret Matkal recruits were handpicked, and the group adopted the same motto as the British SAS: "Who Dares Wins." One early recruit was Ehud Barak, who went on to become chief of the general staff and then prime minister. In 1972, they got their first practice in hostage rescue when Palestinian Black September terrorists hijacked an incoming plane at Tel Aviv airport. Sayeret Matkal stormed the plane, freeing the passengers (see Chapter 3).

After the massacre in Munich, the Israelis took their revenge. In April 1973, the Sayeret Matkal landed in Lebanon and killed a number of Palestine Liberation Organization (PLO) leaders living there. The leader of the assault team was Jonathan Netanyahu, the brother of future prime minister Benjamin Netanyahu and leader of their most famous Special Operation—the 1976 raid on Entebbe.

On June 27, 1976, Air France flight 139 en route from Tel Aviv to Paris was hijacked soon after it took off from Athens. There were 248 passengers on board, along with 12 crew members. The hijackers were two Palestinians from the Popular Front for the Liberation of Palestine and two Germans, Brigitte Kuhlman and Wilfried Böse, from the militant left-wing group "Revolutionary Cells." They had boarded the plane at Athens carrying variously Ecuadorian, Peruvian, Bahraini, and Kuwaiti passports. Once airborne, they forced the plane to divert to Benghazi in Libya for refueling. There, a woman who pretended to be pregnant and about to miscarry was released. That evening, the plane flew on to Entebbe in Uganda, where more Palestinians awaited them.

The dictator Idi Amin was in power in Uganda at the time. He made no secret of his pro-Palestinian sympathies. While his troops surrounded the airport, ostensibly to keep the hijackers contained, it was plain they were also there to discourage any rescue attempt. Inside the terminal building, the hijackers separated the Jewish from the non-Jewish. Meanwhile, they made their demands. Forty Palestinian prisoners in Israel and others held in West Germany, Switzerland, France, and Kenya were to be released. Otherwise, the hostages would be killed.

As the days passed, the non-Jewish hostages were released and flown back to Paris, but the Air France crew refused to leave while the terrorists continued to hold the Jews. In all, 105 hostages were left behind in the Old Terminal Building at Entebbe. They were visited by Idi Amin, who did little to hearten the hostages when he gave an impromptu speech praising the Palestinians.

Israel's secret intelligence service, Mossad, had interviewed the hostages that had been returned to Paris. This gave them a good idea of exactly where the hostages were being held, along with the deployment of the terrorists and the Ugandan troops. One of the released hostages had military training and gave details of the weapons the terrorists were carrying. Israeli firms had been involved in the building of the airport at Entebbe. With their help, a replica of the Old Terminal Building was constructed. The Sayeret Matkal practiced assaulting it from a C-130 Hercules parked nearby. The Israeli Air Force also experimented to see whether it was possible to land a C-130 safely at night on the runway without landing lights in case the Entebbe airport was plunged into darkness as they approached.

Then the Israeli government agreed to negotiate, asking for the deadline of July 1 to be extended to July 4. It would take time to assemble the prisoners and fly them to Africa, they said. Amin supported the extension as he had diplomatic duties outside of the country to attend to, so the Palestinians also agreed. This gave time for the Sayeret Matkal to put what they were now calling Operation Thunderbolt into action.

A ground task force of around 100 highly trained men was assembled. A 29-man assault force of Sayeret Matkal under the command of Lieutenant Colonel Netanyahu would take the Old Terminal Building and free the hostages. A small command group under Brigadier General Dan Shomron provided communication and support personnel, and a large support element would secure the area against any interference by the Ugandans. Then Netanyahu's deputy, Major Moshe "Muki" Betser, had an inspired idea. He called an officer in Tel Aviv and commandeered a Mercedes-Benz. He could only find an old white one. The engine was fixed and the car was quickly painted black. It was then loaded onto a C-130H, along with the Sayeret Matkal's Land Rovers.

On July 3, Operation Thunderbolt was finally given the go-ahead, and four heavily laden C-130 Hercules cargo planes—some as much as 20,000 pounds overweight—lumbered in to the air at Ophir at the southernmost tip of the Sinai Peninsula. They were followed by two Boeing 707 jets. One, an airborne hospital, would land at Nairobi airport in Kenya. The other, carrying Major General Yekutiel Adam, would circle over Entebbe airport as a command and control plane.

The airborne convoy would be escorted for the first part of their 2,500-mile journey from Israel to Uganda by the Phantom jet fighters of the Israeli Air Force. Much of the way they would fly at under 100 feet to avoid detection by Egyptian, Saudi, Ethiopian, and Sudanese radar. Fortunately, the weather was stormy, confusing the radar, and it was unlikely that any foreign radar station could identify the aircraft as Israeli.

Over Lake Victoria, storm clouds towered from ground level to 40,000 feet. The Hercules had neither the time nor the fuel to go around them. With their windshields blue with static, the planes had to circle inside the clouds so that they would be precisely on time as they lined up with the runway at Entebbe.

As the lead Hercules descended toward the airport, Colonel Netanyahu and his men got into their vehicles and started the engines, while members of the aircrew stood by to release the restraining cables. The plane touched down at 2301, just 30 seconds behind schedule. The vehicles drove down the rear ramp and were on the ground before the Hercules rolled to a stop.

The black Mercedes was the same model as Idi Amin's official car, and Israeli Land Rovers and troops lined up alongside it as if they were an escort. The idea was to make the terrorists think that Amin was paying another surprise visit. They drove toward the Old Terminal Building, where they were challenged by Palestinian sentries, who were immediately shot. Jumping from their vehicles, the Sayeret Matkal stormed the building. The first entrance was blocked, so they raced to a second.

"Muki" Betser spearheaded the assault. As he ran along a walkway, he was fired on by a Ugandan. Muki killed him. A terrorist stepped out of the door of the Old Terminal Building to see what was happening, then ran back in. Muki had no chance to fire at him, as his gun was out of ammunition. He was changing magazines on the run when Lieutenant Amnon came up alongside. Together, they burst through the door into the Old Terminal Building, taking out a terrorist to the left of the door. The hostages were lying on the floor. They had been trying to sleep. A terrorist at the back rose to his feet. Muki took him out with two shots.

Another terrorist loosed off a burst of fire. But he aimed high, shooting a window and showering the hostages with glass. He was silenced quickly with a shot. Amnon then identified the female hijacker in the doorway and fired.

A bullhorn boomed out in Hebrew and English, "This is the Israeli Defense Force! Stay down!"

But a 19-year-old Frenchman named Jean-Jacques Maimoni did not understand either language. He had identified himself as an Israeli Jew and stayed behind, even though he was traveling on a French passport. He got up and was shot and killed by the Israeli commandos, who mistook him for a terrorist. Ida Borochovitch, a 56-year-old Russian Jew who had emigrated to Israel, and 52-year-old Pasco Cohen, manager of an Israeli medical insurance fund, were killed in the crossfire.

But still not all the terrorists were accounted for.

"Where are the rest of them?" called out a commando.

The hostages pointed to a connecting door. The commandos lobbed in hand grenades, then stormed the room. A second assault team was confronted by two men in civilian clothes who walked calmly toward them. Assuming they were hostages, the commandos held their fire. But one of the men raised his hand and threw a grenade. The Israelis threw themselves to the ground, cutting down the terrorists with machine gun fire while the grenade exploded harmlessly.

The third team moved to tackle Ugandan soldiers on the floor above. On the way up the stairs, they met two Ugandans. One fired. Both were shot down. Meanwhile, Colonel Netanyahu had been shot dead by a Ugandan sniper from the control tower. The sniper was quickly silenced.

The assault on the airport was over in three minutes. By then, the other three Hercules had landed. They were carrying armored personnel carriers, which guarded the planes while they were being refueled, a dangerous business with Ugandan soldiers still loosing off tracer rounds. To ensure a clean getaway, the Sayeret Matkal destroyed 11 Ugandan Air Force MiG fighters parked on the runway.

The hostages were then taken out to the Hercules. Meanwhile a pickup truck the Israelis had brought with them was used to carry the dead. The Sayeret Matkal made one last check of the airport building. By 2352, the Hercules carrying the hostages was in the air, heading for Nairobi, where the wounded would receive medical treatment.

The equipment was loaded back onto the Hercules, with the exception of the heavy auxiliary pumps used to take the

Ugandans' fuel. By 0040, the last of the Hercules was making the 30-minute flight to Nairobi. Israeli Prime Minister Yitzhak Rabin had decided not to inform the Kenyan government of the rescue plan on security grounds. However, the Kenyan authorities rendered every assistance and refueled the transports as if they had been commercial flights.

Already, the Israeli Ministry of Defense had called the spokesman for the relatives of the hostages to give him the news. Soon the whole world knew. A stringer for the Agence France Presse in the Ugandan capital Kampala had heard that shots were being fired in Entebbe and filed a report. By 0300 the story was being broadcast by the BBC—and the Israeli planes were still far from home. It was not until midmorning that the transport carrying the hostages landed at Ben Gurion International Airport in Tel Aviv.

Three of the hostages were dead and ten wounded. The Sayeret Matkal lost one dead, five wounded. The seven terrorists were dead and some 45 Ugandan soldiers had been killed. But there was another causality: Seventy-four-year-old widow Dora Bloch, a hostage, had been released on July 2, but was taken to Mulago General Hospital in Kampala when a piece of food stuck in her throat. When news of the Israeli raid came, she was dragged from her hospital bed and murdered.

After the success of the mission, it was renamed Operation Jonathan in honor of Lieutenant Colonel Jonathan Netanyahu.

Uganda complained to the United Nations, and UN Secretary General Kurt Waldheim condemned the raid as "a serious violation of the national sovereignty of a United Nations member state." But the UN Security Council refused to pass a resolution condemning the action. The US and UK praised what they called "an impossible mission," and West Germany described it as "an act of self-defense." It was also noted that the hostages were returned home on July 4, 1976—the bicentennial of the signing of the Declaration of Independence.

CHAPTER 6

OPERATION EAGLE CLAW

DELTA FORCE WAS CREATED by US Army Colonel Charles Beckwith in 1977 in direct response to the growing number of terrorist incidents that occurred in the 1970s. Officially designated the US Army's 1st Special Forces Operational Detachment–Delta (SFOD-D), from its beginnings, it was heavily influenced by the British SAS as a result of Colonel Beckwith's year-long exchange tour with the unit in 1962–1963.

Like the SAS, it is organized into three operating squadrons, A, B, and C Squadron, each of which is divided into three troops, assault, sniper, and reconnaissance. As with the SAS, each troop specializes in scuba, HALO (high altitude, low opening) parachuting, or other skills. These troops can be further divided into smaller units to fit the requirements of a particular mission. Usually the troop breaks down into four five-man or five four-man teams.

Trained for antiterrorist operations, Delta are headquartered—along with the Green Berets and the 82nd Airborne—at Fort Bragg, North Carolina. There it has a $90,000 CQB—close-quarters battle—indoor training range that has earned the nickname "The House of Horrors." The SAS have a similar facility in Herefordshire. Training involves runs through CQB killing houses that have been designed to teach teams and individuals how to assault buildings held by terrorists. To develop their skills, the unit undertakes frequent exchange and training programs with foreign counterterrorist units, such as Britain's 22 SAS, Germany's GSG-9, Israel's Sayeret Matkal, Australia's Special Air Service Regiment, and France's GIGN.

Delta's first assignment was at the Pan American Games in Puerto Rico in July 1979. Along with the FBI, it was part of an antiterrorist team set up to protect the event against a possible terrorist attack. The following year, the men of Delta Force got their first taste of action in the ill-fated Operation Eagle Claw.

In the wake of the Iranian revolution, a mob had stormed the US Embassy in Tehran on November 4, 1979, and took the staff and the Marine Corps security guards hostage. In all, 52 Americans had been captured and were being held by the Iranian Revolutionary Guard. It was unclear whether they were being tortured or held for execution. Within hours, the US Army Special Forces Operational Detachment–Delta (Airborne)—Delta Force's airborne contingent, which had passed its certification exercise just the month before—was on full alert as plans were being drawn up for their rescue.

From the beginning, Delta's commander, Colonel Beckwith, was intimately involved in planning the rescue mission. It was a daunting task. Tehran is deep inside Iran and more than 400 miles from any friendly country. The hostages were not held at an airport but in the middle of a city in turmoil. Iran was still in the throes of a revolution, and good intelligence about what was going on in the embassy, or in Tehran generally, was hard to come by.

Nevertheless, after five months of fruitless negotiations, President Jimmy Carter approved an audacious rescue plan. It involved infiltrating operatives into Iran the night before the assault. They would then move into Tehran, take over the embassy, free the hostages, transport them to an airfield, and fly them home. It would involve all four services—Army, Navy, Air Force, and Marines. Eight helicopters, US Marine Corps Sikorsky RH-53D Sea Stallions, would be used, along with 12 planes: four MC-130 Hercules cargo planes, three EC-130 tankers, three AC-130 Spectre gunships, and two C-141 Starlifters. It would be spearheaded by Delta Force, supported by a contingent of Green Berets.

On the first night, three MC-130s were to fly to a barren spot in the Iranian desert and offload the Delta Force operatives to secure the base, combat controllers to organize the air traffic, and translators who doubled as truck drivers. Three EC-130s following the Hercules would then land and prepare to refuel the Marine RH-53s flying in from the carrier USS *Nimitz*, which was on station in the gulf. Once the helicopters were refueled, they would fly the task force to a spot near the outskirts of Tehran. There they would meet up with operatives already in-country who would lead the task force to a safe house where they would lie low until the assault the next night. The helicopters would fly to another remote site in-country where they would stay, hopefully undetected, until they were called for by the Delta Force operatives.

On the second night, the MC-130s and EC-130s would again fly into the country, this time carrying 100 US Rangers, and head for Manzariyeh Airfield, 115 miles southwest of Tehran. The Rangers would assault the field and hold it so the two C-141s that would ferry the hostages back home could land. The three AC-130 gunships would be used to provide ground support for the Rangers at Manzariyeh, support Delta's assault on the embassy, and suppress any attempts by the Iranian Air Force at nearby Mehrabad Airbase to interfere.

Once Delta Force had assaulted the embassy and freed the hostages, they would rendezvous with the helicopters at a nearby football stadium. Then they and the hostages would be choppered to Manzariyeh Airfield and the waiting C-141s that would fly them to safety. All the fixed-wing aircraft would be flown out of the country, while the eight helicopters would be disabled and left behind.

Detailed planning and training went on in conditions of the strictest secrecy on dummy buildings in the Arizona desert. On the night of March 30, 1980, a CIA Twin Otter flew to the first landing area, a dirt road in the Kavir Desert east of Tehran, code-named Desert One. A US Air Force combat controller rode around the landing area on a light dirt bike, testing the ground and taking soil samples. Having ascertained that the ground was hard enough to take the weight of a fully laden tanker plane, he laid out two runways, one on each side of the road. These were marked with six radio-activated infrared landing lights to help guide the airplanes in when they approached at night. That insertion went well. In his 90 minutes on the ground, the combat controller had seen some trucks pass by. He had even seen the face of a man lighting a cigarette behind the wheel. But he had not been spotted, and no contact had been made. The pilot also reported that, although the plane's sensors had picked up some radar signals at 3,000 feet, there was nothing below that. Low-flying aircraft could enter the country and land undetected.

Even so, on the night of the mission, to be on the safe side, the helicopter pilots were told to fly at or below 200 feet to avoid any radar contact. This caused its own problems. When the helicopters went in at that level, they ran into a haboob, or dust storm, that they could not fly over without breaking the 200-foot limit. Down on the deck, visibility dropped to less than 100 feet.

"It was like flying in a bowl of milk," one pilot recalled.

In the choking dust, cockpit temperatures soared to 93 degrees Fahrenheit. In one of the helicopters, the electrical systems overheated. With no artificial horizon—and no real horizon to be seen—no radio compass, and no flight-control computer, there was no choice but to abort. The Sea Stallion barely made it back to the *Nimitz*, almost running out of fuel. Another helicopter had malfunctioned and had put down along the way, and its wingman had put down to pick up the crew.

Another two helicopters landed to reorientate themselves, but when they heard that the sky over Desert One was clear, they continued. It was a grueling trip, flying low over mountain ranges that rose to 9,000 feet. Finally they made it to Desert One 50 minutes late. The other helicopters came in over the next 35 minutes. But by the time they had refueled, they were an hour and a half behind schedule and there was no chance that they would reach Tehran by dawn.

They were already down to six helicopters—the minimum required for the mission. Then the final blow struck. One of the remaining helicopters lost its primary hydraulic system and was unsafe to use fully loaded for the assault. With only five helicopters serviceable and six needed, the entire mission had to be aborted.

On top of that trouble, in the darkness amid the dust kicked up by its rotors, one of the helicopters drifted into one of the parked EC-130s. Both the EC-130 and the RH-53 burst into flames, lighting up the desert night. The order came to evacuate. There were wounded and dying men to be taken care of, and the aircraft had to be moved to avoid disturbing the burning debris and starting other fires. In the confusion, the remaining helicopters were left intact. When they were found by the Iranians the next day, the top-secret plans were discovered on board, endangering the agents in-country who were waiting to help the Delta Force.

Five Air Force personnel and three Marines were killed in the operation and dozens more were wounded. The Iranians scattered the hostages around the country afterward, making any further rescue attempt impossible. Failure to resolve the hostage crisis cost President Carter the 1980 election, and the US Embassy staffers were only released after President Ronald Reagan was voted into office.

CHAPTER 7

IRANIAN EMBASSY SIEGE, LONDON

ALTHOUGH BRITAIN'S SAS HAD BEEN INVOLVED in covert action during World War II and afterward, little was known about them until the Iranian Embassy siege in London in 1980, when they stormed the building and rescued the hostages being held there while the world's TV cameras looked on.

The siege began at 1132 on the morning of Wednesday April 30, 1980, when six armed terrorists stormed into the Iranian Embassy at 16 Princes Gate in Kensington, west London. They were armed with two Polish versions of the Russian Scorpion machine-pistol, one Spanish .38 revolver, three Browning 9-mm pistols, and a number of Russian RDG-5 fragmentation grenades. Inside the embassy, Trevor Lock, a policeman on diplomatic guard duty, managed to alert his superiors by radio before the terrorists had gotten the embassy and the hostages locked down. Within minutes, specialist squads from the Metropolitan Police had arrived outside. They included the marksmen of D11, the C13 anti-terrorist squad, C7 technical support branch, and the Special

Patrol Group. Meanwhile a former SAS man, then a police dog handler, contacted the regiment and at 1148 the beepers of the Blue and Red teams of the SAS went off. Soon Special Forces operatives in plain clothes were on the scene.

Initially, it was not clear how many people had been taken hostage. It turned out to be 26—19 Iranians and seven non-Iranians, including PC Lock and two men from the BBC who were visiting.

The terrorist leader was named Oan, but he called himself Salim. It seemed that he was the only one who could speak English. He made the demands on behalf of an Arabic organization known as the Group of the Martyr. These included freedom for Khuzestan, an oil-rich part of Iran inhabited by Arabs who have traditionally suffered persecution at the hands of the non-Arabic majority, and the release of 91 Arab prisoners held by Iran who were to be flown to London. He also insisted that an Arab ambassador be brought in to mediate. If these demands were not met by noon the following day, the hostages would be killed and the embassy would be blown up.

The police set up an incident room called Zulu Control down on the terrace and began negotiating with the terrorists. Meanwhile, preparations were made for an armed assault. That night, police carpenters built a scale model of the embassy. The next day, work began on a life-size replica built in timber and burlap in Regents Park Barracks.

Technicians from C7 lowered microphones and surveillance devices down the chimney to monitor the movements of the terrorists. When two hostages were freed—a pregnant woman and a man who had stomach pains—they were debriefed. It was then confirmed that there were six terrorists; previously there were only thought to be five.

As the siege progressed and deadlines passed, the negotiators began to make headway. Plainly, the liberation of Khuzestan was not in their gift. The terrorists were forced to drop their demand for the freeing of the 91 Arab prisoners when it turned out that the men concerned had already been executed. The terrorists then asked for a coach to Heathrow Airport and a plane to take them and their Iranian hostages to a Middle Eastern country.

Although it seemed as if the hostage crisis might be solved peacefully, the debacle of Munich was still on everyone's mind, and the SAS continued making plans of their own. They were briefed by the embassy caretaker, who told them that the windows and the front door were reinforced, so it would be impossible to bust in using sledgehammers. However, C7 men in the building next door had removed part of the adjoining wall brick-by-brick, leaving only a thin layer of plaster. To cover the noise of removing the brickwork, an emergency crew from the gas board armed with pneumatic drills had been called to repair a fictitious gas leak outside, while planes to Heathrow were diverted to fly low over the building. The SAS also discovered an unlocked skylight at the roof that gave access to a bathroom.

After five days, the terrorists were beginning to get desperate. They picked a political argument with the Iranian hostages and began to get suspicious about the noise they heard from outside. The male hostages were moved together into the telex room, and PC Lock appeared at the window to say that the terrorists were going to start shooting the hostages if there was no news of the long-awaited Arab mediator.

At 1331, three shots were heard from inside the embassy. Then at 1850, there were three more shots and the body of the embassy's press officer was pushed out the front door.

Ten minutes later, the police handed over command to the military. The SAS were now going into action.

At 1923, the negotiators got Oan back on the phone so that he, at least, could be located. Then the SAS's Red Team fast-roped in pairs from the roof at the back down onto the balcony and ground floor. Another group burst through the plaster from the building next door. At the front, the Blue Team used frame charges to break the windows. When a terrorist appeared, a sniper killed him with a single shot. Then stun grenades and CS grenades were thrown in. However, the terrorists had put newspapers soaked with gasoline under the windows, so a fire rapidly broke out.

The raiders were wearing black so that they were visible against smoke, their torsos protected with Nomex body armor. Their faces were covered with gas masks, and flash hoods protected them from fire and blast.

However, things were not going as smoothly as planned. Only one of the charges lowered by rope down through the skylight went off prematurely. At the back of the house, one of the troopers got entangled in his ropes so his colleagues could not use their frame charges. He had to be cut down later. Instead, a sledgehammer had be used on the lock of the French windows. Nevertheless, front and back, the SAS were in.

When an SAS man appeared through the front window, Oan raised his gun to fire. But Trevor Lock sprang into action, grappling with the terrorist leader until the SAS man could shoot him.

In the telex room, one of the terrorists started shooting into the hostages. One hostage died, and another was wounded. When the SAS bust into the room, the two terrorists hid among the hostages on the floor. But when they were pointed out by the hostages, they were killed. However, the terrorist guarding the women in another room was spared.

The last terrorist was by the stairs between the hostages when an SAS trooper saw a grenade in his hand. With the hostages at such close quarters, it was not possible to shoot him, so the trooper hit him on the neck with the stock of his MP-5. As he fell down the flight of stairs, he was hit by 32 bullets from four SAS guns, killing him. Fortunately, the pin remained in the grenade.

But the action was not yet over. All the rooms had to be systematically cleared and checked for booby traps. Locked doors were opened with bursts of 9-mm bullets. The SAS men could not be sure that they had accounted for all the terrorists, so the hostages were thrown down the stairs from trooper to trooper and bundled into the back garden. There, everyone was handcuffed and searched for weapons and proof of identity just in case terrorists were hiding among them. Once the SAS were sure that everyone in the garden was a hostage and there were no more terrorists at large in the buildings, command was then handed back to the police.

The action was over in 17 minutes. Of the 26 hostages, 2 died, 5 had been released, and 19 were rescued. Five of the terrorists were dead; the one survivor was sentenced to life imprisonment. The SAS, who were expecting 40 percent casualties, had three wounded. One suffered burns, one had a leg wound, and one had an injured finger.

CHAPTER 8

MIA RESCUE MISSION

AFTER THE VIETNAM WAR, there was a growing lobby that believed that prisoners of war had been left behind in enemy hands. As the North Vietnamese had refused to abide by the Geneva Conventions—on the grounds that there had been no formal declaration of war—no lists of prisoners had been returned. Consequently, all American servicemen in Communist hands were technically "missing in action," or MIA.

The idea that men had been left behind after the formal hand-over of prisoners in February 1973 gained popular expression in the 1985 movie *Rambo: First Blood Part II*, in which Vietnam veteran John Rambo was recruited for a top-secret mission to rescue POWs still held in Vietnam. But there were some real-life Rambos, most notably Lieutenant Colonel James "Bo" Gritz.

Gritz was a genuine war hero. A Green Beret, he spent four years in Vietnam and had more than 100 missions to his credit. He was awarded more than 60 decorations, commanded the Green Beret Mobile Guerrilla Force, and survived numerous operations behind enemy lines. After the war, Gritz was appointed head of the Special Forces in the Panama Canal Zone, and in 1979 he was persuaded by his

71

superior, General Harold R. Aaron, to undertake a little free-lance military work in Southeast Asia.

Before becoming deputy director of the Defense Intelligence Agency, General Aaron had been commander of the Special Forces in Vietnam. He knew Gritz well. As deputy director of the DIA, Aaron was certain that there were live Americans still being held in Southeast Asia. The problem was that there was nothing the DIA could do about it. The politics of the situation were all wrong, and President Carter could not have been less interested in the matter. So Aaron approached Gritz in the Canal Zone to sound him out.

Gritz was sympathetic and found himself posted back to Washington, D.C., in a public relations role for the Green Berets. Aaron approached him again and this time asked him to resign his commission and launch a private mission to rescue the MIAs. When the mission was over, Aaron envisaged no problem for Gritz in resuming his high-flying service career. Although he had intended to complete his 30 years, Gritz accepted the assignment and quit the Army.

He went to work, ostensibly, for Hughes Aircraft in California. There he began to recruit, equip, and train a team for cross-border operations in Southeast Asia. Gritz was to avoid the press and government agencies, and, because of the politics involved, he was only to contact the DIA if he got into a situation in which there was no other alternative. The Director of the DIA, General Eugene F. Tighe, Gritz was told, was well aware of the situation. At that time, Gritz also had the support of Ann Mills Griffiths at the National League of Families, the lobbyist group representing the families of the missing men. He also had meetings with the CIA and the FBI.

By 1981, Gritz was ready to go. He had given his men jungle training in Florida and had enough intelligence to mount a rescue mission into Laos, code-named Operation Velvet Hammer. This immediately ran into a problem. New satellite pictures showed an isolated clearing in the Lao jungle at Nhom Marrot, close to the Thai border. In it was a stockade which resembled nothing so much as a frontier outpost on a Hollywood film set. It quickly became known as Fort Apache.

The prison complex was completely cut off. There were no telephone or power lines leading to it, and no radio mast was visible. It seemed to be self-contained and self-sustaining. Crops were planted in nearby fields, and there was a river close by. But what had caught the eye of the intelligence analysts was that, a short way from the prison, there was the number "52" trampled out in long grass.

The number could not be seen from the prison, because the line of sight was impeded by intervening trees. It could only be seen from above—from a spy satellite or a reconnaissance aircraft.

The DIA studied the photographs long and hard. What could the number 52 mean? Could it be a signal from a downed B-52 crew? Was it the work of members of Detachment B-52 of Special Forces Project Delta who conducted secret, long-range reconnaissance missions into Laos in the mid-1960s? Or did it refer to the 52 American hostages recently released from the US Embassy in Iran? The characters "5" and "2" mean nothing in Vietnamese or Laotian, and the number 52 has no special significance in their cultures. The figures "5" and "2" did correspond to *W* in the tap code used by POWs to communicate between cells, but that seemed to be a blind alley as well. More photographs were needed.

The US spy satellite was directed over the prison site, and the new pictures showed that the clearing had been hacked out of dense jungle. Within the clearing there were two compounds enclosed by a 12-foot-high wire fence topped with concertina coils of barbed wire. At each corner stood a watchtower, and inside the inner compound there were two barracks that were believed to house prisoners.

Men could be seen harvesting crops and cutting down trees. Refugee reports had talked of Americans being used as slave labor in that area to clear forests and build roads.

Detailed analysis of the photographs showed that there were two types of men in the prison, one of which was much taller than the other. This could be deduced from the lengths of their shadows when they lined up in rows or when two men stood together. It was also noticed that when they sat on the ground, the tall men would sit with their legs crossed, while the shorter men squatted, Asian-style. After two months, defense analysts came to the conclusion that the taller group of men were Caucasians—white men, possibly Americans. There were around 30 of them.

Reports from refugees coming out of the area supported this conclusion. One, from a former Royal Laotian Air Force pilot, said that 40 or 50 American pilots were being held there. But proof was needed. While Delta Force prepared a helicopter assault from Thailand, the CIA sent in a team of local Hmong tribesmen to photograph the site. The Hmong had been loyal to the Americans during the war, and tall Westerners tramping through the jungles of western Laos would stand out too much. The decision was made: If the Hmong came back with pictures of Caucasians, the rescue mission would go ahead. Meanwhile, Gritz and Operation Velvet Hammer were asked to stand down.

When the tribesmen returned, their film was rushed to the processing laboratory. But, when the fixer was washed from the emulsion, no pictures of tall, broad-shouldered white men appeared. Improperly briefed, the Hmong tribesmen had simply taken pictures of the outside of the stockade. They had confirmed the existence of the prison but not that foreign prisoners were being held there. And there seemed to be no way of getting into the prison itself.

The American press had already gotten wind of the planned rescue attempt, but, because of its sensitive nature, they had been persuaded to hold the story. Once the reconnaissance mission had failed though, they decided to publish and, on May 21, 1981, the *Washington Post* broke the story. Any helicopter rescue in the MiG-filled skies of Laos was now impossible.

Politically, the US could not be seen to be violating other countries' sovereignty. Nor could it be seen to be funding secret armies in Laos or backing anti-Communist resistance forces after the debacle of Vietnam. The American public would not stand for any President getting involved militarily in Southeast Asia again.

President Reagan tried another ploy. He got two junior congressmen to go and negotiate with the Lao. Representatives Bill Hendon and John LeBoutillier made several trips to Laos in 1981 and 1982 to negotiate with the Laotian government, including the then deputy minister of public health and, according to intelligence sources, the physician in charge of the POWs' health after the end of the Vietnam War.

Negotiations were coming along nicely. The Laotians acknowledged that they might be holding some Americans. Their attitude was that America was like a hit-and-run driver. It had come in and wrecked their country and left without paying for the damage. Once America was willing to deal, they would go out and look for the missing men. As a gesture of good faith, Hendon arranged for $275,000 worth of medical goods to be sent to Laos. President Reagan was confident enough to tell a public meeting of the National League of Families that their long vigil was over. Then details of this shipment were leaked to the papers. At the time there was a Congressional ban on dealing with any Communist government in Southeast Asia. Reagan was flouting it. Potentially it was another Iran-Contra-gate, and the president had to back off.

However, in June, Gritz was approached by a supersecret Pentagon-level special-operations unit, the Intelligence Support Activity. Few outside a small Pentagon elite knew the Activity even existed. But after the cancellation of the Nhom Marrot mission, the ISA began a bureaucratic tug-of-war with the DIA for authority over the POW-related missions, and it began to win when the CIA sided with the Activity. The ISA gave Gritz $40,000 and furnished cameras, code machines, polygraph equipment, and night sights for the mission. Even Gritz thought the Activity had overstepped their authority in the hope that he would come up with enough solid evidence to win the MIA charter away from the DIA.

With renewed funding, Gritz put together Operation Grand Eagle, another mission to get photographic evidence of Americans being held. Local Hmong tribesmen would be used again, but this time members of Gritz's team would be going along as well. Anti-Communist free Lao forces were made available by General Vang Pao, former head of the CIA's secret army of Hmongs in Laos, who then lived on a ranch in Montana. A meeting took place between Gritz and Vang Pao at Congressman Robert K. Dornan's office in Los Angeles. Another Vietnam veteran, Dornan backed Gritz's Rambo mission.

Laden with sophisticated equipment, Gritz headed for Thailand. He already had DIA live-sighting reports and satellite-reconnaissance photographs. And Vang Pao's free Laos had spent the summer gathering the latest intelligence on American POWs being held. Four camps were selected where, during August, September, and October that year, 39 Americans had been seen, including 17 men being held in a cave. On November 15, two nine-man guerrilla units equipped with Nikon F3 cameras with motor drives and telephoto lenses set off from Thailand.

With one of the groups was Scott Barnes, a private investigator with shady CIA connections, and Michael J. Baldwin, alias Jerry Daniels, a CIA agent. Barnes says that he and Daniels were sent to a triangular prison some 27 kilometers east of the Thai border in the Mahaski region. There were guards in towers and, Barnes says, they distinctly saw two men who were clearly Caucasian. Through a long-range listening device, they heard them speak English.

Between them, Barnes and Daniels took more than 400 pictures of these men, using a variety of exposures and film types, including some taken with infrared film when the light faded. Daniels hand-delivered his film to the US Embassy in Bangkok. Six months later, he died of carbon monoxide poisoning in mysterious circumstances in his apartment in Thailand. Barnes mailed his film directly to Daniel C. Arnold, CIA Station Chief. When he returned to the States, Barnes was told that all the negatives had been accidentally destroyed in processing.

But Gritz and his men did not give up. Over that year, Gritz received reports from Vietnamese agents of live sightings of 62 other American POWs. One had seen 30 Americans in a Laotian prisoner-of-war camp in early November. They were guarded by 150 Vietnamese soldiers, 150 Laotians, and 65 armored vehicles. A defecting Vietnamese army officer said he saw 12 Americans exercising in short blue pants and short-sleeved shirts with the letters "TB" on the back. "TB" stands for *Tu Binh*, Vietnamese for prisoner of war. Other reports mention shirts with the "TB" markings—there were 20 barefoot POWs in a Laotian camp, and American prisoners seen in similar uniforms were fed only rice and beans, held in a wire compound near Mahaski, and guarded by 12 Vietnamese with AK-47s.

Gritz planned to use these Vietnamese agents to launch two more reconnaissance missions to two camps in Laos and two in Vietnam. The mission was due to set out on December 10, but on December 6, Gritz was recalled to Washington by the head of the ISA, a man named Cranston, also known as Jerry Koenig—which doesn't seem to have been his real name either. Apparently, the DIA had gotten wind of Gritz's activities, and Admiral Allan Paulson, the man now in charge of the MIA issue at the DIA, was furious at the ISA's involvement.

The DIA took the matter to a closed "executive" session of the Congressional Task Force on American Prisoners and Missing in Southeast Asia, chaired by Congressman Dornan. Dornan lost his temper at the intelligence community's tactics and accused them of "stonewalling" Gritz's efforts. He was told that the government was now "going another way." It had been decided that the Gritz–Vang Pao rescue plans were not feasible, although Dornan was convinced that initially they had had government approval.

Meanwhile, the CIA took an interest in Operation Grand Eagle. Gritz was summoned to CIA deputy director Bobby Ray Inman's office on December 9. During a 45-minute meeting, they discussed both Operations Velvet Hammer and

Grand Eagle. Admiral Inman said that he would look into the whole situation and get back in touch before the New Year. On January 4, Gritz received a telephone call from ISA chief "Cranston" who told him that Operation Grand Eagle was going to be put back on the shelf as if it never existed. "There are too many bureaucrats here that don't want to see POWs returned," he said.

Cranston offered Gritz the chance to return to active service with the Activity, but Gritz refused. He said he planned to continue his efforts through private means. Cranston said he should keep in touch and assured Gritz that the US government would be interested if events progressed beyond a critical point.

Gritz had to raise money. He approached actor Clint Eastwood, who donated $30,000 and agreed to be the team's contact with President Reagan. William Shatner—Captain Kirk of *Star Trek* fame—gave Gritz $10,000, supposedly for the book and movie rights. Gritz banked the check and tore up Shatner's letter outlining the rights agreement.

Lance Trimmer, Special Forces communications specialist turned private eye, and two daughters of MIAs, Lynn Standerwick and Janet Townley, raised another $10,000. Lynn Standerwick's father, Colonel Robert Standerwick, had been shot down over Laos in 1971. His copilot, Major Norbet Gotner, was told that Standerwick had been shot shortly after his capture, but later he was told that Standerwick had been rescued. A man answering Standerwick's description with a broken leg was seen being paraded through Mahaski, a village close to the crash site, around that time. Ms. Standerwick says that she saw a DIA file that put Colonel Standerwick's last known location as Hoa Lo prison, Vietnam's famous Hanoi Hilton.

Janet Townley's father, USAF Captain Roy F. Townley, was a so-called "civilian" pilot for the CIA's Air America. He was shot down in a C-123 over Laos in 1971. Janet Townley heard a lot about her father after that. She was told that an intercepted Pathet Lao communication in August 1972 stated that they had downed the plane and captured all the crew. A Pathet Lao defector said he had seen the downed C-123 and seen Captain Townley and the other crewmen, Edward Weissenback, George Ritter, and a Lao kicker called Khamphanh being held with four other Americans and several high-ranking Thai and Lao officers in a cave that had a waterfall running over the entrance. The Americans grew their own vegetables, cut their own firewood, and bathed in the river once a week. There were 50 Pathet Lao—Communist Lao guerrillas—within a kilometer of the cave. Townley had broken an arm, the copilot had injured a knee, an American kicker had a gash over his left eye, and Khamphanh had lost a tooth. The Townley family had a photograph that showed Captain Townley lying on a hospital bed with a broken arm sometime before October 1972. Janet Townley says that the DIA showed her some infrared photos of the same man that revealed two moles near the mouth, identical to those Captain Townley had. No prisoners of war were ever returned from Laos.

Re-equipped, Gritz and his team set out for Thailand again. They were done with reconnaissance. This time they were on a rescue mission, which they aptly named Operation Lazarus. On the night of November 27, 1982, four Americans dressed in jungle fatigues waited on the banks of the Mekong River. They were armed with Uzi machine guns with infrared laser "red eye" night sights. They wore night-vision goggles and carried sophisticated communications equipment. Their target was a camp near Tcepone, on the Phu Xun mountain in Laos where Vang Pao's men had reported 120 Americans being held. Their aim was to spring some of them. Meanwhile, Clint Eastwood would contact the president, who they hoped would immediately send the cavalry to the rescue once they had the POWs. The four Americans were James "Bo" Gritz, his Special Forces buddy Charles Patterson, Vietnam veteran Gary Goldman, and Dominic Zappone, a Green Beret who had served with Gritz in Panama but, as far as combat was concerned, was still a cherry. They were accompanied by 15 free Lao.

As Gritz swung his 150-pound rucksack on his back and climbed into the sampan that was going to take them across the river he said, "It's a good night to die." Three of them did, and Dominic Zappone became another name on the MIA roster.

Three days after crossing the Mekong, deep inside Laos, Gritz's raiding party ran into a Pathet Lao patrol. Three free Lao guerrillas were killed in the firefight. When the raiding party regrouped, Dominic Zappone was missing.

When Gritz, Patterson, and Goldman made it back to Thailand, footsore and battle weary, they say they found a message waiting for them. It was from their contact in the States and read, "Clint and I met the president on the 27th. The president said: quote, if you bring out one US POW, I will start World War III to get the rest out, unquote."

Without one POW, and with one of his own men missing, no one in Washington wanted to know about the mission. But things are different in Hollywood. Paramount's publicity for the 1983 MIA movie *Uncommon Valor*—in which retired Marine Colonel Jason Rhodes, played by Gene Hackman, tries to rescue his missing son—acknowledged Gritz, saying "his journey closely paralleled that of Colonel Jason Rhodes and his men in *Uncommon Valor*—although the screenplay had been written 10 months before."

Back in the US, Gritz tried to raise money by selling the top-secret state-of-the-art communications equipment the Pentagon had supplied back to the manufacturer, Litton Industries. When they refused, Gritz put a small ad in the *Los Angeles Times* offering "Electronic equipment, one day only, discreet sale." Litton came up with the $40,000 Gritz was asking for. But the small ad also attracted the attention of reporters on the *Times* who ran a story covering the "secret" hand-over of the equipment and the money in a deserted parking lot at night.

Gritz used $17,500 of the money to ransom Zappone. The rest he used to mount a new foray into Laos, Operation Omega. Again the mission ended in failure. Although Gritz had been a successful soldier, his training had led him to depend on the backup of a massive military machine. Without it, all he had to fall back on was empty bravado.

His colleagues had become increasingly disturbed by his courting of press attention—the Communists read newspapers too—his use of a psychic and a hypnotherapist during training, and his delusions of grandeur. He talked of a ticker-tape reception in New York's Fifth Avenue, styled himself "Lawrence of Laos," and acted out make-believe medal ceremonies.

Charles Patterson, who, like Gritz's other sidekicks, had not been paid for more than a year, sold his story to *Soldier of Fortune* magazine. The *Bangkok Post* also picked it up. With 450,000 Communist troops massed on their borders, the last thing the Thai government needed was Bo Gritz stirring things up.

The FBI began to put the squeeze on the US end of Gritz's operation, pointing out that it was against federal law to raise funds for any private military expedition against a country the United States is at peace with.

In Thailand, Gritz and his in-country team—Lance Trimmer, Scott Weekly, Gary Goldman, and Lynn Standerwick—were arrested for possession of an illegal radio transmitter. The American government denied any involvement with Gritz's team or their rescue mission. They were each fined $130 and given a one-year suspended jail sentence. Gritz then faced federal charges related to the use of a passport bearing a false name during his trips to Southeast Asia. Not that Gritz's fate deterred others from donning the Rambo garb. Veterans of Operation Grand Eagle and Lazarus made further attempts to free the MIAs—as did Gritz himself. It was all to no avail, leading would-be Rambo Scott Barnes to believe that the issue was so potentially embarrassing to successive American administrations—not to mention the military and the intelligence services—that they would rather have the POWs killed than see them come out alive.

CHAPTER 9

THE FALKLANDS WAR

Two years after raising the siege of the Iranian Embassy in London, the SAS was back doing what it had first been devised for in the deserts of North Africa in 1941: blowing up enemy aircraft. Indeed, the Falklands War in 1982 gave the unit an opportunity to practice all the soldierly skills they had acquired in World War II. These would include infiltration for surveillance and intelligence gathering, as well as launching diversionary attacks and seizing key features in front of the main force.

Since 1820, after Argentina declared its independence from Spain, it had claimed sovereignty over the Falkland Islands—or the Islas Malvinas as it called them—which lie some 300 miles off its coast. However, the USS *Lexington* destroyed the Argentine settlement there in 1831 in reprisal for the illegal seizure of three American ships. Two years later, the British took back the islands, which they had first occupied in 1765. Since 1833, the islands' inhabitants have been of British stock and owed their allegiance to the British Crown.

At the beginning of 1982, the Argentine military junta under Lieutenant-General Leopoldo Galtieri gave up on long-running negotiations between Argentina and Britain over the status of the islands and decided to invade, in the hope that the patriotic fervor engendered by the "recovery" of the Malvinas might help prop up his discredited regime. An invasion force trained in secret.

Then, when a dispute blew up between Argentine salvage workers and British scientists stationed on the British Island of South Georgia, 900 miles east of the Falklands, the government in Buenos Aires seized on this as an excuse to move against the British possessions in the South Atlantic. On April 2, 1982, Argentine troops invaded the Falklands, quickly overcoming the small force of Royal Marines garrisoned in the capital, Port Stanley. The following day, Argentine troops took South Georgia.

Diplomatic attempts—largely through the good offices of the United States—failed to resolve the situation, and Britain decided to retake the islands. As the dispute in South Georgia had been the original excuse for the Argentine invasion of the Falklands, it was decided to retake that island first. Its sovereignty was not in contention and it was thought that it could be taken with a small contingent of Special Forces.

Britain's SBS had been engaged in winter exercises in northern Norway when Argentina invaded the Falklands. Although they were due for a break as soon as they returned from Scandinavia, they found their leave canceled when they returned to Britain, and they were put on standby. Twenty-four hours later, 2 SBS and the command team set off by air to Ascension Island, Britain's base in the mid-Atlantic.

They were soon joined by D Squadron of the SAS, making a Special Forces contingent of around 50 men. They were at sea on board the Royal Fleet Auxiliary transport RFA *Fort Austin* before they learned that their destination was South Georgia. Meanwhile, 6 SBS joined the British nuclear submarine HMS *Conqueror* at its base in Faslane, Scotland. It then set off for the South Atlantic. The last section to leave was 3 SBS, which set off with another 12 men on RFA *Stromness*, heading for Ascension. In Poole, 1 SBS remained behind to deal with any counterterrorist emergency closer to home.

The assault on South Georgia was code-named "Operation Paraquat." On the way, the SBS and SAS tested their equipment and practiced launching in the Atlantic swell from the *Fort Austin*. The elderly outboard motors they had been given often failed, and the men found themselves having to paddle back to the ship in these practices. This did not bode well.

On April 12, they sighted HMS *Endurance*, the Royal Navy's Antarctica ice patrol vessel. Over the next day, the SBS and SAS cross-decked to the *Endurance*, along with their equipment and stores, carried by two Wessex helicopters. The *Endurance* and *Fort Austin* were then joined by the destroyer HMS *Antrim*, the antisubmarine frigate HMS *Plymouth*, and the tanker RFA *Tidespring*.

The detailed planning of the reoccupation of South Georgia was done aboard HMS *Antrim*. The *Endurance* was to put the main body of the SBS ashore at Grytviken on King Edward Point. But first the SAS would land on the Fortuna Glacier to establish an observation point and reconnoiter Leith Harbour, Stromness, and Grass Island. On April 21, 1982, a helicopter dropped 16 men of the Mountain Troop— D Squadron, SAS—on the Fortuna Glacier. The weather was horrendous. Weapons froze up, and the men only managed to advance 500 meters before camping for the night. In severe danger of frostbite and hypothermia, they requested extraction the next day. Wessex helicopters were sent. But one of them crashed just after picking up seven SAS men. The only casualty was one SAS soldier who hurt his back.

A second helicopter also crashed. A third helicopter managed to extract some of the men. But when the helicopter returned to collect the rest of them, it was unable to land. Later that day, after five attempts, the pilot managed to set down and pick up the remaining men. Overloaded, and flying in appalling conditions, the pilot crash-landed, but he managed to get the men safely on board a Royal Navy ship. He was awarded a Distinguished Flying Cross for his actions.

The next attempt to reach the island was by boat. Five inflatables set out for Grass Island in a bay on the north side of South Georgia. Only three boats made it to the shoreline. Then there was a delay because the Argentine submarine *Santa Fe* was in the area. She had to be sought out by helicopter and depth charged. Damaged, she limped back to Grytviken, where she was scuttled.

Once that threat was neutralized, a 75-man-strong force was landed by helicopter from the *Antrim*. They faced a garrison of 150 poorly trained Argentine troops. On April 25, the landing party directed naval gunfire on them. Then helicopters inserted another 30 SAS troops. When the men reached Grytviken, the entire place was covered in white sheets, indicating that the Argentineans had surrendered. Just the threat of facing British Special Forces was enough for the young conscripts. South Georgia had been retaken without bloodshed. Next came the Falklands themselves.

The 6 SBS then moved from South Georgia to join 3 SBS in the advance fleet. The SBS would reconnoiter three separate areas of the Falklands and maintain patrols while the main body of the British task force was making its way across the Atlantic. From May 1, patrols from the SBS and G Squadron of the SAS were inserted on the Falklands to look for sites suitable for an amphibious landing. They were usually flown in by Sea King Mk4 helicopters, although in areas where stealth was called for they came ashore in Gemini inflatables, which were dropped half-inflated off the coast. Helicopter movements were only carried out at night, and once dropped off, the Special Forces teams dug into the coverless hillsides and remained hidden for days at a time as the Argentine forces searched for them. The SBS were hampered by the fact that they had to send reports back using Morse code. This system was not sophisticated enough to relay beach recon reports, so SBS personnel had to made a dangerous exfiltration to deliver maps and charts in person before being inserted again.

Eventually, the SBS found San Carlos Bay, which was almost undefended. This was to be the site of the British amphibious landing. Another four-man patrol located the enemy's position and ascertained the weapons and equipment they were using. These patrols were inserted up to 20 miles from their objectives. Heavily laden, carrying stores for up to 14 days, the patrols moved by night and lay up during the day.

Observation posts were set up. As the ground was too hard to dig into, they made hides to lie up in during daylight hours. A fold in the terrain would be covered with chicken wire and burlap netting. This was then covered with local vegetation to blend in. A trio of hides would be built, one for the men and the other two for the substantial supplies necessary for a 14-day reconnaissance. These were so well camouflaged that the Argentines did not discover a single one of them, though they came close on numerous occasions, once even almost falling over one.

On one occasion, two SBS corporals went missing. This caused SBS Control a great deal of worry. The two corporals were part of a team that had run into an Argentine patrol. Although they avoided actual contact, they were split up. Following their standard evasion procedures, the two missing corporals went to ground. Eventually, seven days later, they picked up and returned to the task force.

For the SAS and SBS men, manning the posts was not a pleasant task. The hides were cold, wet, and cramped. Trench foot became a problem. One man would remain on watch as the others tried to cook and get some sleep. It was only possible for them to stretch their legs at night, and even then it was dangerous.

Although they only had rations for 14 days, one patrol lasted 26 days on Beagle Ridge overlooking Port Stanley. Another patrol watching Bluff Cove held out for 28 days.

Air reconnaissance discovered an airstrip and possibly a radar station on Pebble Island, just north of West Falkland. Argentine aircraft using this base could attack the amphibious force landing at San Carlos, so it had to be dealt with. But Falkland Islanders lived nearby, so it could not be bombed from the air.

On May 11, two four-man SAS patrols approached the island in collapsible canoes and made a reconnaissance of the area. They found 11 aircraft and a small garrison housing 114 Argentines. But there was a problem establishing an observation post, as there was very little cover. An all-out attack was called for. Three days later, the rest of D Squadron—another 45 men—were flown in from the aircraft carrier HMS *Hermes* by Sea King helicopters and landed four miles from the airstrip. They had just 30 minutes to reach their objective. The action began with a bombardment by their 81-mm mortars, supported by naval gunfire. Then the Mountain Troop attacked the bunkers on each side of the airstrip, neutralizing them. Two seven-man groups then destroyed the planes with explosives, machine guns, and hand grenades. All 11 aircraft were wrecked beyond repair. There was only one SAS casualty. A land mine blew one British soldier off his feet and injured him slightly with shrapnel. The job done, helicopters extracted all the SAS men safely. It was a classic SAS raid, but there was trouble ahead.

On May 19, during a night cross-decking operation from *Hermes* to *Intrepid,* disaster struck when a Sea King helicopter dropped from an altitude of 400 feet into the freezing water of the South Atlantic. It is thought that an albatross flew into the engine's air intake. Eighteen SAS men from D and G Squadrons were killed, though 10 men survived the crash. It was a severe blow for the regiment as experienced soldiers lost their lives. However, the commanding officer of 22 SAS, Lieutenant Colonel Michael Rose, said at the time, "The regiment has taken it well and are getting on with the fighting." But he added that he would be happier when all his men were ashore and their lives were in their own hands.

Meanwhile, the SBS were sent to take over an Argentine fish factory ship. But while 2 SBS was en route, the ship was attacked by two British Harrier jets and was listing badly by the time the SBS arrived and boarded her. The SBS discovered charts and operational orders showing that she had been shadowing the British fleet. They took off the crew before setting charges and blowing up the vessel.

Immediately before the landing of the main British ground forces at San Carlos, an Argentine company moved into the area and the SBS were sent to clear them out. Using a thermal imager, the SBS located the Argentine position from one of *Antrim*'s Wessex helicopters. HMS *Antrim* bombarded the position with 4.5-inch naval shellfire for two hours, while the Wessex landed the SBS nearby. The SBS then moved in, calling for the Argentines to surrender. Their answer was a volley of small-arms fire. The SBS men gave the Argentines one more chance to give up before moving forward. They killed 12, wounded 3, and took 9 prisoners.

The Argentines they had taken out had been on Fanning Head manning antitank guns and mortars. These would have been able to inflict considerable damage on the British landings if they had not been put out of action. However, the rest of the Argentine company were hiding in houses in Port San Carlos and were not discovered until after the landings began. In the meantime they had shot down two Royal Marine Gazelles.

The SAS's next task was to stage a diversionary attack on East Falkland. D Squadron was inserted to simulate an attack on Darwin and Goose Green. After a 24-hour approach, they set about making a lot of noise, attacking the 1,200 Argentines there with 81-mm mortars, machine guns, and Milan antitank missiles. The enemy returned sporadic fire but, thinking they were under fire from a much larger force, did not dare counterattack. This also diverted their attention from the other San Carlos Bay, where the main British ground forces landed on May 21, untroubled by the enemy.

As the landings at San Carlos continued unopposed, 6 SBS were inserted from HMS *Fearless* to establish a forward base on the north coast ahead of the Royal Marine Commandos' advance out of the beachhead. This section also carried out a reconnaissance of Port Louis and Green Patch before the Commandos arrived. Then 2 SBS joined them, operating in the Teal area. After the 3rd Parachute Regiment reached Teal, they moved on to observe an enemy company on Long Island Mountain, overlooking the route to Port Stanley. Then the SBS set about removing an enemy observation post. During the operation, the team leader strayed into the SAS operational zone and was killed by fire incident. From then on, there was closer cooperation between the two outfits.

G Squadron of the SAS put an observation post on Mount Kent, a key strategic position overlooking Port Stanley. When they reported that the mountain was not manned by the Argentines, D Squadron moved 36 miles across enemy-held territory to seize it. They held the mountain against Argentine attack for almost a week until the Royal Marines arrived there in force.

To replace battle casualties, B Squadron was flown in from Britain. After a 12-hour flight from Ascension Island, they joined the Royal Navy Task Force by parachuting into the Atlantic to be picked up by HMS *Glamorgan*.

On the night of June 13, 2 Para were attacking Wireless Ridge. One of their companies was commanded by a former SAS man. As the attack was in danger of getting bogged down, the SAS decided to help their old comrade out by launching an attack on an enemy ammunition dump between the eastern edge of the ridge and Port Stanley. They planned to go in on board helicopters, but as the weather closed in this proved impossible. Instead they requisitioned four Royal Marine Rigid Raider assault craft, along with the coxswains, and launched an attack on Port Stanley itself, accompanied by 3 SBS.

Before the attack, the SBS team spent a day in an observation post overlooking the objective before moving across the Murrell River in Rigid Raiders with a troop from D Squadron of the SAS. Ferried by men from the Royal Marines' 1st Raiding Squadron, they waited off Kidney Island until darkness fell and they were ready for the assault.

Port Stanley was defended by around 8,000 Argentine soldiers armed with armored cars, antiaircraft guns, and 155-mm and 105-mm artillery. The attack force was just 60 men—three SAS troops and a six-man SBS section. However, they were supported by other SAS troops on the northern shore who descended from their positions on Murrell Heights to lay down machine gun and Milan missile covering fire.

As the raiding force approached the target area, they bypassed the Argentine hospital ship *Bahia Paraiso* berthed in the bay. As they did so, the hospital ship turned on its searchlights. Spotting the raiders, the Argentines opened fire with everything they had, certain they were facing a full-scale seaborne assault. The British force did not open fire on the hospital ship but were not displeased when it was hit by Argentine artillery fire.

Thinking they were facing a full-scale amphibious assault, the Argentine defenders—including those on Wireless Ridge—turned the fire on the raiders, who had to turn tail. Despite the withering fire, only an SBS corporal and two SAS troopers had been slightly wounded, though the Rigid Raiders were badly holed. Nevertheless, the attack provided a much needed diversion for the Paras attacking Wireless Ridge, and the British quickly overcame the opposition.

This was the SAS's last action in the Falklands, but not their last contribution. On June 14, with a general cease-fire in place around Port Stanley, it was the SAS commanding officer Lieutenant-Colonel Michael Rose who helicoptered into the capital with a Spanish-speaking officer to broker peace. The Argentine commander General Mario Menendez offered to surrender the forces under his control on East Falklands, but he said that he could not speak for the garrison on West Falklands. This would have been acceptable to the commanders of the British Task Force, as the army was now down to six rounds per gun and was suffering other shortages. Rose bluffed it out. A partial surrender, he said, was no surrender at all. He insisted that Menendez instruct all forces on the Falklands to lay down their arms. After two hours, Menendez gave way.

The following day, when Menendez and the commander of the British Land Forces, Major General Jeremy Moore RM, signed the instrument of surrender, the SAS hoisted the Union Jack on Government House alongside their own regimental flag. The SAS and SBS had made a huge contribution to the victory in the Falklands at the cost of 20 of their men.

There also seem to have been SBS operations on the mainland of Argentina. However, for the time being, the details remain classified. The SBS have drawn up plans to counter any future attack or invasion of the Falklands by the Argentines.

CHAPTER 10

OPERATION URGENT FURY

ON OCTOBER 13, 1983, there was a coup d'état on the Caribbean island of Grenada after the Marxist Deputy Prime Minister, Bernard Coard, had Prime Minister Maurice Bishop arrested. Then Grenada's People's Revolutionary Army, under General Hudson Austin, took over. They murdered Bishop, along with a number of civilians. To restore order and protect the lives of US citizens on the island, the United States decided to invade in Operation Urgent Fury, which kicked off on the night of October 24. While the US Marines would take the north of the island, Special Forces would take the capital and the air base in the south.

The first American troops to land on the island were with US Navy SEAL Team 4, whose mission included prelanding beach reconnaissance to prepare the way for the 24th Marine Amphibious Unit. Then SEAL Team 6 was sent in to reconnoiter Point Salines airfield. The 16-man reconnaissance group was to arrive off the island's southern coast in two C-130 transports, parachute into the sea, climb aboard Boston Whaler rescue craft, and rendezvous with the destroyer USS *Clifton Sprague*. Another SEAL squad, accompanied by USAF Combat Controllers, would join them after their own

95

sea jump. After that they would move to the airfield, check the runway's serviceability, remove any obstacles, place homing beacons, and await the US Rangers. But the operation began to go wrong from the start.

The SEAL Team 6 parachute jump was scheduled for dusk, but delays pushed it back a full six hours. This hazardous nighttime jump was then made even more dangerous by a wind gusting to 25 knots—well over the recommended 18-knot limit. Two teams of eight jumped, each carrying the maximum combat load of over 60 pounds. This was done without the benefit of a "dip test" to check for buoyancy. After hitting the sea, only five of the first eight men surfaced. Even though the surviving members had released their equipment as soon as their parachutes opened, they dived 60 feet below the surface when they hit the water. Then they could not find their Boston Whaler and had to bob in the sea in their life preservers until they were recovered by a launch from the *Clifton Sprague*. The other eight-man team did a little better. They lost only one man and found their Whaler.

After the rendezvous with the *Sprague*, they picked up the six-man SEAL–USAF team and set off, undermanned, for the Point Salines airfield. Having lost a vital six of their number, the SEALs were unable to fight their way through to the airfield and carry out their mission, despite two attempts.

SEAL Team 6's next objective was the radio station Radio Free Grenada. They took the radio station successfully, but then they came under fire from Soviet weaponry and were forced to retreat into the surf a mile offshore or be overrun. In the end, the radio station was destroyed in an air strike.

Their next task was to rescue the British governor-general, Sir Paul Scoon, and his staff who were being held hostage in Government House. However, the two TF 160

MH-160Ks helicopters transporting them could not find the governor-general's mansion, which was hidden by trees. While circling the area, the helicopters began to take hits. Ignoring the ground fire, they finally located the objective, but as they approached, they found the ground sloped too steep to land. The SEALs hot-roped to the ground, but the helicopters were forced to retreat before dropping the SEALs' equipment, which included a vital satellite radio.

The 22 SEALs on the ground quickly disarmed the police guard and released the 14 hostages. Then the former hostages and their rescuers had to shelter as Grenadian troops in Soviet BTR-60 armed personnel carriers lay siege to Government House. Without their satellite radio, the SEALs had no easy way to call in backup. Eventually they managed to establish communication with the task force command via a relay of short-range radios. After four hours, an AC-130 Spectre gunship arrived to lay down suppressing fire.

Delta Force was also involved in Operation Urgent Fury. Their primary objective was the liberation of civilians incarcerated at Richmond Hill prison, moving on to capture General Austin and his senior advisors at Fort Rupert. The rescue missions were aborted twice due to poor intelligence and interservice rivalry. But the Fort Rupert mission was a success. Then they were assigned to assist in the capture of the airfield at Point Salines.

At 0534 on October 25, the 1st and 2nd Ranger Battalions arrived in four-engine turboprop C-130 Hercules aircraft over Salines. To avoid the antiaircraft fire, the Rangers jumped from a very low altitude—just 500 feet. Nevertheless, machine-gun fire raked the aircraft and the Rangers, both in the air and on the ground. But US Air Force AC-130 Spectre gunships moved in to silence the hostile fire. Less than two hours after the first drop, the last unit was on the ground at a little after seven in the morning.

By early afternoon, the Point Salines airfield was secured from all but sporadic mortar and small-arms fire. Already the Rangers had moved on to evacuate American students at the True Blue campus of St. George's Medical Center, located at one end of the 10,000-foot runway the Cubans had been building. A second campus at Grand Anse was more than a mile away, and the route was blocked by retreating Cubans and units of the People's Revolutionary Army.

With the airfield secure, the Rangers began moving northward against PRA positions near St. George's, the island's capital. Other Rangers removed obstacles from the runway to allow 800 men of the 82nd Airborne Division to fly in with heavier weapons. Throughout the night, PRA positions were pummeled with gunfire from ships and aircraft. Then at first light on the second day, Marine armor and Navy attack aircraft supported the Rangers and the 82nd Airborne as they began their final assault on positions around St. George's. At 0712, they relieved the SEALs, taking shelter in Government House, and evacuated the governor-general and his staff.

With close air support from the carrier USS *Independence*, the Rangers joined the Marines attacking the heavily fortified positions at Fort Adolphus, Fort Matthew, and Richmond Hill Prison above St. George's, which had put up a torrent of antiaircraft fire that had brought down three helicopters. One of the heavily defended positions in the area later turned out to be a hospital.

Then the 82nd Airborne, with close air and naval gunfire support, moved against the Calivigny military barracks east of Point Salines. The assault completed the last major objective for the invasion forces. Afterward, the Rangers were airlifted out of Grenada. On November 2, hostilities were declared to be at an end.

During Operation Urgent Fury, 19 US servicemen lost their lives and 116 were wounded. The PRA lost 45 killed and 358 wounded, while the Cubans lost 25 killed, 59 wounded and 638 captured.

The Ranger battalions were so impressive in action that the Department of the Army announced in 1984 that it was activating another Ranger battalion and a Ranger regimental headquarters, increasing the size of the active-duty Ranger force to its highest level in 40 years. These new units—the 3rd Battalion, 75th Infantry (Ranger) and Headquarters and Headquarters Company, 75th Infantry (Ranger)—received their colors on October 3, 1984, at Fort Benning, Georgia. These color ceremonies took place at the same time as the first reunion of the Korean War–era Rangers, some of whom were still on active duty. These veterans, both current and retired, took their place alongside distinguished visitors to witness the inauguration of the new 75th Ranger Regiment.

Also on hand in Grenada were the 193rd Special Operations Group of the Air National Guard. They played a significant role in the psy-war with their new EC-130s that acted as an airborne radio station to keep the people of Grenada and US citizens on the island abreast of the US military action.

During the action, a 1st Special Operations Wing Combat Talon crew earned the Mackay Trophy, instituted in 1911 for the "most meritorious flight of the year," and a Spectre crew earned the Lieutenant General William H. Tunner Award, an Air Force prize for the most outstanding airlift crew.

CHAPTER 11

ACHILLE LAURO

ON OCTOBER 7, 1985, the Italian cruise liner SS *Achille Lauro* was hijacked in the Mediterranean by four Palestine Liberation Front terrorists, who demanded the release of 50 Palestinians being held in Israeli prisons. In all, 454 hostages were taken. Some 350 of them were crew members, mostly Italian; 670 passengers had disembarked at Alexandria, leaving just 104 on board. Fifteen of them were US citizens. Consequently, Special Operations were alerted.

At Fort Bragg, North Carolina, Major General Carl Stiner, head of the Joint Special Operations Command, mustered two platoons from the Navy's counterterrorism unit, SEAL Team 6, and Army commandos from Delta Force, and put them on transport aircraft bound for Europe. The ship had been on its way from Alexandria to Port Said when it was hijacked. But it may have changed course, and no one knew precisely where it was. However, it was clear that any rescue operation needed to be based in the eastern Mediterranean, and the British allowed the American team to use their base in Akrotiri on the island of Cyprus. The Italian government also sent 60 paratroopers, four helicopters, and experts on the ship's layout to Akrotiri. Together they made plans to storm the *Achille Lauro* and free the hostages.

On the morning of October 8, the hijackers began separating the hostages. Looking for Americans and Jews, they asked everyone to identify themselves. When no one responded, they took everyone's passport. Twelve Americans were pulled aside, along with six female British dancers who were on board to entertain the passengers. An elderly Austrian man who admitted to being Jewish was knocked to the floor and beaten repeatedly with a rifle butt. Then Leon Klinghoffer, a wheelchair-bound American Jew, was shot in the head and the chest, and thrown overboard.

Under the command of the hijackers, the *Achille Lauro* had been heading to Tartus in Syria, but she was refused permission to dock there. So she headed back to Port Said, where after two days of negotiations the hijackers agreed to surrender the liner in exchange for safe conduct to the airport and a flight to Tunisia. On October 10, they boarded an Egypt Air Boeing 737 at Port Said, escorted by men from Force 777, Egypt's counterterrorist unit.

However, President Reagan had ordered the Sixth Fleet into the Mediterranean. Four F-14 Tomcats from the USS *Saratoga* intercepted the terrorists' plane and redirected it to Sigonella Naval Air Station, a NATO base on Sicily. On the way, the pilots of the Tomcats noted two unidentified radar blips heading west. These were US Air Force C-141 Starlifter transports flying without lights or electronic identification. Unbeknownst to the Tomcat pilots, they were carrying General Stiner and his special-operations team.

Other Special Forces were already on the ground. As the 737 carrying the hijackers taxied to a halt, members of SEAL Team 6 drove out to the taxiway and surrounded the aircraft. Minutes later, the two Air Force transports landed and blocked the runway.

Stiner then called the Egyptian pilot on the radio and informed him that his plane was now in the custody of US Special Forces. The pilot told Stiner that an Egyptian ambassador who wanted to talk with him was on board. A ladder was then lowered from the forward door, and the pilot, Captain Ahmed Moneeb, came down, followed by Egyptian diplomat Zeid Imad Hamed. They were greeted by Captain Bob Gormly, commanding officer of the SEAL team. He examined Hamed's credentials, then escorted him into the base, where he allowed Hamed to phone Egypt's foreign minister.

Major General Stiner then boarded the plane with one of Gormly's officers. They found the four terrorists led by the notorious Abu Abbas, leader of the Palestine Liberation Front, which had made frequent attacks on Israel. Ozzuddin Badrakkan, chief of PLF military operations, was also on board. They were thought to have joined the terrorists at Port Said, and, along with the other terrorists, they were protected by 10 armed men from Egypt's Force 777. Although Stiner had orders to arrest the terrorists, he made no attempt to do so.

The plane was surrounded by 80 SEAL and Delta Force operatives. But they, in turn, were surrounded by 300 armed men from the Carabinieri, Italy's national police force. Italian trucks also blocked the runway. It was a standoff.

Stiner and Gormly informed the Pentagon of the situation. The White House then called the Italian government and told them that the US special-operations team intended to arrest the hijackers. However, the Italians argued that since the hijacking had taken place on Italian territory—the *Achille Lauro*, an Italian ship—and the hijackers were now on Italian soil, even though they regretted the death of an American, Italian law took precedence.

President Reagan then called Italian Prime Minister Betthino Craxi, but he would not back down. The president then informed the prime minister that the US would seek the extradition of the hijackers to face charges in American courts.

While this discussion was taking place, Stiner's special-operations team was eyeball-to-eyeball with 300 armed Italians.

"I am not worried about our situation," said Stiner. "We have the firepower to prevail. But I am concerned about the immaturity of the Italian troops....A backfire from a motorbike or a construction cart could precipitate a shooting incident that could lead to a lot of Italian casualties. And I don't believe that our beef is with our ally, the Italians, but rather with the terrorists."

It was then decided that, while the special-operations team could take the terrorists, they might not be able to get them out of Italy, and at 0400 the next day, Stiner's men were ordered to stand down.

The Italian base commander, Colonel Annicchiarico, then entered the plane with Hamed, the Egyptian diplomat, who explained to the men from Force 777 that the Egyptian government had agreed to hand the terrorists over to the Italians. However, Abbas and Badrakkan refused to leave the plane, claiming diplomatic rights. Then the Egyptians changed their minds and asked the Italians to allow the plane to leave with the hijackers on board. When the Italians refused, the Egyptians denied the *Achille Lauro* permission to sail from Port Said.

Eventually, the four hijackers were removed from the plane and taken to jail. The plane was then allowed to fly to

Rome with Abbas and Badrakkan on board. But Stiner was worried that, once airborne, the plane could fly anywhere—even back to Cairo. So he readied a T-39 Navy executive jet and put his best men on board. When the Egyptian 737 took off, the Italians denied the T-39 the use of the runway, so the jet took off from the runway alongside.

Reacting to this act of bravado, the Italians sent in jet fighters. According to Michael K. Bohn, a staffer of the National Security Council who was in the White House Situation Room at the time, "Pilots on board the US and Italian jets exchanged colorful epithets over the radio about their respective intentions, family heritage, and sexual preferences."

When the 737 approached Rome's Ciampino airport, Italian air-traffic controllers denied the Navy jet permission to land. But the pilot of the T-39 then claimed there was an "inflight emergency," which gave them the automatic right to land the US jet, and it touched down immediately after the Egyptian plane. Pulling alongside the 737 on the ramp, Stiner's men watched as Abbas and Badrakkan disembarked.

While attempts were made to extradite Abbas and Badrakkan, they escaped over the border to Yugoslavia. However, the Italian courts convicted Abbas of hijacking and sentenced him to five years in jail in absentia. Youssef Majed al-Molqi was sentenced to 30 years for the murder of Leon Klinghoff. The other two terrorists were also jailed and were paroled in 1991.

Badrakkan was also sentenced to imprisonment in absentia. Meanwhile, he continued his life of terrorism alongside Abu Abbas. However, Abbas eventually apologized for the hijacking and murder of Leon Klinghoff and spoke out in favor of peace talks between the Palestinians and Israel. He lived in Baghdad under the protection of Saddam Hussein.

After the American invasion of Iraq in 2003, he was captured by US forces while trying to flee to Syria. He died in US custody the following year and is buried in the Martyr's Cemetery in Damascus.

CHAPTER 12

OPERATION JUST CAUSE

IN DECEMBER 1989, Special Forces were to serve alongside conventional Army units in Operation Just Cause—the invasion of Panama. Despite support from the US, Panama's president, General Manuel Noriega, had also been taking money from drug traffickers. Several drug-related indictments were outstanding against him in US courts. Noriega was asked to stand down but refused. He then blatantly fixed an election. President George H. W. Bush asked him to abide by the will of the Panamanian people, to no avail. The US Ambassador then complained that Noriega's soldiers had shot and killed an unarmed American serviceman. Another had been wounded. A third had been arrested and badly beaten, while his wife was threatened with sexual abuse. These were the reasons President Bush gave for going to war.

Soldiers from the 7th Special Forces Group were already stationed in Panama. They were designated Task Force Black and supported the entire invasion by conducting surveillance and implementing blocking tactics. At H hour, the time the attack was to begin, Task Force Black secured a bridge over the Pacora River and engaged Panama Defense Forces in an intense firefight. Despite being outnumbered, they prevented the PDF from reaching the incoming US Rangers.

The entire Ranger regiment participated in Operation Just Cause. They spearheaded the action with two important operations. The 1st Battalion, reinforced by Company C, 3rd Battalion, and a regimental command and control team, made an early morning parachute assault onto Omar Torrijos International Airport and Tocumen Military Airfield, neutralizing the Panama Defense Force's 2nd Rifle Company and securing airfields for the arrival of the American 82nd Airborne Division.

The 2nd and 3rd Ranger battalions, along with a regimental command and control team, then conducted a parachute assault onto the airfield at Rio Hato to neutralize the Panamanian 6th and 10th Rifle Companies and seize General Noriega's beach house. Following the successful completion of these assaults, Rangers conducted follow-up operations in support of Joint Task Force South. In all, the Rangers captured 1,014 enemy prisoners of war and more than 18,000 arms of various types. In the action, the Rangers suffered 5 killed and 42 wounded, while the 7th Special Forces Group suffered no casualties.

The US Navy SEALs were also deployed in Operation Just Cause. Elements of SEAL Team 4 were tasked with cutting off General Noriega's possible escape routes as part of Task Force Bayonet. SEALs aboard two Navy PBRs and two Army landing craft closed the harbor at Colon, firing across the bows of any craft trying to leave. At H hour minus one hour and 15 minutes, four SEALs left Rodman Naval Air Station and swam toward the patrol boat *President Porras*, which was tied up at Balboa Harbor. They attached satchel charges. At H hour—0100—there was a loud explosion and the vessel sunk.

Meanwhile, the SEALs also made an assault on the airfield at Punta Paitilla, where Noreiga kept his Learjet. Swimmer scouts had already been sent ashore to reconnoiter the bay end of the airfield. However, having been notified that H hour had been moved up by 15 minutes, Lieutenant-Commander Toohey decided to move in with his men without waiting for the scouts' report. At about midnight, a US Navy patrol boat launched 15 Zodiacs, containing three 16-man platoons and a US Air Force combat command team to communicate with the AC-130 Spectre providing air support. Meeting with the scouts, the SEALs moved stealthily on their objective.

Toohey then received a report saying that a helicopter thought to be carrying Noriega had left Colon en route to the airfield. As they ran across the field, a detachment of SEALs ran into some Panamanians. Intelligence reports had warned them that there would be security guards at the airfield, and they ordered them to surrender. But the men they had run into were soldiers from the Panama Defense Force who had been dispatched to guard the Learjet after news of the invasion had leaked. With their first volley, the PDF brought down seven of the nine SEALs, killing one. In the minute-long firefight that ensued, more SEALs were wounded and three of those wounded were killed. Three PDF troopers were killed, and eight wounded had been carried off. It took nearly two hours to evacuate the SEALs due to heavy air traffic following H hour. However, during the action, a 40-mm grenade blasted a hole through the Learjet, rendering it useless.

A Delta Force team was assigned the task of capturing Noriega. They went into action in civilian clothes. Sporting

Heckler & Koch MP-5 9-mm machine pistols under their jackets, they searched the city and harbor for the disgraced dictator. On one occasion, an eight-man Delta Force team burst into a brothel where Noriega was purportedly hiding. Dashing upstairs, they caught a whiff of his characteristic cigars and found that the bed was still warm. They were told that he had left less than an hour before.

As a counterterrorist group, one of Delta Force's main functions is hostage rescue. During Operation Just Cause, Delta got their chance to practice their skills. Kurt Muse, an American businessman who operated an underground radio station had been jailed in the city of Modelo. A 160th Special Operations Aviation Regiment MH-6 Little Bird helicopter transported a Delta Force team to the rooftop of the jail. The team fought its way down to the second floor and blew the door to Muse's cell, freeing him without injury. As the team and Muse made their way back to the roof and the waiting MH-6, Kurt Muse counted at least five bodies and one terrified guard handcuffed to a staircase railing. As the Little Bird lifted off, the helicopter was hit by small-arms fire and fell into the street below. The pilot then slid the aircraft along the ground to a parking lot and attempted to take off again. The aircraft was hit by ground fire once more and hit the ground again, this time permanently. A passing UH-60 Sikorsky Black Hawk spotted the infrared spotlight held up by a Delta Force trooper, and soldiers from the 6th Infantry Regiment came to their rescue. Four Delta operators were wounded, but they had successfully rescued Kurt Muse and probably saved his life.

From the brothel, Manuel Noriega sought sanctuary in the embassy of the Papal Nuncio. US forces surrounded the building, but it would be a violation of international law to enter it. Psychological warfare units were brought in. They played "Welcome to the Jungle" by Guns and Roses and "I Fought the Law" by The Clash endlessly at high volume. But the pope complained to President Bush, who ordered the music stopped. Soon after, thousands of Panamanians turned up, demanding that Noriega stand trial for human rights violations. He surrendered on January 3, 1990. Detained as a prisoner of war, he was flown to the US, where he was tried on eight counts of drug trafficking, money laundering, and racketeering. Convicted, he was sentenced to 30 years.

However, Noriega's sentence was reduced to 17 years for good behavior in 2010. He was then extradited to France, where he was sentenced to a further seven years for money laundering. France has already announced its intention to extradite him to Panama, where he faces more charges, when his sentence is finished.

CHAPTER 13

SOMALIA

DURING THE 1980s, SOMALIA was torn apart by a civil war. The government was defeated, and President Mahammad Siad Barre was forced into exile while the country collapsed into anarchy with as many as 12 clans competing for control. In the midst of this, Americans and other foreign nationals sought refuge in the US Embassy. Then on January 1, 1991, the US Ambassador, James Keough Bishop, asked for military assistance to evacuate the embassy. The next day, Operation Eastern Exit began.

The US Navy sent the amphibious assault ship USS *Guam* and the transport USS *Trenton*, along with the 4th Marine Expeditionary Brigade. Meanwhile, the US Air Force sent an AC-130 Spectre gunship. Initially, the plan had been to evacuate the embassy though Mogadishu's international airport. But it soon became clear that not even Air Force planes could land there safely. Besides, it would not be possible to transport the evacuees safely through the war-torn land to the airport. So, despite the buildup to the First Gulf War that was going on at the time, Special Forces helicopters were put on the alert, and a nine-man US Navy SEAL team was brought in.

At 0247 on the morning of January 5, two CH-53E Super Stallions took off from the *Guam*, carrying a 60-man security force that included the SEAL team. On the 536-mile flight, the helicopters had to be refueled in the air twice: once just to get to the embassy compound and a second time before they set down so they would have enough fuel to start the return journey.

As the CH-53Es approached the compound, those on board could see 100 armed Somalis with ladders outside the walls. They scattered as the helicopters came in to land at 0710. Overhead, the special-operations Spectre gunship circled in case fire support was needed. The security force quickly disembarked. The SEALs moved out to protect the ambassador and the chancery, while the Marines secured the rest of the compound.

An hour later, the two CH-53Es took off carrying the first 61 evacuees. By this time, the compound was coming under small-arms fire, but the Marines did not shoot back. A convoy was sent out to rescue four American officials and some foreign nationals from the Office of Military Cooperation a few blocks away. Meanwhile, more foreign nationals seeking refuge arrived at the embassy.

The *Guam* and *Trenton* arrived off the coast at 0043 the following morning and sent in four waves of five CH-46 Sea Knights with pilots equipped with night-vision goggles. The first three carried out the civilians; the last withdrew the security force. In all, 281 people from 30 different countries were rescued. Five days later, they were landed in Muscat while the bloody civil war in Somalia continued.

Operation Eastern Exit had been carried off without a single casualty. However, Somalia was to go on to take many American lives. The following year, CIA Paramilitary Officer Larry Freedman with their Special Activities Division was killed on Operation Restore Hope, an attempt to bring food and humanitarian aid to the starving people of the benighted country.

As a Green Beret in Vietnam, Freedman had won two Bronze Stars and a Purple Heart. He served with Special Forces, officially and unofficially, in every conflict the US had been involved in since Vietnam. He had been at Desert One and, from 1986 to 1990, he helped train Delta Force. After that, he signed on with the CIA's counterterrorism unit. Then, forever searching out risky assignments, he volunteered for Operation Restore Hope.

Freedman always carried a Colt .45 with its grip customized to fit his hand. He had it retooled so the clip would feed faster—"tuned to combat," he called it. Ten days before he shipped out to Somalia, he bought a tactical scope for his .308 rifle, a 10-power scope built to click each time he adjusted his aim for distance. He had ordered it from specialty weapons maker Gale McMillan.

The day before Freedman left for Africa, he and McMillan had a long talk.

"Look in the mirror and see the silver in your temples," said McMillan. "That ought to tell you it's time to slow down and let the young guys take the risks and do the dirty work. You've already done everything expected of you."

Freedman laughed and said, "If there's any way I want to go, it's doing it."

He got his wish. He was inserted prior to the US invasion on a special reconnaissance mission. Near the town of Baardheere in southern Somalia, Freedman drove over a Russian-built mine. Death was instantaneous. His body was medevaced out to the USS *Tripoli*, where a medical officer filled out the death certificate. The blast had caused severe head trauma, blown off his lower right leg, and opened his chest. The three men with Freedman, all listed as "State Department Security Personnel," were also wounded. Freedman was awarded the Intelligence Star for "extraordinary heroism" and buried in Arlington National Cemetery, Virginia, though the exact nature of his mission was never disclosed.

The Green Berets and the US Air Force Special Operations Command, with their AC-130H Spectre gunships, were also deployed in Somalia during Operation Restore Hope and its successor Operation Continue Hope. But, in truth, there was no hope for Somalia. In January 1995, a United Nations peacekeeping force made up of some 2,500 troops from India and Bangladesh was to be withdrawn from Somalia. The withdrawal was to be safeguarded by a 4,000-man international task force in Operation United Shield. The operation would be American-led, and the task force would include the US Special Forces.

The Combined Task Force would arrive off Mogadishu on board USS *Belleau Wood* on February 7. Twenty days later, just before midnight, they made an amphibious assault on the beach there. In under five hours, 2,150 soldiers and their equipment were put ashore. The following day the withdrawal began. By March 3, 2,422 UN and 3,800 CTF troops had been withdrawn without loss of life.

CHAPTER 14

DESERT SHIELD AND DESERT STORM

On August 2, 1990, some 100,000 Iraqi troops, with six divisions of the elite Republican Guard, invaded neighboring Kuwait. The Kuwaiti forces were unable to repel the invaders, and within a few hours Saddam Hussein had achieved his object of seizing the small oil-rich state, which he considered to be a province of Iraq taken by the British after World War I. Possession of Kuwait would also greatly expand Iraq's short coastline. Meanwhile, Saddam Hussein and his henchmen began looting Kuwait of its considerable financial resources. Even the hospitals were stripped of medical equipment. When the United Nations Security Council passed a resolution demanding that Iraq withdraw, Saddam Hussein refused to comply. As the invasion posed a threat to Saudi Arabia, the world's largest oil exporter, which lay next door, the United States, its NATO allies, Egypt, Syria, and other Arab nations put together a coalition to expel Saddam Hussein from Kuwait. With a military buildup of 700,000 men, they began Operation Desert Shield.

This greatly annoyed one Osama bin Laden, who had returned to his native Saudi Arabia as a hero of the jihad against the Soviets in Afghanistan. It was said that he and his Arab legion had expelled the Red Army and had ultimately brought down the mighty superpower that had been the Soviet Union—though, in fact, his foreign fighters had made only a minor contribution to the struggle. With the Iraqi Army in Kuwait, bin Laden met the crown prince and offered his Arab fighters to King Fahd to defend Saudi Arabia. Instead, King Fahd had turned to the US and NATO. This meant that during Desert Shield, foreign, non-Muslim troops would be stationed on Saudi territory. Bin Laden was appalled. The presence of infidels, he argued, defiled the sacred soil of the "land of two mosques"—meaning, the holy cities of Mecca and Medina. His vocal criticism of the Saudi monarchy provoked government attempts to silence him, and he eventually fled to Sudan.

Meanwhile, Saddam Hussein continued to defy the United Nations, so the coalition launched Operation Desert Storm to kick the Iraqis out of Kuwait forcibly in what would become the First Gulf War. The coalition commander, General Norman Schwarzkopf, was an old-fashioned soldier who had little time for Special Forces. However, the commander of the British Forces, Lieutenant-General Sir Peter de la Billière, was a former commander of 22 SAS and tried to convince General Schwarzkopf that their special skills would be useful.

Two squadrons of the SAS were already in the Gulf and, by August 31, 1990, the headquarters unit of the 5th Special Forces Group from Fort Campbell, Kentucky, had moved to Saudi Arabia to support the Saudi Arabian forces. The 1st Battalion, lead by Lieutenant Colonel Jerry Thompson, fol-

lowed. By September 14, the 2nd Battalion[...]
ant Colonel "Ironman" Davis was in-country[...]
3rd Battalion under Lieutenant Colonel Mik[...]
Battalion was based on the east coast, near[...]
operated out of the King Fahad International[...]
plex, while the 2nd and 3rd Battalions were stationed at King
Khalid Military City.

As the buildup of British and American Special Forces in
Saudi Arabia continued apace, the possibility of their exten-
sive use behind enemy lines before the main ground forces
were ready for offensive action was raised. However, the US
high command seemed to have no task for them in the short
term except for a number of "penny packet" operations. This
was thought to be because General Schwarzkopf had formed a
poor impression of Special Forces during his time in Vietnam.

"At first Norman Schwarzkopf had opposed the idea
of deploying Special Forces behind enemy lines," said General de la Billière, "on the grounds that there was no task
that could not be carried out by the Allies' overwhelming air
power or, later, by the conventional armored forces."

Nevertheless, Special Forces began setting up their forward operating bases and arranging their living quarters and
their operational, communications, and support centers.
They needed firing ranges and maneuver areas to acclimatize
the troops and prepare them for combat. They had to develop
defense and evacuation plans for the base. This presented a
problem, as the King Khalid Military City was isolated and
there was a shortage of heavy weapons.

On October 13, 1990, Special Operations Team-A 505
under Captain Ken Takasaki was the first Special Forces unit
into action. They deployed along the Saudi–Kuwait border
with a Saudi Special Forces unit under Captain Prince Fahd,

graduate of the US Special Forces and Rangers course. They patrolled the border from the town of ArRuqi approximately 37 miles eastward, setting up bases in border forts called *mazekahs*. The rest of the border was patrolled by US Special Forces and coalition units using Humvees armed with Mark 19 machines guns and carrying night-vision devices and communications equipment. These units were the eyes and ears of the entire coalition force. The *mazekahs* also provided outposts where Iraqi deserters could surrender. Leaflets and loudspeakers were used to lure deserters over the border, where they were then interrogated, providing invaluable intelligence.

The 5th Special Forces Group continued their border missions until February 10, 1991, when they were replaced by Scouts and lead elements from regular units that were then in the theater. Even when Operation Desert Storm was underway, this border mission was no soft option. There were several firefights with the enemy and some close calls. On one occasion, Captain Dan Kepper's detachment was forced to make a quick exit from their *mazekad* and flee in their Humvee under intense ground fire. They managed to escape without loss of life, though their vehicle was damaged. However, even this hasty retreat provided valuable intelligence on the tactics employed by the Iraqis.

Special Forces played another vital role. They acted as liaison with the Arab members of the coalition. Every Arab unit that went into action had Special Forces troops with them. Thanks to their language skills, they were able to provide General Schwarzkopf with vital information about the coalition force's ability and willingness to fight. Stationed on the brigade and battalion boundaries between Egyptian, Syrian, and Saudi units, they played a valuable role in integrating units from different nations into a single force.

On January 13, airborne intelligence discovered that Iraqi forces were moving up to the border, and General Schwarzkopf ordered the US 1st Cavalry Division to move up to counter them. This meant moving through Syrian positions at night. The 2nd Battalion of the 5th Special Forces Group was called in to expedite their movement without the two coalition partners mistakenly coming to blows. Young American soldiers could easily have mistaken the Syrians for Iraqis, especially as they were both equipped with Soviet T-62 tanks.

Once Operation Desert Storm got underway, there were many other incidents in which units had to pass through the positions of different nations. Thanks to the Special Forces, not one incident of fratricide was reported.

Special Forces men also provided Arab troops with protective measures against the supposed threat from Saddam Hussein's chemical weapons and coordinated fire support and tactical operations. A Special Forces detachment was sent to the 35th Kuwaiti Armored Brigade to train them in mine clearing, Iraqi defensive tactics, aircraft and armored vehicle identification, and tank-killing techniques. When the Kuwaitis received Yugoslav M-84 main battle tanks, Special Forces troops taught them how to operate and maintain them and, as the Kuwaiti 35th Brigade led Joint Force Command north into their homeland, Special Forces soldiers went along as advisors.

The 2nd Battalion of the 5th Special Forces Group turned their three line companies into four companies to divide themselves between Egyptian and Syrian armored and commando divisions. In action, they claim to have been responsible for the capture of 8,700 Iraqi prisoners of war.

British Special Forces also found themselves a role, thanks to General de la Billière. When Saddam Hussein had invaded Kuwait in August 1990, D and G squadron of 22 SAS were on maneuvers in Oman, using their time there to perfect their desert-warfare skills.

"We had been operating in Oman with a batch of our new four-wheel-drive vehicles called Light Strike Vehicles—or LSVs—which were designed specifically for rough terrain," one SAS man recalled. "We had spent weeks putting them through a series of punishing tests. They were good, although their suspension could not survive a fall from a Chinook helicopter from an altitude of 100 meters, which we discovered when one was accidentally dropped. Still, there isn't much kit that can survive that kind of treatment. We were roughly acclimatized by the time we touched down in Saudi, though none of us was prepared for the piss-poor weather we would encounter later on operations."

Nevertheless, they were on hand to put their training to good use.

"So there we were," he said, "a motley crew with weapons walking across the tarmac to a group of waiting trucks. Around us, an army of multinational Air Force personnel worked feverishly on their aircraft. We didn't know what the high command had in store for us, so all we could do was train for any likely operation that might crop up."

No immediate role was seen for the SAS, as the Green Berets had already taken on the role of border reconnaissance. It was then proposed that the SAS join Delta Force in rescuing the hundreds of foreign nationals being held hostage as part of Saddam Hussein's "human shield." Thousands of citizens of the UK, US, and other foreign nations were being held around vital Iraqi military, government, and industrial targets, whose loss to allied air attack would have severely damaged Iraq's ability to wage war. By mid-November, Special Forces command had earmarked some men from the SAS, SBS, and an RAF Special Forces section to join US units for the evacuation raids, although no formal plan had been approved. Helicopter insertion and extraction and amphibious raids were all considered, but all had huge risks involved. In fact, any plan would have proved impractical because the hostages were spread out all over the country. Then suddenly, on December 6, 1990, Saddam Hussein released the hostages. It seemed that the SAS would no longer be needed. This increased their frustration.

"I myself was not prepared to recommend Special Forces unless two conditions were fulfilled," said General de la Billière. "One was that there must be a real, worthwhile role for the SAS to perform, and the other was that we must have means of extricating our men in an emergency."

Nevertheless, more men were brought in. After being on standby for months, men from A and B Squadrons of the SAS arrived in the Gulf shortly after Christmas 1990. It was the largest deployment of the regiment since World War II.

"By late December 1990, the majority of the regiment had been deployed in the Gulf, including some blokes from R Squadron, the reserve," said one man who was there. "However, because no specific role had been assigned to us, patience began to wear a little thin."

By mid-January 1991, General de la Billière had persuaded General Schwarzkopf that the SAS could be effective in creating diversions ahead of the main attack, destroying Iraqi communications facilities, and tracking down the mobile

Scud missile launchers which so far had eluded both satellite reconnaissance and air strikes.

Heavily armed desert fighting columns were formed. These were to infiltrate Iraqi territory to carry out search-and-destroy missions. By destroying just about anything they could find, they aimed to force the Iraqis to deploy large forces to track them down. Each squadron was divided into two fighting columns, and they underwent intensive training in the United Arab Emirates. Each column consisted of between 8 and 12 type 110 Land Rovers, armed with a Browning .50 caliber heavy machine gun, GPMGs, American Mark 19 40-mm grenade launchers, and Milan antitank missiles. They would carry some 30 men and be flanked by motorcycle outriders. With them would be a Mercedes short-wheelbase Unimog open truck that was used as the mother ship. It carried the bulk of the supplies, fuel, ammunition, NBC equipment, and spare parts. There were four columns in total—two drawn from A Squadron and two from D Squadron. These columns would go into action at night, laying up in the day to avoid detection. All the SAS columns stayed inside Iraq for the full duration of the war and would operate under the control of the Special Operations Command of Central Command (SOCCENT), which was an Allied organization coordinated by the US.

Just before dawn on January 17, eight Apache attack helicopters destroyed the Iraqi air-defense radars, creating safe corridors in which Allied aircraft could fly. The coalition Air Forces then targeted the Iraqi command and control infrastructure. Iraq, completely unprepared for such an attack, suffered substantial damage to its infrastructure and a devastating blow to its morale. Desperate to retaliate, Saddam

Hussein turned his Scuds on Israel and launched 12 missiles into the suburbs of Tel Aviv.

The missiles carried conventional warheads. However, the idea that the next batch might carry chemical or biological agents caused widespread panic. Israel threatened to invade Iraq and destroy the Scud sites. It also threatened to respond with a nuclear strike on Baghdad if Iraq used unconventional warheads. For United Nations commanders, this posed a nightmare situation. If Israel became involved in the war, it would cause a massive split between the Western members of the coalition and their Arab allies. The whole war plan would be destroyed—something Saddam Hussein was acutely aware of.

The SAS was immediately ordered to find and destroy the mobile Scud launchers, and set about their task using road watch patrols and mobile fighting columns. Eight-man SAS patrols were dropped by helicopter far behind enemy lines. One of the first patrols wanted to survey their surroundings and requested that the helicopter that had carried them into Iraq wait on landing. They decided that the flat terrain offered too little cover, making it dangerous to continue their mission, and they returned to the waiting helicopter.

A second patrol did not ask their helicopter to wait but again, surveying the surroundings, concluded that it was too risky to stay there and decided to drive back to the Saudi border in the vehicle they had with them. But before they departed, they requested an air strike on a nearby mobile radar station. The US A-10 aircraft that had been called in mistook them for the target. However, realizing his mistake at the last moment, the pilot managed to pull away and went on to destroy the designated target instead.

Other teams were more successful. They set up static observation posts to survey the main supply routes for the movement of Scud launchers, then called in air strikes to destroy them. As a result, Israel put on hold its threat to retaliate.

The area the SAS was working in was suffering its most severe winter weather on record, and the SAS men were ill-prepared for the conditions they faced. Standard-issue desert kit gave them little protection from the snow, sleet, rain, and freezing nighttime temperatures. The men developed frostbite and hypothermia.

The desert units were resupplied by a temporary formation known as E Squadron. This was a resupply convoy, comprising ten Bedford four-ton trucks and a heavily armed SAS Land Rover escort that met up with the fighting columns at a rendezvous point some 86 miles inside Iraq. The convoy left Saudi Arabia on February 10 and reached the RV at 1500 on the 12th. This was a huge operation. Behind enemy lines, more than 390 NCOs attended a mess meeting called by the regimental sergeant major. The vehicles were serviced or repaired, and prisoners were handed over. The supply convoy then returned to Saudi Arabia, reaching base on February 17.

There was no amphibious role to assign to the SBS, but they were determined to get involved anyway. A line was drawn down the middle of Iraq. The SAS's area of operation was to the west and the SBS's was to the east. Besides searching for mobile Scud launchers, the SBS had a special mission to perform. Their sector contained a mass of buried fiber-optic cable that provided the Iraqi high command with intelligence and frontline reports. The location of the main junction was just 32 miles from Baghdad.

On January 22, with barely time for their usual workup, 36 SBS men embarked on two Chinook helicopters from

No. 7 Squadron's Special Forces flight and flew into Iraq where they were joined by US Special Forces. The team was heavily armed and carried 400 pounds of explosives. They were venturing into an area full of nomads and desert spies, close to Iraqi air and ground forces. As the helicopters landed, they disengaged their rotors but kept their engines for a quick escape.

The SBS men quickly found the communications cables. Digging down, they pulled out a length to take back, then placed explosives along the exposed area. When the charge was detonated, it took out a 40-yard section of the cable. In an operation that took just 90 minutes, the SBS had destroyed what was left of the Iraqi communications grid while suffering no casualties. The lieutenant leading the team grabbed one of the cable route markers and presented it to General Schwarzkopf on their return. According to an after-action report, this was "a totally successful operation in that the infiltration and exfiltration was perfect and no enemy activity was encountered."

The most famous SAS patrol of the First Gulf War had the call sign Bravo Two Zero. On the evening of January 22, 1991, eight SAS men, loaded with equipment and supplies for an extended stay, were flown into Iraq by Chinook. Besides hunting down Scuds, their task was to observe the main westerly supply route and sever underground communications cables that ran between Baghdad and Jordan. Once on the ground, the patrol traveled some 12 miles from the landing zone. After finding shelter in a small cave, they discovered that their radio was not working. Soon after, they made contact with the enemy. After vicious firefight, the patrol was forced to withdraw and headed for the Syrian border some 75 miles to the west. On the way, the patrol suffered hypothermia and injury, and the men became separated. As a result, three died, one escaped, and the four who were captured endured weeks of beating and dreadful torture. However, at the end of the war, they were released with the other POWs and returned to the regiment. The patrol was immortalized by two books: *Bravo Two Zero*, written by its sergeant-commander under the alias Andy McNab, and *The One That Got Away* by Chris Ryan, the patrol member who reached the Syrian border.

Other SAS units were not so unlucky. They engaged targets of opportunity and used laser designators to mark targets for air strikes, ensuring pinpoint accuracy. By the end of the war, they had helped take out numerous communications facilities and, it is estimated, destroy about one-third of Iraq's Scud launchers.

General Schwarzkopf also sent US Special Operations teams deep into Iraq to look for Scuds once the air war started as a backup to British Special Forces who were providing intelligence and briefings on the conditions there. These missions were extremely dangerous as the entire country was an armored camp, and even areas that looked empty on the map turned out to be heavily patrolled by Iraqi units sent out to capture downed coalition pilots. As the war progressed, US and UK Special Forces formed into fighting groups that constantly harassed the enemy and tied up large numbers of Iraqi soldiers who otherwise would have been available to face the main forces as they came across the border.

While the 2nd Battalion of the 5th Special Forces Group moved forward with their Egyptian and Arab units, the battalion's main headquarters stayed behind in King Khalid Military City to collate incoming intelligence. During the Allied offensive, the Special Forces detachment also coordinated close-area support. The entire Arab force was dependent on US air cover, and they needed English speakers to call in air strikes.

Two Special Forces medical sergeants performed a combat amputation on an Egyptian soldier while under intense indirect fire. Another Special Forces soldier crawled into a minefield to drag wounded Egyptian soldiers to safety under artillery fire. One Special Forces Battalion Commander, with two of his officers, made a close-quarters battle assault on an Iraqi command post, clearing the position. They later received awards for their valor.

Ahead of the main force there were Special Forces on reconnaissance missions hundreds of miles deep into Iraq. These teams, supported by the XVIII Airborne Corps and the VII Corps, were placed near the highways to report any attempt by Republican Guard reserves to counterattack or retreat. Special Reconnaissance units had been in training for this task since early October 1990 in flat areas outside the cities in Saudi Arabia that resembled Iraq. The teams worked on their patrolling techniques, immediate-action drills, and reconnaissance procedures. The construction of hide sites was a primary concern. Due to the barren terrain the teams would be operating in, they would have to rely on ground observation posts dug rapidly during the hours of darkness. Problems soon became obvious. Where would they put the dirt and sand they had excavated? What could they cover the hide sight with once it was almost finished? What materials best camouflaged the viewing ports? But as they conducted mock infiltrations and rehearsals, these problems were gradually solved, team by team.

Special Reconnaissance teams also infiltrated by helicopter on Scud hunts in areas where they were hundreds of miles from friendly forces and surrounded by enemy troops.

They were ferried in on the MH-60s and MH-47s of the 3rd Battalion of the Special Operations Aviation Regiment. Their pilots were old hands at special-operations flying. They came in 20 feet off the desert floor at 140 knots in the dead of night and dropped the teams at isolated landing zones. Beforehand they had pored over dozens of aerial reconnaissance photographs, looking for power lines, towns, and areas where dogs and camels might alert their owners.

After they had been set down, the teams had the problem of finding somewhere to hide as daylight approached. In some places there was no vegetation, hills, or small folds in the ground for miles. The ground was usually hard, covered with just a dusting of sand. But where the ground was softer, along the Euphrates River, for example, there were other problems. Soft ground and water meant agriculture, and teams deployed there found themselves surrounded by inquisitive farmers.

On February 23, the day before the ground attack, eight more Special Forces teams flew into Iraq. They were unable to find hide sites in the barren terrain. Some were extracted. Others were captured. One MH-47 delivered two Special Forces A-teams. One radioed for immediate extraction. The area where they had landed was completely featureless and nothing like the terrain they had prepared for. The others hung on for three days, communicating via satellite.

Also on February 23, three soldiers from Detachment A-532 of the 1st Battalion under Master Sergeant Jeffery Sims were dropped off by an MH-60 from the 160th SOAR, which crossed the border at 2100. They landed at 2200 at a position north of the Euphrates River less than 100 miles from Baghdad. The rest of the detachment would also infiltrate to a position 15 miles to the south. They would have less than five hours to prepare their hide sites. Unfortunately, the helicopter landed in a plowed field with furrows almost three feet deep, and their boots sank into the loose earth. They were greeted by the sound of barking dogs, though it seemed to alert no human interest. There was less than eight hours to go before the XVIII Airborne Corps and the VII Corps would cross the border.

By first light, Master Sergeant Sims and his men had hiked to their hide sites and dug in. On their way, a 50-car railroad train had rolled close by their position, a fact that they communicated by satellite directly to the XVIII Airborne.

When the sun came up, the local people awoke. Farmers and sheep herders began walking around near the hide site. No one had expected so much foot traffic. One shepherd walked within a foot of the hide's peephole but took no notice and walked on. They had another close scrape when another sheep herder with a dog came dangerously close.

Then around 1400, their luck got worse. A small girl and a man who appeared to be her grandfather stopped in their tracks, staring in the direction of the hide site. The old man edged closer. Then the girl bolted toward the hide site. Slowly lifting the lid, she stared wide-eyed at the Green Berets inside. The three-men aimed their 9-mm pistols, fitted with silencers, at the little girl's head, and the old man began screaming. But the team had already been compromised. Shooting two civilians would serve no purpose, especially as one of them was a little girl.

Other shepherds were close by, and the old man started yelling, "The Americans are here! The Americans are here!"

The Green Berets let the girl and the old man go and radioed for extraction. Then they ran to a ditch some 500 meters away, where they intended to make a stand. Within 30 minutes, Iraqi troops began arriving by truck along the highway. The team then began firing at the enemy soldiers, knocking them down one by one. Their rifles were set on single shot to preserve precious ammunition.

Then two busloads of troops arrived while armed civilians began moving around their flanks. Several village men stood on an old masonry wall surrounding a stone house nearby, waving their hands to indicate Sims's position. The Green Berets picked one of them off. Soldiers and villagers were now creeping up the irrigation ditches. The team hit several of them and they retreated. More buses carrying soldiers arrived. It was plain that the Green Berets could not hold them off forever.

An hour and a half after they had been discovered, an F-16 Eagle roared overhead, and at Sims's direction, the plane dropped cluster bombs and 1,000-pounders into ditches just 300 yards from Sims's position. Then an MH-60 flown by Chief Warrant Officer Randy Stephens and Chief Warrant Officer John Crisufulli arrived, having crossed 240 nautical miles in broad daylight. Under an intense barrage of small-arms fire, Sims and his men dashed for the helicopter and got on without injury. The MH-60 whisked them back to Saudi. It was the only hot extraction in daylight carried out during Desert Storm.

Another Special Reconnaissance mission was led by Chief Warrant Officer Chad Balwanz, commander of Detachment A-525. His eight-man team was inserted on a tributary of the Euphrates River. Their mission was to monitor traffic along Highway 8 from Baghdad to An-Nasiriyah. After infiltration they dug to hide sites. But by morning the area was swamped by civilians, including throngs of small children playing nearby. At one point these children found themselves right on top the hide sites and, meeting the Green Berets eye-to-eye, screamed and fled. The team had plainly been compromised.

They relocated to a new position and, at nightfall, planned to move farther south and establish another temporary hide site. For two hours, they carried out surveillance on the road. Then the children returned. Adults followed. Some were carrying weapons. After them came Iraqi soldiers. Four large trucks came screeching down the road. More Iraqi soldiers poured out. Balwanz counted more than 100. He and his eight-man team managed to pick off some 40 enemy soldiers in the next 10 minutes. Then a US Air Force F-16 came into the attack. Soon Balwanz was directing air strikes dangerously close to his own position. Nevertheless they held out and, at 2000, an MH-60 of the 160th SOAR managed to pull them out. Not one member of Balwanz's team was killed or wounded.

Between them, Master Sergeant Sims's Detachment A-532 and Chief Warrant Officer Balwanz's Detachment A-525 accounted for an estimated 250 to 300 enemy dead and wounded.

Other special reconnaissance missions were not so dramatic. All the other teams infiltrated without any fuss, dug their hides and counted vehicles and soldiers. It was tedious work, and they remained undiscovered.

US Special Forces also conducted few direct action missions during Desert Storm. Most were of a sensitive nature, and details remain classified. General Schwarzkopf took a dim view of the Special Forces sneaking into enemy territory before the air war started and rejected many proposed operations after the bombing started. The main objective of the few direct action missions that were launched involved disrupting enemy communications.

One direct action Special Forces mission followed a request by the two Army Corps for soil samples so they could assess the capacity of the area to carry heavy traffic. The CIA had warned General Schwarzkopf's generals that the tanks and trucks they wanted to send across Southern Iraq for the "Hail Mary play" might become bogged down in the sandy terrain.

General Schwarzkopf recognized that he was short of detailed intelligence on the weather and terrain in the region and allowed six-man Special Forces teams to be helicoptered covertly into Iraq to scoop up soil samples for analysis in Riyadh. The teams also carried camcorders and digital cameras that transmitted photographs back to headquarters. The soil samples showed that the ground was firm enough for tanks, and the pictures gave commanders a close-up view of their intended battlefields.

US Special Forces were also tasked with search-and-rescue missions to recover downed pilots. The 2nd Battalion of the 5th Special Forces Group took it upon themselves to train for this role in September and October, and took over combat search and rescue (CSAR) from the US Air Force, which did not have a tangible and effective program.

As aircraft were needed for CSAR, Special Forces again called on the 160th SOAR for assistance since their MH-60 Black Hawks and MH-47 Chinooks were equipped for deep insertions. They began training together, developing new tactics and maneuvers. Their plan was to infiltrate a rescue team and a Humvee up to 200 miles behind enemy lines with the MH-47 setting down while the vehicle made the recovery.

Special Forces teams established a good rapport with the pilots of the 160th SOAR as they spent long hours practicing rescuing downed airmen. They sawed down stretchers to fit on the MH-60s and procured communications devices for the Special Forces security teams.

When the air war began, CSAR units positioned themselves in forward operating bases. On February 17, a US F-16 suffered engine failure 40 miles behind enemy lines and crashed. At 1815, the Airborne Warning and Control System (AWACS) aircraft in charge of the operation put out the call. Within minutes, two modified MH-60 Black Hawks from the 3-160th SOAR were in the air. They were equipped with night-vision devices and carried security teams from the 2nd Battalion of the 5th Special Forces Group armed with AT-4 handheld rocket launchers and M16/203 assault rifles. By 2000, Chief Warrant Officer Thomas Montgomery located the pilot as enemy vehicles were closing in on him. Montgomery called AWACS for support. He then went and picked up the pilot, Air Force Academy football star Captain "Spike" Thomas. As they made their escape, Iraqis fired surface-to-air missiles at the retreating helicopter, but on-board jamming devices and emergency evasive action left the missiles far behind. Minutes later, an F-16 was on station to take out the enemy vehicles. This was the only CSAR mission conducted at night using night-vision guidance.

The Special Forces did not have to carry out as many CSAR missions as they expected. It had been predicted that 40 aircraft would be lost on the first night of the air war. In fact, only three were downed. The entire coalition only lost 52 planes during the entire war. Twenty-two pilots and crew survived their shoot-downs. Of those, 14 were captured immediately, while 8 evaded capture—2 for more than 24 hours. Of the seven CSAR missions launched, only three were successful. Nevertheless, knowing that the Special Forces were on hand to ride to the rescue boosted the morale of the aircrew.

US Special Forces also played a key role in liberating Kuwait City. The plan was for the US Marines to hold their position on the outskirts while a vanguard of Kuwaitis, Syrians, Egyptians, and other Arab forces drove into the capital. This meant that the only American troops into the city in the first wave were the Green Berets attached to the Arab units. One of the Special Forces' responsibilities was to see that the Kuwaitis did not retaliate against Iraqi prisoners for the atrocities that had been committed during the occupation. The coalition did not want any atrocities of its own on its hands.

As the Allies entered the city, the Special Forces expanded their role beyond merely "advising" the Arab forces. With the help of Kuwaiti resistance fighters who had remained in the city during the occupation, Special Forces troops began clearing areas of booby traps and mines. Members of the resistance also guided Special Forces teams to key Iraqi headquarters building and torture facilities, where they collected five truckloads of documents indicating violations of the Geneva Conventions.

With Special Forces teams accompanying Arab units, who certainly overstepped the mark when it came to retaliation, the Special Forces came under criticism by the international press who had then arrived. As a result, they were withdrawn from the Arab units, but not before the Special Forces helped the Egyptians secure their embassy. US Special Forces also retook the US Embassy in Kuwait City.

The SBS were chosen by General de la Billière to reclaim the British Embassy in Kuwait. On February 27, 1991, they flew into Kuwait and set up a temporary base at the Kuwait Airport. The SBS worked on the assumption that the embassy buildings might be booby-trapped or even harbor a suicide squad of Iraqi troops. They went in the next day. As two Chinooks hovered over the embassy, the SBS team fast-roped down to the roof. They threw stun grenades through the windows and blew down the famous front door designed by the well-known architect Edwin Lutyens.

At a press conference at the end of the war, General Schwarzkopf singled out Special Forces for special praise. This surprised his staff, as he was known not to be a fan. As it was, he had left half of the Special Forces commands back in the US. At the beginning of the war, he had also doubted the usefulness of the SAS. Now he thanked them personally.

"What you've done is never going to be made public, and we can't make it public," he said solemnly. Then he had added, "You kept Israel out of the war."

General Schwarzkopf conveyed more fulsome praise privately in a letter dated March 9, 1991, 10 days after the cease-fire. It was written on the headed notepaper of the "Office of the Commander-in-Chief Operation Desert Storm, United States Central Command, APO New York 09852-0006" and marked "SECRET." It was addressed to "Sir Patrick Hine, Air Chief Marshal, Joint Headquarters, Royal Air Force Wycombe, Buckinghamshire HP14 4U" and was sent "Thru: Sir Peter de la Billière KCB, CBE, DSO, MC, Lieutenant-General, British Forces Commander Middle East, Riyadh, Saudi Arabia." It read:

Subject: Letter of Commendation for the 22nd Special Air Service (SAS) Regiment

1. I wish to officially commend the 22nd Special Air Service (SAS) Regiment for their totally outstanding performance of military operations during Operation Desert Storm.

2. Shortly after the initiation of the strategic air campaign, it became apparent that the Coalition Forces would be unable to eliminate Iraq's firing of Scud missiles on Israel.

The continued firing of Scud on Israel carried with it enormous unfavorable political ramifications and could, in fact, have resulted in the dismantling of the carefully crafted coalition. Such a dismantling would have adversely affected in ways difficult to measure the ultimate outcome of the military campaign. It became apparent that the only way the Coalition could succeed in reducing these Scud launches was by physically placing military forces on the ground in the vicinity of the western launch sites. At that time, the majority of available Coalition forces were committed to the forthcoming military campaign in the eastern portion of the theatre of operations.

Further, none of these forces possessed the requisite skills and abilities required to conduct such a dangerous operation. The only force deemed qualified for this critical mission was the 22nd Special Air Service (SAS) Regiment.

3. From the first day they were assigned their missions until the last day of the conflict, the performance of the 22nd Special Air Service (SAS) Regiment was courageous and highly professional. The area in which they were committed proved to contain far more numerous enemy forces than had been predicted by every intelligence estimate, the terrain was much more dif-

ficult than expected, and the weather conditions were unseasonably brutal. Despite these hazards, in a very short period of time the 22nd Special Air Service (SAS) Regiment was successful in totally denying the central corridor of western Iraq to Iraqi Scud units. The result was that the principal areas used by the Iraqis to fire Scuds on Tel Aviv were no longer available to them. They were required to move their Scud missile firing forces to the northwest portion of Iraq, and from that position the firing of Scuds was essentially militarily ineffective.

4. When it became necessary to introduce United States Special Operations Forces into the area to attempt to close down the northwest Scud areas, the 22nd Special Air Service (SAS) Regiment provided invaluable assistance to the US forces. They took every possible measure to ensure the US forces were thoroughly briefed and were able to profit from the valuable lessons that had been learned by earlier SAS deployments into western Iraq. I am completely convinced that had the US forces not received these thorough indoctrinations by SAS personnel, US forces would have suffered a much higher rate of casualties than was ultimately the case. Further, the SAS and US joint forces immediately merged into a combined fighting force where the synergetic effect of these fine units ultimately caused the enemy to be convinced that they were facing forces in western Iraq that were more than tenfold the size of those they were actually facing. As a result, large num-

bers of enemy forces that might otherwise have been deployed in the eastern theatre were tied down in western Iraq.

5. The performance of the 22nd Special Air Service (SAS) Regiment during Operation Desert Storm was in the highest traditions of the professional military service and in keeping with the proud history and tradition that has been established by that regiment.

Please ensure that this commendation receives appropriate attention and is passed on to the unit and its members.

Signed:
H. Norman Schwarzkopf
General, US Army
Commander-in-Chief

CHAPTER 15

BLACK HAWK DOWN

IN OCTOBER 1993, 40 DELTA FORCE joined elements of the 75th Ranger Regiment and the 160th Special Operations Aviation Regiment (Airborne)—aka "The Night Stalkers"—to form Task Force Ranger. Their job was to capture Somali warlord Mohammed Farrah Aidid. On October 3, intelligence indicated that Aidid was meeting with his aides in a building near the Olympic Hotel in downtown Mogadishu. The plan was that the Delta Force would attack the target building using MH-6 Little Bird helicopters and round up the wanted men, while the Rangers would fast-rope down from UH-60 Sikorsky Black Hawk helicopters and establish a perimeter around the building. Then a convoy of 12 Humvees and trucks would drive the three miles from the Rangers' base near the beach and pick up the assault team and their captives. The entire operation was supposed to take no more than 30 minutes.

But things went wrong from the beginning. The ground-extraction convoy that was supposed to arrive at the target building minutes after the operation began was delayed by barricades of burning tires blocking the streets. Then, while fast-roping from the helicopter, 18-year-old Ranger Private

Todd Blackburn fell 70 feet and lay unconscious and bleeding from the mouth, nose, and ears on the street below. It was too late to abort the mission, as the Delta Force commandos had already leaped from their Little Birds and were storming the house where the meeting was being held.

A medic quickly attended to Private Blackburn, while 26-year-old Staff Sergeant Matt Eversmann mustered the rest of his 12-man squad, designated Chalk Four. Bullets were already flying, and they took cover behind two parked cars. Eversmann tried to call the Ranger commander, Captain Mike Steel, who had roped in with Chalk One, to get Blackburn medevaced out. But a bullet had severed his radioman's antenna.

By this time, armed insurgents were pouring into the streets. More barricades were being erected, and Somalis were setting fire to tires to summon the militias. Men were firing at them, but the Rangers were loathe to return fire because the gunmen surrounded themselves with women and children.

Eversmann had already noted that they had landed 100 meters from where they should be. Getting back in position with a wounded man under intense fire would be an impossible task. If Blackburn did not reach a hospital soon, he was going to die.

One of the Humvees, carrying more Delta soldiers and Navy SEALs, managed to get through to join the assault force, which had, by then, stormed the house and arrested 24 Somalis. Aidid had left minutes before, but they had taken two important clan leaders. As the Humvee approached the house, one of the men on board, SEAL John Gay, was shot in the thigh, but the bullet hit his combat knife, shattering it. Delta medic Master Sergeant Tim "Grizz" Martin picked out bits of the shattered blade before the limping Gay took cover and began returning fire.

Spotting the Humvee arriving, Chalk Four's Sergeant Casey Joyce ran down the road after it. He jumped in and explained they had a wounded man. The Humvee then raced back to pick up Blackburn and take him back to base, joining an escort of two other armed Humvees on the way. As they rammed though the barricades blocking the streets, they kept up a constant blaze of fire with their 50-caliber roof machine guns and M-60s. On the way, one of the gunners, Sergeant Dominick Pilla, was shot in the head and killed.

Chalk Four were still 100 meters from their designated position at the northwest corner of the target block. Worse, two of Eversmann's men, Sergeant Jim Telscher and Sergeant Scott Galentine, were trapped behind cars across the street under heavy fire. As they returned fire, hundreds of Somalis bore down on them. Then Galentine was hit, a bullet almost severing his left thumb. He grabbed the thumb, pushed it back in position and ran across the road under withering fire before lapsing into shock.

Chalk Four was now under fire from RPGs as well as AK-47s. A huge mob of armed Somalis approached. But at that moment, a Black Hawk flew over and raked the insurgents with its minigun. The Somalis stopped firing, but not for long. Private Anton Berendsen was hit in the arm but continued firing his M203 barrel-mounted grenade launcher one-handed.

Two men from Chalk One, Sergeant Aaron Williamson and Sergeant Mike Goodale, were also taking cover behind a car when a bullet severed the end of Williamson's finger. The next time the militiaman came out to fire, Goodale took him out. Another militiaman was shot down as he fled. By then the Rangers had abandoned their rules of engagement, which said they could only fire at someone who was actually pointing a gun at them.

First Lieutenant Larry Perino was taking cover across the alley when children walked up the street and pointed out his position. He threw a flash-bang at them so they would scatter. When that did not work, he fired his M-16 at their feet. Then a woman approached the position where Staff Sergeant Chuck Eliot had set up his M-60. Eliot called out to Perino, saying that he could see that there was a man behind her with his gun tucked under her arm. Perino gave Eliot permission to fire, and the man and woman fell dead.

Chalk Two was at the northeast corner of the target block, where Specialist Shawn Nelson had set up his M-60. He could see a number of Somalis taking aim at the southwest corner of the target block where Chalk Three had fast-roped in. A burst from his "pig" sent them scattering. But one old man with white hair continued walking toward him. As he walked, he put a new magazine into his AK-47. Nelson put a dozen bullets in him. One went right through him, chipping the wall behind. Although the murderous burst of bullets knocked the old man off his feet, he got up, retrieved his gun and kept on coming. Another burst knocked him down again, and he crawled behind a tree. He did not return fire, but still he was not dead, so Nelson fired another burst into him. He had never realized how hard it was to kill a man.

Nelson saw the barrel of another AK-47 poking between the legs of two women who were kneeling in the dust. The rest of the gunman was completely covered by four children who were sitting on him. Nelson threw a flash-bang. The women, children, and gunman fled so fast that the gun was left behind.

Taking cover from a hail of bullets, Staff Sergeant Ed Yurek ran into a tin shed which, he found, was filled with terrified children. The shed was an improvised schoolhouse. Yurek calmed the kids' teacher and got them all to lie flat on the floor. Then he got Chalk Two's medic to guard the door in case anyone mistook the occupants for combatants before moving on.

A cow appeared in the street with an armed man riding on its back. Another eight men were hidden behind it. The Rangers began firing. Then a Black Hawk came over, its minigun turning the cow into mincemeat.

Crowds began closing in. Not all of them were armed, but the Rangers found they had no choice but to fire on them. They were only dispersed when a Little Bird swooped in, firing. Then Black Hawk *Super 61* flew over. It was piloted by Chief Warrant Officer Cliff "Elvis" Wolcott, a veteran of the First Gulf War who had flown missions behind enemy lines in Desert Storm, taking out Scud missile sites.

In the alley below, a Somali militiaman with an RPG dropped to one knee and fired upward, hitting a Black Hawk as it flew overhead. The grenade hit the tail, cracking it. Wolcott and his copilot, Donovan "Bull" Briley, could not hold it. The helicopter began to spin, hit the roof of a house, flipped over, and crashed into the alley. The two pilots were killed and the two crew chiefs badly wounded.

On the radio, the call went out: "Black Hawk Down."

An 18-year-old youth who lived in the house, now partially destroyed, managed to get the rest of his family out. He then hid under a car in case he was mistaken for a militiaman. Other Somalis began running toward the wreckage. Fearing for the safety of any survivors, Nelson fired a burst from his M-60 at them, then ran toward the stricken helicopter himself. The commander of Chalk 2, First Lieutenant Tom DiTomasso, ordered half his men to stay in position to maintain the perimeter, while he and the other eight headed off after Nelson.

Chief Warrant Officer Keith Jones, pilot of Little Bird *Star 41*, also headed toward the downed Black Hawk, guided by Chief Warrant Officer Mike Goffena in Black Hawk *Super 62* hovering above. The Little Birds were small enough to land in the narrow streets of Mogadishu, and Jones put *Star 41* down next to the smoking wreckage. But before they could attend to any survivors from *Super 61*, Jones and his copilot, Chief Warrant Officer Karl Maier, had to hold off the Somalis with handguns.

Delta Force sniper Sergeant Jim Smith clambered out of the wreckage dragging his injured Delta buddy, Staff Sergeant Daniel Busch, with him. As he propped Busch against a wall, Busch was shot again in the stomach, and Smith got a bullet in the shoulder.

As Jones and Smith dragged Busch back to *Star 41*, DiTomasso and his men arrived. Nelson put a couple of bullets in the wounded Somali, while DiTomasso threw a perimeter around the wreckage. It was clear to Jones that Busch needed immediate medical attention. Smith was also badly wounded. Now that they were safely on board Star 41, he decided to pull out before they got caught on the ground in the crossfire.

Black Hawk pilot Chief Warrant Officer Mike Durant and his copilot, Chief Warrant Officer Ray Frank, also with the 160th SOAR, were circling over the scrubland to the north of the city in *Super 64* as an airborne reserve when they heard Super 61 had gone down. They were then called to take over *Super 61's* position, while another Black Hawk fast-roped a rescue team into battle zone.

On the ground, Yousuf Dahir Mo'Alim and his band of 26 bandits—know as *dai-dai*, or "quick quick," for the jumpy nerves chewing *khat* gave them—began to close in on the downed helicopter. They were essentially mercenaries who would fight for any side that paid. But they fought Americans for free, calling themselves "revengers."

They heard the rotors of *Super 64* beating overhead. Then came the bullets. A 40-year-old bandit they called "Alcohol" fell dead. Another bandit knelt and aimed his RPG at the helicopter. He pulled the trigger. There was an explosion high above as the grenade hit the helicopter's gearbox. Oil sprayed out.

Mike Goffena on *Super 62* had seen the RPG hit and alerted Durant by radio. Durant checked the crew and his instruments. From where he sat, everything looked okay. Lieutenant Colonel Tom Matthews, the air mission commander, had also seen the impact from the command and control helicopter circling above and told Durant to put his bird on the ground.

As *Super 64* turned for home, Goffena decided to follow. But as he turned, he saw *Super 64*'s gearbox tear itself to pieces, taking part of the tail fin with it. The nose dipped, and the helicopter began to spin. With the tail rotor out of action, there was nothing Durant could do to stop it. As Frank cut the engines, Durant shouted to the crew that they were going down hard.

At the last moment, the nose lifted, the spin slowed, and the helicopter came down flat. Inside, the four crewmen, though shaken, were alive—for now. *Super 64* had not hit one of Mogadishu's stone houses, like *Super 61* had. It had landed on a patch of flimsy tin huts that cushioned its fall. However, the downed helicopter was in bandit country more than a mile away from where the Rangers and Delta Force were slugging it out on the ground. The airborne rescue team had already gone to the aid of *Super 61*, so the crew of *Super 64* were on their own.

Somali militiamen were already on their way to the new crash site. Mike Goffena could see them from above. The gunners opened up as Goffena took the helicopter in low so the wash from the rotors would force the Somalis back. He depended on the three Delta Force snipers on board to take out anyone with an RPG before he could loose off a grenade. Even so, *Super 62* was taking a lot of small-arms fire. Other helicopter gunships came to help. But what Durant and his men needed was help on the ground—and fast.

So it was Delta Force to the rescue. Goffena took *Super 62* to five feet, and two of the Delta snipers jumped to the ground. Master Sergeant Gary Gordon and Sergeant Randy Shughart were both veterans in their mid-30s. They reckoned that, with accurate and concerted fire, they could hold off a disorganized rabble of militiamen. A crew chief then popped a smoke marker on the downed Black Hawk, and the two Delta Force men made for it.

When *Super 64* hit the ground, Durant had been knocked unconscious. When he came to, he found he had broken his thigh. Frank had a broken leg. Crewman Staff Sergeant Bill Cleveland was bleeding and delirious. Sergeant Tommy Field was also a stretcher case. There had been no one in the hut they had landed on, but a two-year-old girl in the next hut had been hit in the forehead by a piece of flying metal and lay unconscious and bleeding, while her mother had been badly scalded on the legs and face by hot engine oil.

Durant, a veteran of the First Gulf War and the invasion of Panama, cleared the debris from his broken windshield and grabbed his short-barreled Heckler & Koch MP-5K. Frank clambered out of the doorway. It was the last Durant would see of him. Then Gordon and Shughart turned up. They pulled Durant out of the wreckage and propped him up against a tree. The Delta Force men then went to help Fields. By then the Somali militia had arrived. Durant loosed off a few shots to keep them back, but his gun kept jamming.

Jones and Maier had also come to the rescue. They had set *Star 41* down nearby, while Goffena continued to circle above. He could see that there was no way the injured crewmen from *Super 64* were going to make it to *Star 41* without a large ground force in place. By then Little Bird was running low on gas, so Jones and Maier reluctantly asked permission to head off and refuel.

Gordon and Shughart set up a perimeter as best they could and held the crowd back with automatic fire. Many fell dead. Assessing the situation, Mo'Alim mustered his men to make a coordinated attack.

The end came quickly. Gordon was hit. Durant only realized this when Shughart handed him Gordon's loaded CAR-15, a shortened version of the M-16. Then Shughart clambered into the stricken helicopter to get more weapons and make a distress call. In reply, he was told that a rapid reaction force would be there soon. As the Somalis closed in, Durant picked them off. On the other side of the helicopter he could hear Shughart firing. There was a final burst, then silence.

Over the radio, Durant heard those overhead saying that indigenous people were closing in. Then the sound of the radio was overwhelmed by the roar of the mob. Durant was now out of ammunition, except for in the pistol strapped to his side. He did not even reach for it.

As the crowd closed in, they hacked the Americans' bodies to pieces. Finding Durant still alive, they beat him with their fists and sticks. They tore his clothes off and carried him away in triumph above the heads of the crowd. While they continued beating him, they did so less brutally. Durant realized that they wanted him kept alive, perhaps for propaganda purposes or exchange. Eventually, Mo'Alim shoved Durant in a car, and he was taken to see the warlord whose intended capture had started this fiasco—Mohammed Aidid.

Eventually, a nine-vehicle extraction convoy turned up to evacuate the Delta Force assault ream and the 24 prisoners they had taken from the target house. That done, they were to move on to the downed *Super 61* and pick up the survivors. After that, they were to make their way to Durant's crash site. To find their way through the narrow streets, they would be guided by Delta Colonel Gary L. "Shooter" Harrell in the command helicopter circling above.

On the ground, the convoy was taking heavy punishment. An RPG hit one of the five-tons, disabling it, and wounding Staff Sergeant Dave Wilson in the legs. Private Clay Othic, gunner on the rear Humvee, was hit in the arm. Sergeant Bob Gallagher was also hit in the arm and Sergeant Bill Powell in the leg. There were now not enough vehicles to carry all the Rangers and Delta men back to base.

Even with guidance from above, the convoy still got lost. They came upon Sergeant Eversmann and Chalk Four, who had been pinned down since the operation began. Aiming to consolidate at the crash site of *Super 61*, they hitched a ride. But this was no easy option. Along the way the convoy was shot at from every alleyway, window, and rooftop.

In one alleyway, they saw a woman in a purple robe. The driver of the second truck pulled a pistol.

"Don't shoot!" cried Specialist Eric Spalding. "She's got a kid."

When she turned, they could see that she had a baby in one arm. But in the other hand she had a gun. Spalding shot her. It took four rounds to down her. Spalding could only hope that he had not hit the baby.

Now hopelessly lost, the convoy kept stopping to try to get its bearings. This left the vehicles behind halted dangerously exposed at intersections. At each stop, men jumped out to provide security, leaving them vulnerable to gunfire, and frequent U-turns took the convoy back across the same field of fire they had just traversed. One RPG went through the side of a vehicle and exploded, blowing the men out of the back. The five-ton truck behind ran over them. The transports were filling up with wounded.

Things became even more confused when a second convoy set out for the crash site of *Super 64*, who were also given directions from the aircraft above. Instructions became confused. Eventually, as the sun set, there was no choice. The first convoy left off looking for the crash site of *Super 61* and headed back toward base. Along the way, they ran a series of murderous ambushes at almost every intersection.

The second convoy was also pummeled with RPGs and raked with small-arms fire. Avoiding the worst of the ambushes, it took a circuitous route, eventually running into the first convoy, which was loaded with dead and wounded Rangers and Delta Force men. After torching one of the damaged Humvees, the two convoys headed back to base together.

As the search-and-rescue team fast-roped down to the crash site of *Super 61*, the last man out, Sergeant Tim Wilkinson, had noticed that they had left behind their vital medical kits. He had to wait until the other men were safely on the ground and clear before he threw them down, then fast-roped down himself. This delayed the departure of the helicopter by crucial seconds. It was enough time for a Somali militiaman to take aim and hit the Black Hawk with an RPG.

With Wilson and Master Sergeant Scott Fales hanging on the ropes below him, pilot Chief Warrant Officer Dan Jollata held the Black Hawk steady. He could hear the rotors whistling above him where the blades had been holed by shrapnel. His training taught him to move away as soon as he was hit, but he continued to hover a few seconds more to allow Wilkinson and Fales to get safely to the ground. Once they were on terra firma, he pulled away and limped back to base, where he landed heavily but safely.

As soon as Wilkinson hit the ground, he heard bullets snapping around him. Grabbing the medical bags, he ran around the corner to the downed helicopter. Delta Force and the Rangers had already set up a tight perimeter. Several Somalis lay dead. He saw Ranger Sergeant Alan Barton shoot two Somalis—a man with an M16 and a woman—as they rounded a corner. Barton calmly picked up the man's rifle and clicked a new magazine into it.

Fales was already at the downed helicopter, peering inside to check for survivors, when he was shot in the leg. The bullet had passed right through the calf muscle, but the bone was not broken. He took cover and dressed the wound himself.

At the front of the helicopter, Delta soldier Sergeant James McMahon, who had survived the crash with bad facial injuries, was pulling out the body of copilot Donovan "Bull" Briley. Wilkinson lent a hand. They carried his body to a hastily established collection point.

McMahon then climbed into the cockpit to check on Wolcott. It was clear that he was dead. His body was trapped, and

McMahon was unable to extricate him. Meanwhile Wilkinson tended to an injured crew chief, then checked inside the main cargo area. He could see no one. His next job was to remove or destroy weapons and sensitive equipment or paper. Then, under the pile of debris he found the left gunner, Staff Sergeant Ray Dowdy. He was disoriented but alive. With the help of Delta medic Sergeant Bob Mabry, he was freed.

The insurgents were closing in with a blizzard of gunfire. Wilkinson was hit in the face and arm, Mabry in the hand, and Dowdy lost the tops of two fingers. They took shelter under bulletproof Kevlar floor paneling and began burrowing out of the other side of the helicopter. Once they had gotten Dowdy out, Wilkinson returned to the job of destroying sensitive equipment, while Mabry took the Kevlar panels to shelter the position under the tail where Fales had set up a makeshift casualty station. But nowhere was safe. Bullets came at the casualty station from all directions and, with a pressure dressing on his leg and an IV in his arm, Fales returned fire as best he could.

In the midst of this mayhem, there was humor. Wilkinson recalled the scene in *The Jerk* when Steve Martin finds oil cans being shot at all around him. Wilkinson said, "They hate the cans! Stay away from the cans!"—Martin's line from the movie. Despite their perilous situation, Wilkinson and Fales cracked up.

Once the ground convoy with their prisoners had left the target house, Staff Sergeant Ed Yurek and his half-dozen Rangers at the northeast corner of the perimeter had to move from cover and braved Somali fire to make their way to the crash site of Super 61. Guns appeared around every corner and out of every window. Miraculously, the small party caught up with the rest of Chalk Two without casualty.

But Yurek found himself pinned down behind a Volkswagen with Lieutenant DiTomasso as heavy-caliber rounds sliced through the vehicle. Yurek was carrying a light antitank weapon. He aimed it at the big gun on a tripod up the street, but the antitank round fell short, and the gun resumed firing soon after. Next he fired an M203 grenade from the grenade launcher on his M16. This time his aim was better. The two insurgents firing the gun lay dead, but the gun itself was not put out of action. No one else came to man it, but it remained a danger.

At the crash site, a fierce firefight was underway. They tried to clean away the Somali gunmen with grenades. But one of the Rangers forgot to take off the safety strap when he threw his grenade. A Somali threw the grenade back, badly injuring 22-year-old Specialist Rob Philips, the youngest of the search-and-rescue team.

As the Delta men and the Rangers pulled back to the crash site of *Super 61*, the Ranger formations began to break down, with some of the Rangers preferring to stay with the more experienced Delta Force. Communications also broke down and, at one point, they even exchanged friendly fire.

After an RPG hit the wall near Sergeant Paul Howe's Delta team, peppering them with shrapnel, Howe kicked in the door of a Somali house to take cover. Casualties mounted. The Rangers under Captain Mike Steele were also taking casualties. He had little idea of where most of his 60 men were. The rest of Rangers and Delta men also got themselves off the streets and took cover in the courtyards and houses around the crash site, handcuffing the occupants. There was no sign of the ground convoy that was supposed to extract them. The situation looked grave. They were now fighting for their very survival.

Sergeant Howe felt that the Rangers did not realize the hole they were in. They were not aggressive enough. He was also angry at the Army's new 5.56 green-tip ammunition. It was furnished with a tungsten carbide point that could penetrate steel. But that also meant it would pass right through flesh, doing little real damage. If the first shot did not hit the target in the head or the spine, it would take five or six rounds to bring a man down.

By this time, just 90 minutes into the mission, 8 of the 13 men in Lieutenant Perino's Chalk One were injured. Several men needed urgent hospitalization. Captain Steele called for medevac. The reply from command was that the area was too hot and they could not risk losing another helicopter.

As dusk fell, men ran out into the streets to drag the wounded to cover. Although they were in a concentrated area, the courtyards and houses they occupied were separate, and they had little idea where the others were. It was clear now that the ground convoy was not coming, and with darkness falling, they would have few of the normal advantages. As they had been sent on a daylight mission, the men had not brought their night-vision devices with them. Some had come without their canteens, figuring that they could do without water for an hour. After a hard day's fighting, they were also running low on ammunition.

Although they had taken cover inside buildings, they were still being hit with small-arms fire and RPGs. Casualties continued to mount. They could fight back, inflicting casualties on the enemy, but there was no escape. Orders came that they should consolidate their position, with the Rangers moving up to join Delta Force. But the Rangers refused to go out on the streets carrying the wounded through withering crossfire. This caused more friction between Delta Force and the Rangers. Captain Scott Miller, head of Delta Force on the ground, then ordered those of his men who were taking cover with Captain Steele's Rangers to move up and join him. They tried. But when the four D-boys ran out of the door, there was a huge explosion of fire, and within seconds they were back inside again.

To improve their cramped position, the Rangers blew a hole in the wall to get into the next house. A woman in an orange robe appeared. She started screaming, attracting more gunfire. One of the Delta Force men shot her.

Lieutenant Perino had two men desperately injured. He begged for a medevac. But a helicopter that had dropped fresh ammunition and medical supplies had been badly shot up and had barely made it out. Delta Force's Lieutenant Colonel Harrell, who was observing the situation from a Black Hawk above, asked for a quick-reaction force. But the ground convoys had been shot up, too. Now Aidid's men had dug trenches and erected burning barricades, cutting all roads that led to the crash site where the remains of the assault force were trapped.

One of the seriously wounded men was Corporal Jamie Smith, who had been shot in the groin. Perino was taking turns with medic Kurt Schmid to put pressure on his severed femoral artery. They could feel Smith's life ebbing away. Not long after being told that no helicopter would be coming, Perino radioed Steele, telling him that the medevac was no longer necessary. Smith was dead.

Although two ground convoys had failed, a third was now assembled. It would be a massive armored column with 28 Malaysian armored personnel carriers and four Pakistani tanks from the UN peacekeeping force, along with those Humvees and flatbed trucks that were still serviceable after the last foray into the city. The convoy's commander, Lieutenant Colonel Bill David, mustered the 150 men of C Company of the 10th Mountain Division's Quick Reaction Force. A platoon of Rangers volunteered, along with the rest of Delta Force.

At the last moment, the Pakistani commander received orders that he was not to lead the convoy. However, he agreed to let his tanks escort the convoy for the first few miles. But as the two-mile-long convoy headed into the city, it was attacked from all sides and returned thousands of rounds. The men under cover around the crash site saw the sky light up. Suddenly, there was hope.

Again the convoy took a wrong turn, then it was brought to a halt when the lead APC was put out of action by an RPG. The men who leaped out to provide security suffered more casualties, some fatal. The convoy got underway again, but it was soon halted once more when the Malaysian driver of the lead vehicle refused to plow through a barricade that he feared was mined. He did not respond even to the threats of the D-boys, who eventually had to dismantle the barricade by hand under heavy fire.

The security force had to fire into a crowd to keep the Somalis back. Under concentrated fire from a building that overlooked them, they soon had more dead.

Painfully slowly, the convoy edged its way toward the crash site. The men there could hear them coming. But it was not until 0200 the following morning that they got the word to ready themselves. In the meantime, they were to stay away from the doors and windows. Finally the column arrived and the Rangers identified themselves.

The 10th Mountain Division tried to extricate Wolcott's body from the wreck of the downed Black Hawk. But the cockpit was lined with Kevlar, and they saw they had made little impression. Eventually, they had to physically tear the body out.

The wounded were loaded into the APC and the dead laid on the roof. But there was not enough room in the APCs to carry all the men. Those who were still ambulatory had to run back down the convoy to get a ride. One man was badly injured on the way.

The convoy then returned to the soccer stadium that served as the Pakistani headquarters. A field hospital had been set up there. Helicopters marked with red crosses then ferried the most badly injured to the main hospital.

Some of the dead had been left behind at the crash site. Their bodies were dragged through the streets. Eventually they were returned in a terrible condition. One had its head severed. After 11 days in captivity, Michael Durant was returned alive, along with a captured Nigerian soldier.

Six members of Delta Force were dead, along with six Rangers and five men of the 160th Special Operations Aviation Regiment. Two men from the 10th Mountain Division were also killed. Three Malaysians were dead, one captured. He was released after nine hours. Two Pakistanis were wounded. Aidid claimed that only 315 Somalis died, some 133 of whom were members of his militia.

The following March, US forces pulled out of Somalia, followed by the rest of the UN troops. The story of the mission later became the basis of the 2001 movie *Black Hawk Down*.

BATTLE OF QALA-I-JANGI

FOLLOWING THE ATTACK ON THE UNITED STATES on September 11, 2001, the Taliban government in Afghanistan refused to hand over Osama bin Laden and other the al-Qaeda terrorists responsible. Consequently, it was necessary for the US and its allies to go in there and get them. The action would be led by the Special Operations Command, which would help the Northern Alliance—a group of dissident warlords in northeastern Afghanistan—oust the Taliban regime from power. The US Special Forces operation would be spearheaded by Task Force Dagger. They would be joined by Britain's SAS and SBS.

On the night of October 19, Delta Force and the SAS flew into Afghanistan from Task Force Dagger's base in Uzbekistan and attacked a house owned by Mullah Mohammed Omar, the Taliban leader who had refused to hand over Osama bin Laden. The only daughter of Mullah Omar's tenth wife was married to bin Laden. According to Pulitzer Prize–winning journalist Seymour Hersh, writing an article in the *New Yorker* magazine, the operation was a "total goat fuck." Mullah Omar was nowhere to be seen. Members of his family were killed. Twenty or more Delta Force men were wounded. The SAS also took casualties. One man lost a foot and at least three more were seriously wounded.

The tactics then changed. Instead of making raids from outside, it was decided that Special Forces needed a secure base in-country. The SBS were sent. Instead of making a HALO insertion the manner of Delta Force and the SAS, they simply landed on the runway at Bagram in their C-130 and took over the air base. This did not please the Northern Alliance. The British had tried to take over Afghanistan three times before—in 1839–1842, 1878–1880, and 1919. So the Afghans demanded that the British leave the air base immediately.

During the night, the Americans had presented the Northern Alliance with an ultimatum.

"The Brits are our allies," the US commander said. "They are part of the equation. They're here to stay."

Either the Northern Alliance let the British stay in Bagram or the British and Americans would stop their air strikes against their enemy, the AQT, al-Qaeda–Taliban. This would leave the anti-AQT troops without close air support. The Northern Alliance backed down, but to sweeten the deal the US sent Delta Force into Bagram to make an ostentatious show of taking over the air base from the British. Meanwhile, the SBS went on to conduct operations with the US Navy SEALs in the Naka Valley.

Then on November 23, an eight-man SBS team was deployed by Chinook to Mazar-e-Sharif. The fourth largest city in Afghanistan, it had fallen to the Northern Alliance under General Rashid Dostum, with the help of US Special Forces. After the city had surrendered, there had been a massacre of approximately 520 suspected Taliban supporters.

For diplomatic reasons, the SBS went into Mazar-e-Sharif in plain clothes and driving Land Rovers painted arctic white, as if they belonged to the UN—even though they had general-purpose machine guns mounted on them. Reporting to the US military headquarters housed in a schoolhouse closed down by the Taliban, they were seconded into the US quick-reaction force.

Their first task was to observe the surrender of 600 Taliban to General Dostrum out to the east of the city. It was a sensitive operation, so the SBS men wore jeans and T-shirts and hid their faces behind shemags. Heading out on the road to Kondoz, which was still under siege by the Northern Alliance, they stopped at a fortified mound that housed a Northern Alliance checkpoint around a mile from where the surrender was going to take place. They were not to go any closer, as General Dostrum feared that the Taliban might change their minds about surrendering if they saw British and American observers there.

Through binoculars, they could see tense negotiations going on between the Taliban and Northern Alliance soldiers. After several hours, the Taliban began handing over their rifles, machine guns and RPGs, but they were not searched to see if they were carrying any other concealed weapons. A US Special Forces officer explained that this was not deemed necessary. The Afghans took each other at their word. If, as a good Muslim, a Taliban soldier said he had no concealed weapon, that was good enough. It was the Afghan way.

The 600 Taliban were to have been held at the airport, along with other detainees. But US units were now flying military missions out of the airport and were, understandably, reluctant to have the place teeming with the enemy. Instead, the prisoners were to be held in the old fort of Qala-i-Jangi—which means "The House of War"—eight miles to the west. It was a hexagonal building, 500 feet from end to end, with towers at each corner. Its sloping ramparts rose 60 feet above the desert. On top of them, a mud wall rose another 10 feet with battlements along the top. It was an impressive sight.

The joint US–UK quick-reaction force waited at the checkpoint to see a truck laden with surrendered arms—Kalashnikovs, heavy machine guns, and rocket launchers—drive by. The surrendered weapons were headed for General Dostrum's armories at headquarters in Qala-i-Jangi. They were followed by truckloads of prisoners.

The following day, carrying only sidearms, the quick-reaction force was sent out on a bodyguard mission to protect a US Navy admiral who was flying in to inspect a hospital that had been damaged in an air strike. On their way back to Mazar-e-Sharif, they heard the sound of gunfire from the direction of Qala-i-Jangi. It seems that the Taliban prisoners had had concealed weapons with them. They overpowered their guards, stormed the armories and re-armed their comrades. Two CIA men had been in the fort at the time, interrogating the prisoners, and were thought to be hiding somewhere within the labyrinthine fortifications.

The US contingent went back to Mazar-e-Sharif to arm themselves. But as their presence in Mazar-e-Sharif was supposed to be discrete, the SBS team had only brought their Diemaco assault rifles and 9-mm Sig Sauer pistols. They loaded up with 15 30-round 5.56-mm magazines for the Diemacos and 3 magazines each for their pistols, giving each man a total of 500 rounds. They had no grenades, machine guns, or heavy weapons. Nine 5.56-mm magazines were hung on their webbing. The rest slung in a grab bag with the pistol magazines, a knife, a flashlight, night-vision goggles, field dressings, a 24-hour ration pack, and water. They also carried a communications kit and laser target designators in case they had to call in an air strike.

The briefing was sketchy. The Taliban, it was known, were now well armed. The two CIA men had been at the southern end of the fort when they had been attacked. One of them, Dave Tyson, had made a call on a satellite phone, but he did not know what had happened to his colleague, Johnny Michael Spann. After that the satellite phone went down. Although they could no longer communicate with him, it was presumed that the man who had called, at least, was still alive, so the initial operation was primarily a rescue mission. Once the CIA men were rescued, the next priority would be to contain the enemy and stop the prisoners from breaking out. However, the quick-reaction force numbered just 21—hardly enough to take a fort.

The good news was that some other CIA men and Northern Alliance soldiers still held the entranceway to the fort. The bad news was that they could not expect any reinforcements. At the time, Task Force Dagger's Delta Force contingent and the rest of the Northern Alliance were still fully committed in the battle for Kondoz.

The quick-reaction force was also going into action without proper intelligence. The SBS did not like this. It was not their way of doing things, but lives were at stake. The odds were not good either. There were 13 US Special Forces operatives, 8 SBS men, a handful of CIA agents, and some 50 to 100 Northern Alliance soldiers against 600 Taliban holed up in a seemingly impregnable fort. While the SBS men had no heavy weapons apart from the general-purpose machine guns on their Land Rovers, and US Special Forces were little better equipped, the Taliban were armed to the teeth. The consensus was that they were on a suicide mission.

It was 1305 when the quick-reaction force left Mazar-e-Sharif, giving them just six hours of daylight. As they approached the fort at Qala-i-Jangi, they could see tracer and the occasional trail of an RPG. From half a mile away, they could hear explosions and the crump of mortars. Battle was raging all over the ancient fort. When they left the paved road and took to the track leading up to the entrance to the fort, large 80-mm mortar rounds began slamming into the ground around them. The SBS white Land Rovers made an easy target. One hit and it would all over. The drivers gunned the engine and began weaving. Minutes later the two Land Rovers, followed by the US Special Forces Humvees, slammed to a halt under the shelter of the 40-foot arch of the entranceway to the fort. Their vehicles were full of bullet and shrapnel holes, but amazingly no one had been hit.

They were greeted by a CIA man who gave them a quick briefing on what he knew about the situation, shouting to make himself heard above the noise of battle. The CIA man did not know which parts of the fort were still in friendly hands, apart from the entranceway and the tower above it. However, this offered a good view over both the fort's north and south compounds. The prisoners had been held in the south part of the fort, although the fighting had originally broken out in the north. There may have been some beleaguered North Alliance men holding out in small enclaves, but it was impossible to communicate with them as they had no radios. The CIA also had no long-range communications with them at the fort and had been returning to the US military center in Mazar-e-Sharif each evening to file their reports.

By then, the uprising had been going on for some 18 hours. It had begun when one of the Taliban prisoners had grabbed a senior officer of the Northern Alliance and pulled the pin on a grenade, killing both of them and injuring a number of other Northern Alliance men. Northern Alliance soldiers had then herded the prisoners into the dungeons beneath the fort but, in their haste, had once more forgotten to search them. Later, another suicidal Taliban pulled the same trick with a grenade. The following morning, while Mike Spann and Dave Tyson were interviewing John Walker Lindh, an American who had been with the Taliban, all hell broke loose in the dungeons. Spann had headed for the entrance to the dungeon, shooting wildly in an effort to quell the riot. When he ran out of ammunition, he was brought down by a crowd of escaping prisoners and beaten savagely by the mob. It was thought he had died, but no one could be sure. Tyson loosed off a few shots. With the help of the National Alliance soldiers, members of the International Red Cross there to oversee the fair treatment of the prisoners, he managed to escape. Tyson had raised the alarm. He had found refuge in General Dostum's headquarters at the north end of the fort. As he was not certain what had happened to Spann, he urged headquarters not to send in an air strike. Then the batteries in his satellite phone ran out, and the line went dead.

Key to holding the fort was the eastern tower above the entranceway. From there they could cover both the northern and southern compounds. The SBS were tasked with securing it. They rushed up the stairs to find the top of the tower held by half a dozen National Alliance men who were pleased to get some help, though they were a little bemused by the fact that the SBS men were in T-shirts and jeans rather than proper uniforms. The SBS joined in a furious firefight with the enemy below and quickly proved their worth. The prisoners from the south compound had broken through into the north compound and were heading for General Dostum's headquarters. They had to be stopped. From there, they would be in position to dominate the fort. This, too, was Tyson's last known position, and the quick-reaction force's primary mission was to find the CIA men.

The men on the tower began firing on the escaped prisoners, who were heading for Dostum's HQ. The SBS, like all Special Forces men, fired off two shots at a time, making every round count. The Northern Alliance men, like regular infantrymen, fired in long bursts. Too long. This allowed the enemy time to take aim. One Northern Alliance man fell dead with a bullet through his forehead. Another fell back with a bullet through his right shoulder.

The SBS team leader tended the wounded man. But with two casualties, they were now having trouble stopping the Taliban from reaching Dostum's HQ. What they needed was more firepower. Two SBS men ran down to the Land Rovers and unbolted their GPMGs. Then they hauled the two guns and a crate of ammunition up the tower. Meanwhile, the US Special Forces captain arranged an air strike.

As the SBS got the GPMGs to the top of the tower, a second wave of Taliban broke through into the north compound and made for General Dostum's HQ. The machine guns mowed them down. The intense volleys of fire the enemy returned chipped away at the baked-mud battlements, robbing the defenders of essential cover. Soon there would be nowhere to hide on the top of the tower. But if they had to abandon the tower, the battle was lost.

The Taliban had taken cover behind three Toyota pickups and were well protected. The SBS men had no grenade launchers or antitank weapons to take them out. Instead they aimed the GPMGs at the trucks' fuel tanks. One burst into flames and they exploded. For a moment, the enemy fell silent. Then the fighting began again with renewed vigor.

Despite the intense firefight, the SBS team leader kept his eyes peeled and spotted a Taliban fighter with his Kalashnikov slung over his back, attempting to scale the tower with a wooden ladder. He squeezed off a shot with his Diemaco sending the climber tumbling to the ground. A second man started the climb, followed by a third. Both were dispatched the same way. Then he put a couple of rounds into the ladder's upright, smashing it in two and putting it out of action.

While the SBS held the tower, US Special Forces mounted a rescue mission intent on General Dostum's HQ—Tyson's last known position. This would entail a dash across the north compound, where they would be exposed to enemy fire. But like Special Forces, the CIA made it a point of honor not to leave their men behind. Even if Spann and Tyson were dead, their bodies would have to be recovered. It would be a risky mission, but an SBS man and his oppo, or opposite number, a SEAL seconded into the regiment, volunteered to go with them, and some Northern Alliance men came too.

The rescue mission was more dangerous than they imagined. Just as their dash across the north compound had begun, mortar rounds began falling. They threw themselves to the ground. When they got up again and resumed their flight, a National Alliance fighter put a foot down wrong and was blown into the air with one leg shredded.

They had run into a minefield. Everyone froze. But standing still was not an option. Mortars began walking toward them again. Mindful of where they were falling, they hurled themselves to the ground. Then they got lucky. A couple of mortars that had zeroed on their position sunk into the soft earth and failed to explode. But this was merely a fluke. Stuck out in the middle of the compound, they were sitting ducks.

There was nothing for it. The SEAL jumped to his feet and ran toward General Dostum's HQ. The others steeled themselves and ran after him. Somehow they all made it to the comparative safety of a doorway. After catching their breath, they started scaling the wall with Taliban bullets pinging around them. When they reached the top, two RPGs smashed into the wall below them, injuring two Northern Alliance men and sending them tumbling to the ground. The SBS man and his fellow SEAL quickly returned fire, killing the men who had fired the RPGs.

Close air support was now on its way. Two of the SBS men on the tower crawled forward under intense RPG and mortar fire with their laser target designators. They illuminated the gateway the Taliban were using to get into the north compound and the pink building they were coming from. Then the team leader radioed through the target coordinates to the pilot. Following American procedure, they also supplied their own "friendly" coordinates. This was against SBS SOPs—standard operating procedures—but without providing them, the US Special Forces men explained, there would be no air strike.

As they were dangerously close to the target, the SBS man asked the pilot not to use their 2,000-pound GPS-guided JDAMs, only their 500-pound laser-guided bombs. Just as the US pilot lined up for this bombing run, the Taliban began to break out through the gateway again. The SBS tried to contain them with their GPMGs. Then the F-18 Super Hornet wheeled into sight. They watched the bomb drop and threw themselves to the ground. The 500-pound bomb smashed into the gateway, silencing the Taliban there. The

SBS men felt the shock wave as it rolled over them, followed by rumble and shrapnel. Then they jumped to their feet and finished off the remaining men who had made it through into the north compound.

The fort fell silent. But after 30 seconds, the firing began again with renewed intensity. Taliban reinforcements had reached the bombed-out gateway and were pouring fire onto the men who had called in the air strike. It seemed there was no stopping the Taliban. Actively seeking martyrdom, they were happy to make suicidal attacks. Sooner or later they would get through. The SBS men shared a last cigarette and prepared to die. Death they did not mind. In these circumstances, it was preferable to being captured alive. Taliban zealots were happy to torture those they considered *kaffir*, or lowly infidels.

As the Taliban burst through the ruins of the gateway again, the two SBS men on the tower alternated bursts of 60 to 80 rounds. This ensured that both guns did not jam or run out of ammunition at the same time. It also allowed the guns to cool down, preventing rounds "cooking off" in the chamber. If one of the GPMGs failed on them, it would be all over. They had been fighting now for about an hour. Their only hope lay with a second air strike that was now on its way.

Meanwhile, the US Special Forces–led team was infiltrating General Dostum's headquarters. But first they had to make another quick dash over open ground on an upper tier. What they needed was close air support. The air strike was still five minutes out. They held their position. In the meantime, all they could do was return fire.

Then they heard an F-18 roar overhead. When the bomb hit the gateway, the order came: "Go! Go! Go!"

They hit the ground running and raced across the open ground to Dostum's HQ. When, after the initial shock of the air strike, the Taliban opened up again, they caught the rescue party in the open. The highly trained Special Forces men fell flat on the earth and quickly turned to making short fire-team rushes to continue their advance. The Northern Alliance men had not been taught this maneuver. They fell like flies.

The SBS man shouted at the remaining Northern Alliance men, encouraging them to make for a baked-mud wall that offered some little cover. He inched his way on his belly toward it as bullets kicked up dust all around him. Some Northern Alliance men followed. They too reached cover, but then they were stranded. The intense Taliban fire was also chipping away at their mud wall, which provided them their only protection. Their only hope lay in another air strike, which was still six minutes away.

Pinned down, the Special Forces rescue team began crawling on their bellies in the direction of Dostum's HQ. They were halfway there, then the mortar barrage started up again. The SBS man radioed to his colleagues on the tower to take the mortar crew out. They could not locate them. But then relief was at hand.

The rescue team saw flying above them the second 500-pound bomb. As it hit, they were on their feet, sprinting the last 10 yards to the comparative safety of the stout mud wall outside the entranceway to Dostum's HQ. Moments later, the Taliban machine guns opened up again. The enemy was unstoppable.

They were just contemplating the last dash to the entranceway itself when 30 Taliban came hurtling across the compound with cries of "*Allahu Akhbar.*" The SBS man and his SEAL colleague turned and fired. The oncoming Taliban returned fire from their Kalashnikovs held at waist level. Although the Special Forces men picked off the enemy one by one, they were relieved when a GPMG opened up, scything the enemy down.

One man who fell had pulled the pin on a grenade. When it went off, it detonated the others he was carrying. The rescue team leaped for cover. When they looked up, all that was left of the man was his pelvis and legs. His fellow Taliban lay dead around him.

In the lull that followed, the rescue team contacted headquarters in Mazar-e-Sharif. Nothing more had been heard from Mike Spann and Dave Tyson, the two CIA men who had been under attack in the fort. Then they heard from the SBS team leader on the tower who was acting as forward air controller. The next air strike was 10 minutes away. They decided to postpone their final dash to General Dostum's HQ until then.

After what seemed like forever, they saw a 500-pound bomb falling from the sky, jumped to their feet, and started running. The Northern Alliance men, who were not so heavily laden with equipment, forged ahead. Their reward was a burst of machine-gun fire. The Taliban had a .50-caliber heavy machine gun zeroed in on the door to Dostrum's HQ. The Special Forces men reacted quickly, diving for what little cover there was. Now they were between a rock and a hard place, caught out in the open with bullets pinging around them.

The Special Forces team had now been fighting for two-and-a-half hours and the Taliban, despite their losses, still showed no sight of flagging. The SBS team leader called in four more air strikes on the gateway, then another two on the southern compound of the fort. One laser-guided bomb hit the pink building where most of the Taliban were taking shelter. After each attack, there was a brief period of silence. Then the gunfire started up again. It was plain that no amount of air strikes was going to deter the Taliban.

It seemed to the SBS team leader that the Taliban were managing to reinforce the men at the gateway from some hidden source. They must have a pool of men waiting in the dungeons beneath the fort, where they were safe from the effects of the 500-pound bombs that hit their fellow believers up above.

However, the bombing was having some effect. As the sun set, a Taliban ammunition dump began to cook off. For around half an hour, there were no further attacks. But it seemed they had more caches of weapons. Mortar fire and gunfire then concentrated on the men on the tower. It seemed plain to the SBS that, for the mortar crew to zero in on them, the Taliban must have a spotter on some elevated position overlooking them. They looked but could not find him. Nor could they find the mortar crew, who moved between each round to avoid being located. However, this meant that the fire was not as accurate or as deadly as it could have been.

Nevertheless, it was time to move on. They headed around the battlements toward the tower on the northeast of the fort, halfway to General Dostum's HQ. On the way, they picked up more Northern Alliance men. These were reinforcements sent back from Kondoz, where General Dostrum had the Taliban under siege. The SBS zeroed their GPMGs in on the ruined gate again and waited.

The Special Forces rescue team outside General Dostum's HQ then got a message from headquarters in Mazar-e-Sharif. It seems that Dave Tyson had managed to escape from the fort and had turned up back at base. Tyson believed that Spann had been killed, though they had yet to find his body. Anyway, for the moment, the rescue mission was over. However, the situation was growing dire. The rescue team was getting short on ammunition. Dusk was falling. In the twilight, it was going to be difficult to distinguish between friend and foe, so the quick-reaction force decided to pull out for the night and resume the search for Spann's body the next day.

However, the SEAL seconded to the SBS was not happy. There was no proof that Spann was dead, he said. He might be lying injured somewhere, or worse: He might be alive and in the hands of the Taliban. While the other men were pulled out, he raced back toward the western tower. The SBS man had no choice but to follow him. When they realized what was happening, the rest of the Special Forces rescue team also decided to follow suit and turned back toward General Dostrum's headquarters.

Scaling the western tower, the SEAL became involved in a firefight. His SBS buddy quickly joined in. Soon the SEAL was out of ammunition and continued the firefight with a Kalashnikov he had picked up off a dead Taliban. Like all Special Forces men, he had trained on enemy weapons, just in case. Under cover of darkness, the two men edged forward. They knew that on the top of the northwestern tower there was a Taliban position with a Dushka heavy machine gun and a number of men carrying small arms. The Dushka, or DShK M1938, is a World War II–vintage Soviet heavy antiaircraft machine gun that fires 12.7 x 108 mm rounds. Mounted on wheels and with an armor-plated gun shield, it is also used as a heavy infantry machine gun. It takes its name from weapons designers Vasily Degtyaryov, who designed the original weapon, and Georgi Shpagin, who improved the feed mechanism. The *K* comes from *Krupnokaliberniy*, which means "large caliber." Its nickname, *Dushka,* means "dear" or "sweetie" in Russian. The gun was their objective.

They had gone just 15 yards when the machine gun opened up. But it seemed to be aiming at the wall behind them. Perhaps, in the darkness, the Taliban had not spotted them, so they got to their feet and ran for the base of the tower. Covering each other, they made their way up the stairs. It was the sort of maneuver they had been trained for. Above them, they could hear the machine gun squirting off, presumably loosing off suppressing fire into the gloom. As they burst out of the stairwell, they took the three Taliban fighters completely by surprise. The machine gunner tried to turn his Dushka on them but took a bullet to the head. The other two were dispatched before they could react. It was a perfect Special Forces hit.

The SBS man took over the machine gunner's seat, ready to give cover to the SEAL who moved along the top of the wall. He was still hell-bent on finding Mike Spann. The SEAL was about 150 yards away when the SBS man saw a figure lurking in the dark. He loosed off a burst from the Dushka to distract attention from his buddy. It worked. However, the burst of fire alerted the Taliban to the fact that the machine-gun post was in enemy hands. The SBS man now came under Taliban fire. But with the Dushka in his hands, he had enough firepower to take on anything they could throw at him.

When the enemy fell silent, the SBS man listened intently between squeezing out the odd burst of suppressing fire. He heard sporadic gunfire from the direction of his SEAL buddy and grew worried. After a while, the SEAL returned, his face ashen. He had found a body he took to be that of Mike Spann, but, on his own and under fire, there was nothing he could do about it.

The two men then withdrew to meet up with the rest of the Special Forces rescue party. They had been searching General Dostum's headquarters building. Finding nothing, they decided to return to base in Mazar-e-Sharif for the night and leave the Northern Alliance to contain the enemy.

In the ride back to town, everyone was quiet. They had been fighting for six hours and were exhausted. They were relieved to have survived—on several occasions they had thought that they faced certain death. But who knew what the next day would bring or how long the siege would last.

It was dark when they reached the schoolhouse in Mazar-e-Sharif. The first thing they did was break out more ammunition. If something at the fort kicked off during the night, they wanted to be ready. While they refilled their magazines, they assessed the day's fighting. The enemy they had been facing, they realized, were not Afghans. They were what the mujahideen used to call Arab Afghans—Egyptians, Saudis, Chechen, Pakistanis, Yemenis, Algerians, Sudanese, and even assorted Europeans and Americans—foreigners who had rallied to the Taliban's cause. Nor were they prisoners in any normal sense of the word. They had only pretended to surrender so that they could mount this attack from inside the fort where the weapons were stored. They had not handed over all their arms, nor had they refrained from further fighting after they had agreed to surrender in the honorable Afghan way. Some of them were skilled fighters, leaving cover to deliver a couple of shots, then disappearing before you could detect them. The others were so suicidally fanatical that the ordinary Afghans among the Northern Alliance could not understand them. However, what had saved the day for the quick-reaction force was their Special Forces training.

After a cup of tea, there was a debriefing. Dave Tyson was on hand. He explained that he had escaped through a window at the back of General Dostum's headquarters, scaled the outer wall, then scrambled down the ramparts. It was the same way the Red Cross workers had gotten out before, but he had left it until the last moment when darkness was falling and he was certain that there was nothing more that could be done for Mike Spann.

It was generally assumed that Mike was now dead. This meant the quick-reaction force could change strategy. The Taliban, they knew, had more than enough weapons and ammunition, both those they had surrendered and the other weapons in the arsenal that General Dostum stored there. Irrigation ditches ran under the walls, so they had water, and they had food in the shape of General Dostum's horses that had been killed in the crossfire. This meant they could hold out for weeks. However, as the Taliban had gone to considerable lengths to seize the fort and the weapons in it, this would only make sense if it was part of a greater strategy.

A CIA operative then gave their assessment. There were some 6,000 AQT armed with heavy artillery in Kondoz. If they broke out and linked up with the forces from Qala-i-Jangi, they could take Mazar-e-Sharif. If they succeeded, the Northern Alliance would find themselves trapped between them and the AQT forces still holding the south of their former stronghold, Kandahar. Consequently, the fort and the fighting force in it had to be neutralized.

It was plain that the Special Forces team did not have nearly enough men to storm the fort. Nor did they have enough men to besiege it. The only way they could thwart the enemy was to call in more air strikes. That meant that they would have to go back into the fort the following morning and act as forward air controllers, directing the bombing raids. After liaising with Central Command, it was decided that these would start at 0601. The plan was to set up an observation post on the west tower as it overlooked the whole of the south compound. As they had spent most of the previous day defending the eastern tower, this would give them the element of surprise when they went back in the morning. Taking the tower would be the job of the Special Forces rescue team with the SEAL and his SBS buddy attached. The SBS guys who had occupied the eastern tower the day before would retake it and keep the enemy busy from that side too.

In the morning they awoke to hear that six Taliban had escaped from the fort during the night and raided a nearby village, slaughtering women and children. The men of the village grabbed their guns, tracked down the Taliban, killed them, and hung their bodies from the trees as a warning to others.

At 0510, the US–UK Special Forces team left the US military headquarters in Mazar-e-Sharif. Twenty minutes later they reached Qala-i-Jangi. This time they parked a few hundred yards away from the fort, out of range of the Taliban's weaponry. From there they proceeded on foot, arriving at the walls of the fort just as dawn was breaking.

As the team tasked with retaking the eastern tower approached, they were warned by the Northern Alliance that the mortar crew who had given them so much trouble the day before had zeroed in on the entranceway to the tower. So inside they relocated to the northeastern tower, skirting a large minefield on the way. On top of the tower, they found a Soviet T-55 battle tank with its gun pointing toward the south compound. It had been driven up the ramparts by the Northern Alliance during the night, the crew explained. Although they were happy to have some extra firepower, the SBS were a little worried about having the tank on the tower, as the fort had certainly not been built to carry that sort of weight. They feared that if the tank loosed off a 100-mm round from its main armament, the recoil would bring the whole tower tumbling down.

By 0545, the SBS had set up their GPMGs and their communications equipment on the northeastern tower. The sun was not yet up, nor had the Taliban spotted them. The Special Forces team was now in position on the west tower. They had with them a Northern Alliance soldier who knew the layout of the fort well. He pointed out two targets they should hit. One was the pink building, General Dostum's stables, where the Taliban had taken shelter. The other was the main ammunition store. The SEAL painted them with his laser target designator, while the SBS man relayed the coordinates and identifying features. The stables were 250 yards away; the ammunition store 150 yards. This was dangerously close, especially as the F-18 Hornet was armed with a 2,000-pound JDAM.

Exactly on schedule, they heard the scream of the JDAM falling and took cover. The shockwave rolled over them, sucking the air from their lungs. Then they leaped to their feet and started letting loose with their assault rifles. They were met with an unexpected volley of return fire. Then they realized that the explosion had not been nearly as big as they had expected, given that the JDAM was to have landed so close to their position. But a quick inspection revealed that the target had not been hit. Then they heard an English voice over the radio calling for a medic. When they looked toward the northeastern tower, they saw that it had been hit. Quickly they hit the radio and, in the nick of time, aborted a second air strike.

The situation was confused. The main SBS team was supposed to be on the eastern tower, not on the northeastern one. The SBS man with the rescue team was a medic, so he and his SEAL oppo headed for the northeastern tower to find out what was going on. When they reached it, a terrible scene greeted them. The JDAM had hit the tank on top of the tower, killing the crew and all the Northern Alliance men around it—20 men in all. Fortunately, fearing the weight of the tank would bring the wall down, the SBS and the American Special Forces men had spread out around the battlement away from the tower. The tank itself had shielded them from the full power of the explosion. Nevertheless, they wandered around in a state of shock. One SBS man was plainly suffering from internal injuries. Others were buried under the rubble of the tower that had collapsed with the impact. They were dug out alive.

The SBS man from the rescue team did what he could to patch up the wounded. They called for help. Within minutes, a quick-reaction force from the 10th Mountain Division was on its way. They could not get there fast enough, as the Taliban seized the opportunity to fire on the wounded, who had neither the strength nor the weapons to fire back.

When the 10th Mountain Division quick-reaction force arrived, they quickly set up six M240 heavy machine guns to pump out suppressing fire while the wounded were evacuated. Eleven injured men had to be taken out. The rest of the Special Forces team accompanied them. The walking wounded were taken to Mazar-e-Sharif, while a helicopter was called to pick up the more serious cases. It was to land about a mile outside the fort to medevac the stretcher cases out. As they were getting the stretchers out of the vehicles and ready for the pickup, a news crew coming down the road stopped and began filming them. When asked to stop, the cameraman took the camera down but kept filming surreptitiously. The SBS and SAS are secretive organizations whose members and their families could face reprisals from the terrorist outfits they face. They need to keep their identities hidden and are naturally sensitive to being photographed or filmed. They also went on covert operations, which would be compromised if they had their faces all over the media. So one of the SBS covered his face with his shemagh and walked up to the cameraman with a pistol in his hand. The news crew fled. Asked by a buddy if he would have shot the cameraman, the SBS man said no. He would have taken the man out into the desert to scare the shit out of him, then put a couple of bullets in his camera.

Once the wounded had been dealt with, the team had to decide what to do next. Back at the schoolhouse in Mazar-e-Sharif, they assessed the situation. If things had not been bad enough before, they were now seriously understrength. They had lost 20 Northern Alliance men, along with the firepower of their tank. Half the US Special Forces men were out of action, and two SBS men had had their eardrums blown in.

For the rest of the day, the Northern Alliance managed to contain the Taliban inside the fort unaided. There were sporadic exchanges of mortar and small-arms fire, but no serious attempt was made to break out. Perhaps the foreign Taliban men feared what the Afghan villagers would do to them if they escaped, or perhaps they were waiting for an outside force to arrive from Kondoz or Kandahar.

That night at 2200, the remains of the Special Forces team returned to the fort. They watched as an AC-130 Spectre gunship circled over Qala-i-Jangi. It began pounding targets within the fort with shells and large-caliber machine-gun rounds. In the fort, the mortar crew prepared to respond, only to receive a barrage of 20-mm rounds for their pains. Then the AC-130 hit the main armory, leaving the sky above the fort bathed in white light.

The following morning the Special Forces team returned to the fort again. They found that, although the Spectre gunship had taken out the mortar crew and the armory, most of the Taliban fighters had taken refuge in the dungeons below the fort and survived the gunship's attack.

General Dostum had left the siege at Kondoz to come to Qala-i-Jangi and take charge. He was appalled that the Taliban who had surrendered had not behaved honorably like a good Afghan would. Breaking your word in such a manner was against the tenets of Islam. Two captured Taliban commanders explained that the Afghan Taliban had behaved according to the Afghan code of honor. They had laid down their arms and returned to their villages. Those in the fort, who had broken the code, were foreigners. The Taliban commanders offered to try to re-establish the original surrender deal. But anyone who approached the fort was fired upon. As there was no other way to make contact with those inside the fort, it was impossible to reopen negotiations. There was no alternative. It would now be a fight to the death.

General Dostrum was also concerned about his horses. They were the cream of Afghanistan's cavalry mounts. He was furious when he heard that some had been killed and eaten. The order was passed down that no one should risk killing any more horses in the crossfire.

For the rest of the day, there was little more they could do but contain the Taliban. The SBS men trained a GPMG on the window of a building where the Taliban were holed up and poured bullets through it. But it did little good. The

Taliban kept their heads down when the SBS were firing, but popped up again when they stopped. The day ended with another standoff, and they returned to base at the schoolhouse at Mazar-e-Sharif.

The following morning, back at the fort, the Northern Alliance insisted that there were only a handful of Taliban left inside. Special Forces knew this was not the case. True, only half a dozen appeared above ground at a time. The rest remained down below in the dungeons in case there was another air strike.

General Dostum decided to send his men in on a frontal assault, with the Special Forces team giving them cover. It was a suicidal tactic. Men would be sent across open ground against an enemy that had good cover. Hundreds would be killed, and nothing would be achieved. Special Forces tried to persuade the general that the infantry assault should be led by a tank. That way, his men would have some cover. The general was less than enthusiastic. He had already lost one tank and did not want to risk losing another. However, the only heavy weapon the Taliban now possessed was an RPG. Only a very lucky shot with an RPG could take out a tank, especially if the tank was front-on to the enemy positions. If it kept its distance, it could hammer the Taliban with shells, which would at least keep their heads down until the Northern Alliance infantrymen got to them. Finally, the general saw the logic of this plan, and a second tank was brought up.

As the T-55 trundled forward with Northern Alliance men taking shelter behind it, the Taliban rose to the bait, peppering the heavy armor plating on the front of the tank with small-fire and RPGs—to no effect. Every time a Taliban put his head up to fire, a Special Forces sniper was on him. When the tank entered the south compound, it stopped and fired a shell into the main building where the Taliban had been taking refuge. It reloaded and fired again. The Taliban now had no choice but to launch a desperate counterattack. But it was too late. The shelling of the building blocked the entranceway to the dungeons below. Their main force was now trapped underground.

Anyone emerging from the rubble was cut down by Special Forces marksmen. Then the Northern Alliance troops moved in. Clearing away the rubble, they tried to enter the dungeons below, but anyone attempting to descend the stairs was shot dead. By the time a dozen men had been hit, they pulled back behind the tank, then withdrew to tend to the wounded.

The following day, the Special Forces team resumed their positions on the battlements of the fort. The Northern Alliance began a second sweep, this time trying to locate the body of Mike Spann. As they did so, they came under fire from fresh enemy positions. It appeared that the Taliban had taken refuge in other underground chambers some distance from the main stronghold. The Northern Alliance responded by dropping grenades though the ground-level ventilation portals, followed by a burst of machine-gun fire.

Then a truck full of fuel drums was brought up. Diesel oil was then pumped into the basement and a phosphorus grenade was thrown in. A huge flame burst out of the entranceway. The idea was that anyone down below would be burned alive or asphyxiated. However, though many were killed by the grenade, the heavy diesel oil refused to ignite. Still, sporadic bursts of defiant gunfire could be heard. However, the Northern Alliance had located Mike Spann's body and, when they withdrew again, they brought it with them. A fellow CIA man covered it with an American flag and said a short prayer. Then it was loaded on a truck and taken away. That evening at the schoolhouse in Mazar-e-Sharif, the SBS joined a guard of honor for Mike Spann as his body was loaded onto a Chinook and flown out on the first leg of its journey back to the States.

The next morning, day six of the siege, the Special Forces team drove back to Qala-i-Jangi and entered the south compound. It was a scene of utter devastation. Burned and mutilated bodies were surrounded by spent ordinance. Some of the dead still had their hands tied together. Beside them some 30 horses lay dead. The smell of death was overwhelming. The Northern Alliance were looting the bodies, a dangerous pastime since some had been booby-trapped with grenades that went off when you turned the body over.

Nor was the fighting over yet. Northern Alliance soldiers tasked with removing the bodies heard voices from an underground chamber and were cut down by a short burst of fire. Others rushed forward and dropped grenades down the ventilation shafts. There was a boom down below, but then came answering fire. The Northern Alliance emptied the magazines of their Kalashnikovs down the ventilation shafts and dropped in more grenades, but they had no way of knowing how effective this was, as no one was eager to go below to check.

The Special Forces team then figured out how to finish off the siege once and for all. The plan was to fill the entire basement of the fort with water. That way, the Taliban would either have to give up or drown. With the aid of the Northern Alliance, they diverted one of the irrigation ditches so it discharged into the basement. They left it filling the dungeons with freezing water all night and returned to Mazar-e-Sharif.

They returned to Qala-i-Jangi at 0630 on day seven of the siege. An old fire truck had been brought up to pump in more water. Eventually the survivors down below could stand it no longer. At 0700, movement was seen in the entranceway to the basement. A bedraggled Taliban fighter dragged himself blinking up the stairway into the light. Special Forces kept him covered at a distance, fearing that he might have a grenade concealed under his clothing. Two Northern Alliance soldiers forced him to his knees and frisked him. They took his boots and cuffed his hands behind his back. He was followed by 12 more Taliban, making their way hesitantly up the stairway one at a time. Some were still clutching their Kalashnikovs. Others were blackened with diesel oil.

They were disarmed and marched barefoot down a desert pathway to a waiting truck. Some were so exhausted that they could not make it that far and had to be carried on the stretchers the Northern Alliance had been using for removing the dead. Red Cross workers turned up and began distributing food, though most of the survivors were too weak to eat. One Chechen with a shrapnel wound to his leg continued mouthing off about killing the unbelievers, not realizing that some of the Northern Alliance men could understand Russian. They told him in no uncertain terms to shut up. Then he begged for someone to tend his wound. A Red Cross worker stepped forward to do so, but this provoked an angry reaction from the Northern Alliance. Why were these foreign workers feeding and tending these men who had tried to kill them just a few hours earlier? One Northern Alliance soldier threatened to smash the Chechen's head in with the butt of his rifle. The Taliban had killed his son, he said. His comrades restrained him.

At 1000, there was further movement on the stairs. One by one, 50 more Taliban emerged, some exhibiting shocking wounds. One man told his captors that he was an American. This was John Walker Lindh, the so-called American Taliban Mike Spann had been interrogating before he was killed. He had a bullet in his thigh and was taken to Mazar-e-Sharif for treatment and interrogation. Other prisoners taken at Qala-i-Jangi said that they had been present when Mike Spann was tortured and finally killed. Shipped back to the US, Lindh faced 10 capital charges. In a plea bargain, he pleaded guilty to two counts in return for a sentence of 20 years with no parole. He also had to sign a secrecy agreement and drop all allegations of maltreatment and torture at the hands of the American authorities. In court, he pleaded guilty to being a member of the Taliban and carrying an AK-47 and two grenades, knowing it to be against US law. He is now serving his sentence in a medium security prison in Indiana.

In all, 86 Taliban gave themselves up. After the last one emerged, Northern Alliance soldiers went down into the basement to check for booby traps. One Special Forces man also went down to see for himself. At the bottom of the stairs he found corpses floating in the oily scum. It was dark and cold, and the air was foul. No one knows how many men died down there. Just 150 bodies were recovered, and most of the 600 Taliban prisoners held at Qala-i-Jangi remain unaccounted for. Some of the bodies would have been obliterated completely by the bombing. The Northern Alliance lost 50 men, including the 20 killed in the JDAM friendly fire incident. The US Special Forces had five men seriously injured. One had his hip shattered. All lost their hearing temporarily but regained it after their ruptured eardrums healed. They had black eyes from concussion and lacerations from shrapnel. Only one American, Mike Spann, was killed. All of the SBS men lived to fight another day.

When the world's media, which had been covering the siege of Kondoz, reached Qala-i-Jangi, questions were asked. Some accused Special Forces of being complicit in the massacre of the Taliban prisoners. Amnesty International called for an enquiry. There were also questions about the efforts made to rescue Mike Spann. His father believes that his son might still have been alive when the SEAL first spotted his body, and if a greater effort had been made then, he might have survived. The suggestion has also been made that Mike Spann committed suicide rather than fall into the hands of the Taliban. The official story is that Marine Johnny Michael Spann had been alive when he fell into the hands of the Taliban. Both legs had been broken below the knee in a fashion known to be a favorite al-Qaeda torture method. He was kept alive for some time. He had been shot twice in the small of the back, on each side of the spine, in a way that would deliberately cause pain rather than be life threatening. Sometime later he was killed by a bullet in the back of his neck, thought to have been inflicted when he was kneeling with his arms tied behind his back. His death would have been a long and painful one.

After an exhaustive enquiry, the JDAM friendly fire incident was attributed to human error. However, in the future, the US would adopt the SBS's SOP of only giving the coordinates of the target, not those of the friendly forces giving them, precluding the possibility of the pilot getting them mixed up.

Special Forces officer Major Mark Mitchell was awarded the Distinguished Service Cross, the first to be awarded since the Vietnam War, and Chief Petty Officer Stephen Bass was awarded the Navy Cross for his actions while attached to the SBS. Mike Spann was awarded the Intelligence Star for his "extraordinary heroism" in fighting off the prisoners long enough to allow his colleagues to escape. As the Intelligence Star is the equivalent of the Silver Star, Span was buried at Arlington National Cemetery.

For their part in the action at Qala-i-Jangi, the SBS men were awarded the American Congressional Medal of Honor. The British are more secretive about their awards to Special Forces soldiers, rarely naming names unless the man concerned is dead. The SBS commander and another man received high gallantry awards, and two were mentioned in dispatches. Chief Petty Officer Bass was also awarded the British Military Cross, which he received personally from the Queen.

CHAPTER 17

BATTLE OF TORA BORA

IN DECEMBER 2001, DELTA FORCE were given the job of taking the Tora Bora cave complex where Osama bin Laden was thought to be hiding. Central Command in Florida again asked the British SAS and SBS to assist. The Australian and New Zealand SAS would also be involved in the operation, with the German KSK guarding the flanks. The KSK—*Kommando Spezialkräfte*, or Special Forces Command—is a unit in the German army formed in 1996 to take over antiterrorist operations from GSG-9. It saw action in Bosnia and Herzegonia, the Kosovo War and Afganistan.

Tora Bora lay in the Tangai Mountains that separate Afghanistan from Pakistan. It is a lawless region, home to bandits and smugglers. The narrow roads there were cut into the sides of the mountains and are dangerous for sure-footed pack animals and impassable for four-wheeled vehicles. The cave complex at Tora Bora had been used by the mujahadeen as a base during their war with the Soviets. Just 50 kilometers west of the Khyber Pass and 10 kilometers from the Federally Administered Tribal Areas of Pakistan, the labyrinthine underground fortress has been compared to the complex built by Hitler under Berlin. According to US intelligence, there were underground ammunition dumps, command and control rooms furnished with the best communications equipment bin Laden's millions could buy, sleeping quarters, dining facilities, and everything else an army needed to survive.

As Taliban resistance collapsed throughout the rest of Afghanistan, intelligence came in that al-Qaeda and the Taliban's foreign fighters planned to make their last stand at Tora Bora. It had been bin Laden's headquarters during the jihad against the Soviets, and it was where he had started al-Qaeda with his mentor, the radical cleric Sheikh Abdullah Azzam. It was Azzam who had invited bin Laden to come to Afghanistan from his home in Saudi Arabia in 1979, though the two man had fallen out when bin Laden set up his own force of foreign fighters in 1988. Azzam was killed by a car bomb soon after. Bin Laden's foreign fighters became al-Qaeda, which means "the base." The base was Tora Bora.

Despite the might of the Red Army, the Soviets had never managed to dislodge the mujahadeen from Tora Bora. The US Army feared it would do little better. Taking the fortress would involve heavy casualties. Since the Vietnam War, the American public was particularly sensitive about body bags being returned home, so no US politician was likely to sanction a full-scale onslaught. If bin Laden were in Tora Bora, he could continue to thumb his nose at the West indefinitely. However, while US firepower might not succeed against Tora Bora, Special Forces might just be able to take it. And as their activities are largely covert, if they failed it would not be catastrophic—in public-relations terms at least.

As they moved into the area of Tora Bora, the anti-Taliban Afghan forces recruited by the Green Berets took the ridgeline and a small village called Milawa where caves used by al-Qaeda for storing weapons were discovered. Four al-Qaeda men were killed by Special Forces snipers. From their position overlooking the valley, Special Forces identified targets that were then bombed. It was thought that some 600 al-Qaeda men were killed, though it is hard to get accurate casualty figures after air strikes. However, it is known for certain that large numbers of al-Qaeda men were killed by snipers.

By December 10, there were 50 US Special Forces operatives on the ground in the region. The Green Berets manned high-altitude observation posts, while Delta Force advanced with the anti-Taliban Afghan forces. However, although they made substantial advances against al-Qaeda during the day, the Afghans fell back in the evening, allowing the enemy to reoccupy their positions at night.

The commander of Delta Force decided to detach his men from the Afghan forces and send dedicated teams of snipers and forward air controllers to hold the positions that the Afghans abandoned. However, a local warlord, Ghamshareek Zaman, supposedly an American ally, opposed this. There was a tense standoff when his men refused to let Delta Force move into position. Zaman then claimed that al-Qaeda had put out peace feelers. On the night of December 11, they had sent a radio message to the Northern Alliance offering to surrender. Zaman then enforced a cease-fire, and negotiations dragged on. It was plain that al-Qaeda were only stalling for time, so the commander of Delta Force insisted that, come what may, the bombing of Tora Bora would begin at 0800 on December 12. Even then, al-Qaeda tried to lay down conditions. They said they would only surrender to the United Nations. Nor would they give up their guns. Meanwhile they tried to make another backroom deal and attempted to persuade Zaman's men to withdraw so they could fight the Americans and British. They had no wish to kill fellow Muslims, only the infidel.

Neither deal worked. America would not accept any conditional surrender, and it was footing the bill. Local anti-Taliban leader General Hazrat Ali, who outranked Zaman and had 8,000 seasoned men in the area, then stepped in. He told al-Qaeda that he would indulge their foreign fighters' most fervent wish and arrange for them to visit Allah personally. He then added his own personal condition to any continued cease-fire: al-Qaeda must hand over bin Laden.

Hazrat Ali's intervention was not necessarily helpful. He was one of a number of local warlords competing for the $25 million reward the US had offered for the capture of bin Laden. Unfortunately, the reward had rather confused things. Junior commanders held good intelligence back for fear that they would not get a slice of the reward and that all of it would be taken by the senior warlord. CIA and Special Forces men on the ground pointed out to Washington that a cash reward was of little incentive to most Afghans, who measured their wealth in sheep, goats, and Toyota Land Cruisers. It would have been better to offer to equip and supply any faction that caught bin Laden. That way everyone in the force that caught up with him would get a share.

To make absolutely clear to al-Qaeda that they were in no position to put conditions on their surrender, when the 0800 deadline arrived, B-52s dropped smart bombs into the mouths of the cave where they were sheltering. Special Forces snipers were on hand to pick off those fleeing over the surrounding mountains.

For good measure, at 1000, a 15,000-pound BLU-82 "daisy cutter" bomb was dropped at the entranceway of a cave complex, filling the valley with smoke and dust. This sent the surviving al-Qaeda men scuttling over the frozen mountaintops with everything they could carry. Once over the ridgeline, they ran straight into an SAS team who were doing strategic reconnaissance along the eastern slope facing Pakistan.

To avoid further "blue-on-blue" incidents, anti-Taliban forces were cleared from the area at night, giving Special Forces equipped with night-vision equipment a free-fire zone where they could kill anyone they came across. They were armed with M24 7.62-mm sniper rifles accurate up to 900 meters and Barrett Light 50s that could fire heavy .50-caliber bullets 1,000 meters. Even at that range, the heavy shell could knock out a truck.

On December 12, the fighting flared again, possibly initiated by a rear guard buying time for the main force's escape through the White Mountains into the tribal areas of Pakistan. Once again, tribal forces backed by US special-operations troops and air support pressed ahead against fortified al-Qaeda positions in caves and bunkers scattered throughout the mountainous region. Twelve British SBS commandos and one British SAS Royal Signals Specialist accompanied the US special-operations forces in an attack on the cave complex at Tora Bora.

Meanwhile, as American intelligence continued to monitor al-Qaeda radio traffic, they could hear the terrible toll the air strikes were having on the enemy. On December 13, bin Laden was heard on the radio saying, "The time is now, arm your women and children against the infidel."

But after a few more hours of bombing, he became disheartened. Breaking radio silence again, he said, "Our prayers were not answered. Times are dire and bad. We did not get support from the apostate nations who call themselves our Muslim brothers. Things might have been different...I'm sorry for getting you involved in this battle; if you can no longer resist, you may surrender with my blessing."

At 0200 on December 14, bin Laden was overheard on the radio one last time. He was still in Tora Bora, though he was preparing to leave. A two-man sniper team was sent in. At 1400 on December 15, they radioed back that they had a positive identification on bin Laden. The entire team could have been there in half an hour, but the team leader refused to give the order without consulting high authority. When the request climbed the chain of command, it was denied. The operation was considered too risky. It could have been a trap. Bin Laden was lost again.

As the fighting around Tora Bora intensified, the British sent another 60 SAS men into Afghanistan, bringing their numbers up to 110. Alongside the Green Berets and Delta Force, they helped clear out the remaining caves. They made surgical strikes using the close-quarters battle skills they had learned in the counterrevolutionary war training. At night, SAS snipers would pick off anyone making their way over the mountain passes. At least once, they claim to have had bin Laden in their sights, trapped in a small valley near Tora Bora. They planned to send one squadron into the valley to flush him out. When he headed for the farthest pass in an attempt to escape, the other squadron would be waiting to kill anyone who crossed their path. Delta Force were eager to join in, and they were promised close air support.

Although everyone involved in the planning of the operation was confident that it would succeed, the US commanders back in the States pulled the plug. Al-Qaeda, they knew, had SAM missiles, and they would not risk any planes coming in at below 12,000 feet. At that time, they did not have any attack helicopters or A-10 Warthogs—the first US plane to be designed specifically for close air support—in the country. This was extremely frustrating for the Special Forces, who felt that they were not being allowed to do their job.

The next time overflight surveillance spotted enemy activity—45 men entering a cave thought to be al-Qaeda's command control center—Task Force Dagger's HQ contacted the SAS and sent them maps and pictures. The SAS men quickly prepared their kit. As they were going into a cave, they replaced their ball ammunition, which would ricochet off the walls, with ceramic rounds, which would shatter. They also abandoned their flash-bang stun grenades for the more deadly high-explosive fragmentation variety. Two Delta Force men would accompany them as liaison officers.

They planned to enter the cave at first light. That meant a long trek during the hours of darkness. Nevertheless, with the help of GPS, they were in position as dawn broke, having identified four tunnel entrances. One or two four-man teams were to enter each, with additional teams remaining outside to guard the rear. They checked to make sure there was a round in the chamber, flicked off the safety, and went in. Once inside, they switched on their weapons' lights. The first team made contact immediately. Two sleeping al-Qaeda men awoke and grabbed for their guns. A third man was also cut down. By then every al-Qaeda man in the place was awake.

There were more al-Qaeda men than they had expected. Others were sleeping in bunkers on the other side of the slope. They took on the teams who were waiting outside the caves. The first SAS man to be hit inside the cave was dragged out, only to find himself under heavy fire from al-Qaeda on the next ridge. A second SAS man went down with bullet wounds in his leg and hip. They called for air support, then canceled their request as al-Qaeda closed in. A 500-pound bomb on the al-Qaeda position would have hit the SAS too.

MD-500 Little Birds brought 24 more men with 7.62-mm belt-fed GPMGs. But the only nearby landing zone that was not under fire was two miles away, leaving the men with a long trek over rocky terrain. Then two more Little Birds came in. Once they had al-Qaeda in sight, they gave the order for the SAS to take cover. After scything through the enemy with their mini-guns, risking small-arms fire and RPGs, they finished off the attack with a couple of rockets each. Then they made off with requests for more ammunition ringing in their ears.

The fighting lasted for four-and-a-half hours. At the end, 38 al-Qaeda lay dead; 50 were wounded, and 21 were captured, mainly Arab, Chechen, and Pakistani. Besides the two wounded SAS men, 10 more had bullets embedded in their armored chest plates. The wounded men were flown back to Britain, while the prisoners were taken to the jail in Jalalabad and delivered into the tender mercies of Hazrat Ali.

During the attack on Tora Bora, one SAS man, the regimental sergeant major, won the Conspicuous Gallantry Cross, awarded "in recognition of an act or acts of conspicuous gallantry during active operations against the enemy." The CGC has been awarded just 15 times since its introduction in 1993. Despite having been seriously wounded, the RSM took on the enemy armed only with his commando knife. He had been hit at least twice by enemy fire, yet somehow managed to get back to his feet and continue fighting before resorting to his knife as the conflict descended into savage hand-to-hand contact. The citation praised his "outstanding leadership in drawing his knife and charging the enemy, inspiring those around him at a time when ammunition was running low and the outcome of the battle was in doubt."

Search-and-destroy operations continued, but Special Forces did not find the massive underground fortress they were expecting, only small bunkers and outposts and a few minor training camps. As they cleared out the caves, it became clear that al-Qaeda did not have the sophisticated cave complexes that intelligence imagined. Most of the caves were shallow, sometimes with crude ventilation shafts. Munitions were stacked inside, and there were mats for men to sleep on. Occasionally they found documents or laptops left behind that rendered some useful intelligence. The back numbers of the cases of Chinese, Russian, and American ammunition they found were also a source. The US ammunition, it turned out, had been bought from American manufacturers, using American money, by Pakistan, who had then shipped it on to the Taliban and al-Qaeda.

Despite the success of these missions and the intelligence they produced, the US commanders did not favor missions that put fighting men on the ground. Instead they preferred precision bombing. However, blowing up the cave entrances simply sealed the caves, along with any intelligence material that might be inside. No excavation operations could be undertaken easily in that remote location. Indeed, it would have been almost impossible to get the necessary earth-moving equipment there. Osama bin Laden could have been dead in one of the caves and no one would have known about it. In fact, it is thought that bin Laden and his main force escaped through the White Mountains into the tribal areas of Pakistan.

CHAPTER 18

OPERATION ANACONDA

ONCE THE TALIBAN AND AL-QAEDA had been driven out of Tora Bora, the role of Special Forces changed. They began interdiction and search-and-destroy missions, making commando-style raids, usually under the cover of night, upon villages suspected of harboring the AQT. The Special Forces of all the Allied nations got involved. The SEALs led a unit called Task Force K-Bar that also included German, Canadian, Danish, and Norwegian Special Forces personnel and was involved in raids and surveillance in southern Afghanistan. The British SAS was employed in operations along the Kwaja Amran mountain range in Ghazni and the Hada Hills near Spin Boldak. They went in at night by helicopter, storming villages using stun grenades and grabbing suspects who were whisked away for interrogation.

In early March 2002, the US Special Forces Groups Task Force 11, Task Force Bowie, and Task Force Dagger, along with the Australian and New Zealand SAS, and the German KSK, led elements of the US 10th Mountain Division, 101st Airborne Division, British Royal Marines, Canada's 3rd Battalion, the Princess Patricia's Canadian Light Infantry, and the Afghan National Army in Operation Anaconda.

This Allied push aimed to clear al-Qaeda and Taliban forces out of the Shahi-Kot Valley and Arma Mountains southeast of Zormat.

It began on March 1 when US Special Forces infiltrated the area and set up observation posts. Teams India and Juliet, primarily from the Delta Force, were to take positions at the north and south ends of the Shahi-Kot Valley, where they could watch the approaches from Gardez. The third team, Mako 31, a SEAL unit, was tasked to set up an observation post on a feature known as the Finger where they could observe the landing zone for Task Force Rakkasan. This comprised the 187th Infantry Regiment of the 101st Airborne, who got their nickname, Rakkasan, from the Japanese word for parachute during their occupation of Japan after World War II. On their way to the Finger, the SEAL unit saw a group of Afghan fighters with a Russian DShK machine gun in a position that would have threatened the Chinooks bringing in the first wave of US troops. They made plans to destroy the emplacement at D-minus-1 hours. Any earlier and the enemy would have been able to replace the Dushka and make preparations to resist the attack they knew was coming.

The following day, US and Afghan forces begin to sweep the Shahi-Kot valley area to root out rebel forces regrouping in the valley. Around midnight, the units of Task Force Hammer loaded into their vehicles and left their base in Gardez for the Shahi-Kot Valley. Task Force Hammer consisted of a large-force Afghan militia led by Zia Lodin and the Special Forces A-team Texas 14/ODA 594. The road was in poor condition, and several soldiers were injured when their trucks overturned in the dark. It was then decided that the trucks should switch on their headlights to see where they were going, though this would destroy any element of surprise.

Farther down the road, a convoy led by Army Chief Warrant Officer Stanley L. Harriman of the 3rd Special Forces Group split off from the main force and set out for its observation point. Overhead, an AC-130 aircraft called *Grim 31*, providing fire support and reconnaissance for the assault, spotted Harriman's convoy. Due to a problem with the plane's inertial navigation system, the aircrew failed to identify the convoy as American. So *Grim 31* engaged the column, killing CWO Harriman and wounding several US Special Forces and Afghan militiamen before orders were sent telling it to break off.

The main body of Task Force Hammer reached its start line around 0615 and waited for an aerial bombardment, which it had been told would last 55 minutes. In fact, only six bombs fell before one got stuck in the launch bay of the next B-1B Lancer. While the next bomber waited for the B-1B to get permission to jettison the bomb and go around again, both planes and the two F-15E Strike Eagles accompanying them received orders telling them to cease the bombardment. There may have been some confusion, and this order may have been the one telling *Grim 31* to cease fire.

Already demoralized by the lack of air support, Task Force Hammer's trucks were raked with enemy mortar fire that had been registered in advance on key points along the road. Plainly, al-Qaeda had been expecting an attack, and the anti-Taliban Afghans suffered over 40 casualties. Additional air support they had been promised was then assigned to Task Force Anvil on the other side of the ridge, and Task Force Hammer's attack stalled even before they entered the valley.

At 0630 on March 2, the first wave of Rakkasans and mountain troops were landed by helicopter along the eastern and northern edges of the valley. These were blocking positions where they were to await fleeing fighters. However, they came under fire almost immediately and were pinned down by heavy mortar fire throughout the day. Instead of the 150 to 200 fighters they had been expecting, they found there were between 500 and 1,000 dug in on the high ground surrounding the valley. The first wave of American troops had brought just one 120-mm mortar with them. Signalman Martin "Jock" Wallace of the Australian SAS Regiment was with them to prevent friendly fire incidents with the Australian SAS operating in the area.

"We landed early in the morning and walked straight into an ambush," said Signalman Wallace.

They were put down on top of an al-Qaeda stronghold, a tunnel complex that they had no intelligence about. Seconds after touching down, they were caught in a withering crossfire. Wallace had a rocket-propelled grenade fired straight at him. "The round hit the ground and slid through the mud," he said. "It basically chased us up the hill as we ran from it, and it just lay there steaming in the ground as we scrambled for cover."

If it had gone off, he would almost certainly have been killed. But though Wallace and his comrades had survived, there was another problem. The American soldiers with them had dropped their backpacks in the opening attack as they ran for cover. These packs contained their ammunition and radio equipment and were in full view of the al-Qaeda machine gunners. The US troops had no hope of recovering this vital gear.

Fortunately, Wallace had not dropped his pack. He kept hold of his radio, so they could communicate directly back to Bagram. Even so, the odds were not good.

"Al-Qaeda got onto the western ridge," said Wallace, "which meant that they were behind us, so the guys who were shooting at the al-Qaeda on the eastern ridge were now taking rounds in the back."

SAS commander Colonel Rowan Tink, who was listening on the radio link as al-Qaeda closed in, was convinced that they were not going to get out alive. Using their knives and their bare hands, the beleaguered force began to dig in. Al-Qaeda then began mortaring them, targeting the only mortar the Americans had.

"I was just lying there, watching them out of the corner of my eye," said Wallace, "and about five or six of them disappeared in a puff of gray smoke. It was basically a direct hit on the American mortar from the al-Qaeda mortar."

The survivors were badly injured. "We had guys with chest injuries," said Wallace. "There were open fractures, basically fragmentation wounds, some over their entire bodies."

Like all SAS men, Wallace had some basic medical training. It was clear that he would have to go out, pull the injured men to safety, and dress their wounds. Putting himself in harm's way, he moved out under fire, collected some of the wounded, and dragged them back to the comparative safety of the dry creek bed. It was this action that won him the Medal for Gallantry.

Al-Qaeda laid down heavy fire and fought more fiercely than anticipated.

"These guys were definitely committed, and they were there to fight to the death—and we accommodated them," said Wallace.

According to Colonel Tink, the assumption Lieutenant General Hagenbeck, the ground commander of Operation

Anaconda, and his staff had made was that, at worst, his men would be facing a stalemate in that position.

"This was perhaps a little bit overoptimistic," said Colonel Tink. "On the afternoon of the first day, there was no doubt that we knew we had a real battle on our hands."

Even General Hagenbeck realized they were in trouble.

"The medics had called for air evacuations," he said. "In fact, on one occasion the helicopters were en route and I had to turn them around in mid-air to take them back out of there because it was clear to me that they would be shot down."

By then, 30 Americans had been wounded. They lay in a pit in the creek bed that Signalman Wallace had managed to hollow out during the battle to provide them some cover. The situation grew so desperate that a B-52 bomber was called in to hit the al-Qaeda positions, though barely a few hundred meters separated them from the American position.

"I was lying on my back watching the B-52 come overhead," said Signalman Wallace, "and you could see the bomb bay doors open and the bombs as they started to fall. You're just hoping that they're going to be on target and not on your position. When you're dropping things from thirty thousand feet and they are not laser-guided, it's definitely a recipe for disaster."

When the bombs hit, Wallace could feel the initial shock waves coming through the air and the ground. They were followed by the noise of the shrapnel whistling overhead. Undeterred, al-Qaeda continued its attack, and by now the Americans were running low on ammunition, much of which was in their discarded backpacks, which lay exposed to enemy fire. Already they had run out of 7.62-mm ammunition for the heavy machine guns. Their only mortar piece had been taken out, so they were down to personal weapons. Meanwhile, the enemy kept up their withering attack.

"Probably the heaviest fighting was around last light," said Signalman Wallace, "when they managed to dominate both of the ridgelines and launched a ground assault from the north. By the end of that they had set up a machine gun in the south, so they had us surrounded. That was probably the scariest part of the whole day."

For 18 hours, machine-gun fire, mortars, rocket-propelled grenades, and surface-to-air missiles hammered the encircled troops. It was estimated that the Americans were up against a thousand AQT fighters, outnumbered ten to one.

"There was no chance of reinforcements—they would have been cut to pieces by the surrounding force," said Wallace.

American Apache attack helicopters tried to rocket the al-Qaeda positions. But the entire hillside opened up with small-arms fire, and that was the last they saw of the Apaches.

"They copped a caning and then limped off the battlefield," said Wallace.

But when darkness fell, AC-130 Spectre gunships moved in.

"It was a survival situation," Wallace said. "Without air cover, we would have been wiped out."

He helped direct the AC-130 gunships' fire on the enemy. This prevented al-Qaeda from massing their forces and overrunning the American position. At midnight, a fleet of Black Hawks airlifted the American task force out. Twenty-eight Americans were dead. But it was not all bad news. Throughout the day, the Special Forces reconnaissance teams had infiltrated the area. They now called in air strikes from B-1s, B-52s, F-15s, and F-16s, inflicting heavy casualties and killing an estimated 500 AQT fighters.

The SEAL teams, Mako 21 and Mako 30, were sent to establish an observation point on the peak of Takur Ghar, which gave a commanding view over the Shahi-Kot valley. They were to be dropped some 1,300 meters east of the peak and to be in position by dawn; they were to set off at 2323 on March 3. But one of the Chinooks broke down. The resulting delay meant that the SEALs would have to be dropped on the peak itself. An AC-130 gunship reconnoitered the peak and saw no enemy activity, but it was called away before *Razor 03* and *Razor 04*, the two Chinooks carrying the SEALs, arrived.

Around 0245, *Razor 03* landed on the peak and was struck in the left-side electrical compartment by an RPG. As the stricken helicopter took off, Petty Officer First Class Neil Roberts fell out of the open ramp. *Razor 03* tried to return and retrieve him, but the damage prevented proper control, and the helicopter crash-landed some four miles away in the valley.

Roberts managed to activate his emergency beacon. His only weapons were a pistol and two hand grenades; his light machine gun had not fallen out of the chopper with him. The men on the helicopter saw three al-Qaeda fighters beginning to move in on him. Roberts crawled toward cover, engaging the terrorists with the pistol and grenades, but he soon ran out of ammunition. Nobody knows exactly what happened next. Images broadcast by a Predator unmanned aerial vehicle showed the three men dragging him away. A rescue team later recovered his body. Roberts had died from gunshot wounds.

Soon after, *Razor 04* arrived at the LZ to drop Mako 30. As soon as the SEAL team hit the ground, they came under fire. Air Force combat controller Technical Sergeant John A. Chapman was hit, and two SEALs were wounded. Mako 30 was then forced off the peak and called the Ranger quick-reaction force at Bagram Air Base for help.

The quick-reaction force consisted of 19 US Rangers, a tactical air control party and a three-man US Air Force special tactics team. It was carried by two Chinooks, *Razor 01* and *Razor 02*, and led by Captain Nate Self. Due to difficulties with satellite communications, *Razor 01* was directed to the hot landing zone on the peak by mistake. Around 0610, *Razor 01* reached the LZ and immediately came under attack. The right-door minigunner, Sergeant Phillip Svitak, was killed by small-arms fire. Then a rocket-propelled grenade hit the helicopter, demolishing the right engine and forcing it to crash-land. As they left the stricken helicopter, enemy fire cut down Sergeant Brad Crose, Specialist Marc Anderson, and Private First Class Matt Commons, who was posthumously promoted to corporal. The rest of the men took cover behind a hillock, and a fierce firefight ensued.

Fifteen minutes later, the rest of the quick-reaction force and their commander, Lieutenant Commander Vic Hyder, arrived. With the help of close air support, the small force was able to consolidate its position on the peak. However, fog had closed in, in the Shahi-Kot valley rendering the Predator surveillance drones useless. However, they had some backup in the form of a six-man Australian SAS team that had infiltrated the day before, though they were having trouble surviving the bitter cold.

"Quite a few of us are Queenslanders and had never seen snow before until we went to Afghanistan," said one of the SAS men. "The novelty wore off after about five minutes."

On the nearby peak, dozens of Rangers were trapped and under fierce attack. The SEALs were under fire. Undetected by the enemy, the SAS team reported back the situation to the coalition command tent, where the feeling was close to despair.

"These men were way behind enemy lines," said Colonel Tink. "They were isolated on the top of the mountain. Clearly they had been engaged by some heavy machine guns, and at that particular stage, we were unsure how long they'd be able to survive. We knew they had dead and wounded there."

But luckily the SAS team was in place.

"You had to have someone there on the ground," said General Hagenbeck, "that could see and hear and smell and pick up the sense of the battlefield, of what was going on, and we were very much dependent upon the Aussies, certainly in that part of the battlefield."

The Australian SAS team coordinated a constant barrage of bomb and rocket attacks on the advancing fighters. They were able to call in multiple air strikes to prevent al-Qaeda from overrunning the downed helicopter.

The enemy counterattacked at midday, mortally wounding Senior Airman Jason D. Cunningham. Under the direction of the Australian SAS, AC-130 Spectre gunships were brought in to give close air support. Even then the al-Qaeda barrage was so intense that US troops could not be medevaced out during daylight hours. Finally, at around 2000, the quick-reaction force and Mako 30 were rescued from the peak of Takur Ghar. Along with the survivors, the helicopters carried the bodies of seven Americans—Roberts and six of his would-be rescuers. Eleven more were wounded. The ridge was named Roberts Ridge by the US troops in memory of their fallen comrade.

The Australian SAS men continued to provide this niche capability to American forces during Operation Anaconda.

"We were able to remain deep behind enemy positions undetected for long periods of time," said Colonel Tink, "and provide them with valuable information which was very detailed. In fact, in a number of reports I handed over, I remember various Americans being amazed at the detail we were able to provide on dress, equipment, activities, where these people were positioned, et cetera, et cetera."

The value of this specialist support did not go unnoticed.

"I tell you, I would not have wanted to do that operation without the Australian SAS's folks on that ridgeline," said General Hagenbeck. "I mean, they made it happen that day."

But by the time the SAS men returned to base, the word had got around.

"It was almost embarrassing, to the point where the Americans were so glad of our help," said one of the Aussie patrol. "You may go to a meal night in a mess, there might be a hundred people in front of you, all Americans, and all of a sudden they would step aside, maybe even applaud, and push you to the front of the line. We were looking pretty wild and woolly, but we were taken aback by it and a bit embarrassed."

Despite their lack of fancy gadgets, the SAS had proved their worth again.

"I think there's one important lesson I took out of Afghanistan in regard to technology," said Colonel Tink, "and that is, at the end of the day, the technology has to be designed to support the man, not replace the man. And I think we demonstrated that through our reconnaissance and surveillance capacity."

Shortly after the fiasco on Roberts Ridge, the US set up a revenge mission to punish al-Qaeda. US Delta Force troops led the payback mission and invited several men from SEAL Team 6 to join them, as Roberts had been one of their men, along with an SBS man who was on secondment with the SEALs. Their opportunity came when a US Predator spotted an al-Qaeda convoy. An ambush team was dropped on the ridgeline along its route. When the five-vehicle convoy passed by in the valley below, they opened up with everything they had. The AQT fighters on board were hardly able to raise their weapons and return fire before they were taken out.

Once the firefight was over, the Delta and SEAL ambush force went down to search the 20 or so bodies. They noticed that there were few Afghans among them. Most were Arabs or Chechens. Several of the dead were wearing US Army webbing. The American troops angrily ripped it off the bodies. One of the al-Qaeda men was still alive. As a US soldier turned him over, the wounded man detonated a grenade. Luckily, his body took the brunt of the blast, which caused few injuries to the ambush force.

They also retrieved a US Army GPS and night sight from the dead. When the serial numbers were traced, it turned out that they had been taken from US soldiers killed or captured in Somalia during the US military intervention in Mogadishu in 1993. It was clear that these men had been waging their jihad for years.

By March 12, US and Afghan forces swept through the valley and cleared it of remaining rebel forces, and on March 18 Operation Anaconda was declared officially over. But that was not the end of the hunt for al-Qaeda and the Taliban. On April 15, 2002, Operation Mountain Lion began in the regions of Gardez and Khost.

On August 18, the Army Rangers and other coalition Special Forces joined the 82nd Airborne Division on Operation Mountain Sweep. They mounted five combat air assault missions on the area around the villages of Dormat and Narizah, south of the cities of Gardez and Khost. The troops found an antiaircraft artillery gun, two 82-mm mortars and ammunition, a recoilless rifle, rockets, rocket-propelled grenades, machine guns, and thousands of small arms rounds, and detained 10 people during the operation.

A week after the end of Operation Mountain Sweep, reports surfaced in the *New York Times* that some US Special Forces commanders wanted to quit what they saw as the futile search for bin Laden. Indeed, Special Forces were now on the defensive. Their forward operating bases were coming under attack regularly. The base three miles northeast of Sarabagh was under virtually constant bombardment during March. By mid-May, reportedly six rocket attacks had been made against bases in Orgun-e, Khost, and Miran Shah.

A US Special Forces soldier was killed while on patrol in Paktia on May 19, 2002. On June 17, a Special Forces patrol was fired upon near Tarin Kot. The same day, another team of 20 US Special Forces troops and 40 Afghan soldiers came under small-arms fire near Shkin in the Birmal region of Paktika. On June 22, a rocket landed near the US Special Forces base in Khost. Before dawn on September 3, four 107-mm rockets landed close to US Special Forces operating in southeastern Afghanistan. Then on the night of September 15, at least 10 rockets fell upon the Khost bases, where more than 1,000 American troops were based.

The 46 US Special Forces troopers guarding President Karzai did little better when, in early September 2002, ex-Taliban soldiers tried to assassinate him in Kandahar. They managed to wrestle one of the two attackers to the ground, but two innocent Afghans were killed in the fracas.

Eighteen months later, a CBS camera crew was given access to the 19th Special Forces Group's base in the hostile Pesch Valley, an isolated place near the Pakistani border. Osama bin Laden had been seen in the valley a few months before, just before the unit entered the area. But by that time the Special Forces had dropped their aggressive role. Now they concentrated on making friends, although when they met with the local elders, they reminded them that they were still looking for bin Laden and that they would pay good money for him.

When the Special Forces had first arrived in the area, they had been rocketed every other day. After five months, attacks came only every two or three weeks. The Green Berets' medics helped local people who were sick or injured, and they began building schools. The aim, at this time, was to win hearts and minds.

CHAPTER 19

OPERATION IRAQI FREEDOM

DURING THE SECOND GULF WAR, the US, Britain, Australia, and Poland put on the ground in Iraq the largest special-operations force that had been deployed since the Vietnam War. In northern Iraq particularly, there was a huge special-operations presence. At the time of the invasion, as much as 80 percent of the combat forces of the 53,000-strong US Special Operations Command—including Navy SEALs, Army Green Berets and Rangers, and Delta Force operatives—found themselves committed in Iraq and Afghanistan.

After Tora Bora, the SAS had returned home to Britain, but in the run up to the Second Gulf War, America asked for their help again. President Bush particularly wanted the British SAS on board. General Tommy Franks, who was now in command of the invasion of Iraq, was aware how close the SAS had come to nailing bin Laden and the remnants of his al-Qaeda forces in Afghanistan. When they slipped away into Pakistan, he blamed overcaution of the US Special Forces.

The multinational contribution to the invasion of Iraq was the responsibility of Brigadier General Gary L. Harrell.

He had commanded the Special Forces' hunt for Pablo Escobar in Colombia in the early 1990s and had been with Delta Force during their disastrous attempt to capture the warlord Mohammed Farrah Aidid in Mogadishu in 1993, resulting in the notorious Black Hawk Down incident.

By this time, the British element was closely integrated into the US Joint Special Operations Command, alongside the 75th Rangers and the 1st Special Forces Operational Detachment Delta—Delta Force. They were supported by the 160th Special Operations Air Regiment with 14 Chinooks, 18 Sikorsky MH-60 Pave Hawks, seven MH-6 Hughes Little Bird assault helicopters, and Hercules MC-130s, along with other helicopters and air-to-air refueling tankers for search-and-rescue missions. The British component was 215 SAS men from B, D, and G Squadrons along with their Land Rovers, painted pink for desert camouflage, and SAS-trained signalers and support groups, plus M Squadron of the SBS, which was with 3 Commando Brigade of the Royal Marines on board the aircraft carrier HMS *Ark Royal*.

British Special Forces were also supported by the Joint Special Forces Aviation Wing—the 657 Army Air Corps Squadron with six AH-7 Lynx helicopters, along with eight CH-47 Chinooks from the 7th Squadron of the RAF, based at Odiham, Hampshire. The Hercules aircraft of RAF Special Forces Flight of 47 Squadron would carry the SAS to their drop-off points, and a former commander of the SAS, Lieutenant General Cedric Delves, was sent to MacDill Air Force Base in Tampa, Florida, as Special Forces liaison officer with US Central Command.

General Franks also wanted the Australian Special Forces on board. He was well aware of their contribution to the war in Afghanistan after their commanding officer, Lieutenant

General Rowan Tink, had been awarded the US Bronze Star for bravery. The Australians contributed 100 men from their 1st SAS Regiment with the 4th Battalion of the Royal Australian Regiment, a commando unit who would act as a quick-reaction force to extract the SAS if they got into trouble. They were supported by some 250 airmen and women and maintenance crews deployed with a squadron of 14 F/A-18 Royal Australian Air Force Hornet fighter aircraft; about 150 personnel deployed with three RAAF C-130 Hercules transport aircraft; and another 150 deployed with two P-3C Orion maritime patrol aircraft.

The Australian Special Forces Task Group itself comprised some 500 men. These included an advance party of an SAS squadron, CH-47 Chinook troop-lift helicopters, and personnel from 5th Aviation Regiment, as well as specialist troops to deal with the threat of weapons of mass destruction drawn from the Incident Response Regiment—or TIRR—based at Holsworthy, New South Wales. They would also be on hand to rescue downed airmen or evacuate the wounded. The Australian contribution was designated Operation Falconer.

Rather than be integrated into the command structure of the American Special Forces, like the British, the Aussies maintained their own Special Forces Forward Command to ensure that the Australian SAS was always commanded by Australians. However, it was located within the headquarters of the US Special Operations Command.

Other coalition members also supplied Special Forces troops. Poland provided commandos from the Polish Operational Maneuver Reconnaissance Group—the Grupa Reagowania Operacyjno Manewrowego, or GROM—and Canada sent its specialist Joint Task Force Two.

The American contingent comprised three battalions from the 5th Special Forces Group based at Fort Campbell, Kentucky—2,000 men in all—and the US Navy Special Warfare Wing, consisting of US Navy SEALs and DEVGRU, the Naval Special Warfare Development Group, formerly SEAL Team 6. They had their own air arm, the 16th US Aviation Wing, with MH-53 Pave Low helicopters for CSAR missions and Hercules MC-130, some of them kitted out as Spectre gunships. Then there were the 8th US Psychological Operations and the 9th Civil Affairs Battalion (Airborne) tasked to win over the hearts and minds of the Iraqi people.

US Special Forces and the SAS went into Jordan in 2002, using Azraq Air Base as their forward operating base. By October, they were in western Iraq, where they were to undertake an "area denial mission" so that Saddam Hussein could not station his Scud launchers there as he had in the First Gulf War. Under a secret agreement, Israel was to pull out members of the Sayeret Matkal who were operating there. For political reasons, these were replaced with freewheeling teams of Green Berets, British and Australian SAS, and Polish GROM, who were to neutralize any Scud missile batteries threatening Israel. They found little opposition. One officer has called western Iraq a "Special Forces playground." They also undertook covert forward reconnaissance and attacked air bases, roads, and the communications network.

During the initial air attacks, they directed the bombing and undertook "psy-ops"—psychological operations—to encourage those who opposed Saddam Hussein's regime to rise up. In the south, Special Operations personnel gave aid to the invading conventional forces and, in the cities, gave assistance the anti-Ba'athist Shi'ite elements. Meanwhile, the Green Berets, Delta Force, and the CIA were training the Kurdish

Peshmerga guerrillas in the north. US Special Forces also went into battle alongside the Kurdish fighters who were trying to bring down the regime.

The British were determined not to have any repeat of the disastrous Bravo Two Zero mission. Men would not be sent in on foot. The SAS's pink Land Rovers would be airlifted by helicopter or Hercules into the country. Then the SAS would drive to their objectives. They would also have the designated combat air support of two RAF flights of G7 Harriers. Also on call at Azraq Air Base were 10 F-16 Fighting Falcons and a National Guard contingent of A-10 Warthog dedicated ground support aircraft.

Even before the main forces went in, there were already hundreds of Special Operations men in country, laid up in positions where they could observe the Iraqi Republican Guard or key military installations. That figure rose rapidly as the glare of the international media turned to the buildup of the main UK and US ground forces, allowing Special Forces units to conduct a shadowy war in the west and north. Unofficially, US and Allied Special Forces were given freedom of action to operate anywhere inside Iraq.

On March 15, the US Navy SEALs, the SBS, Royal Marine commandos, and US Navy SEALs went in to capture and secure oil platforms in the Gulf and the oil fields around Basra. Dropped into the sea by helicopter at night, they had to swim in full kit to the legs of the platform, then scale them using ropes and magnetic pads. Then with MP-5SDs and stun grenades they stormed the platforms. They did not know whether the platforms were manned, whether those who might be on board were armed, or whether the platforms were booby-trapped. On one platform taken by the GROM, the phone began to ring. The team froze, fearing the telephone might be rigged to detonate explosive charges. After a while it stopped, and the Polish officer commented that it must have been a wrong number—to everyone's great relief.

As the air war began, Special Forces were used to guide air strikes on Saddam Hussein's headquarters and palaces. They also identified and called in air attacks on other key targets. As the coalition forces massed offshore, the US Navy SEALs were joined by the SBS, and Royal Marine Commandos took key positions around the Al Faw peninsula and led the attack on the port of Umm Qasr in the largest SEAL operation ever mounted. The SBS and Royal Marine Commandos occupied the forward observation posts, coordinating naval gunfire on the targets inland. After the fall of Umm Qasr, members of GROM were photographed by Reuters alongside the Marine team Special Warfare Development Group (DEVGRU), formerly known as SEAL Team 6, to the embarrassment of the Polish authorities who wanted their commitment kept secret. The GROM were withdrawn from Umm Qasr and sent to join the Royal Marine commandos attacking Basra, believing the British were less likely to court publicity.

US Special Forces took up positions south of Baghdad, while Delta Force and the CIA's Special Activities unit readied the Peshmerga to attack key Iraqi positions. They were also to attack villages along the Iranian border occupied by Ansar al-Islam, a radical Islamist group thought to be linked to al-Qaeda.

On the night of March 20, 2003, as the main force was attacking from Kuwait in the south, MH-6 Little Bird assault helicopters started attacking the Iraqi positions along the Jordanian border with electronically operated 7.62-mm miniguns and pods of air-to-ground missiles. The defenses quickly crumbled. RAF Chinooks and SAS Land Rovers streamed over the border in the dark and headed for airfields designated H-2 and H-3 after the old pumping stations on the Haifa pipeline. Saddam Hussein still had operational planes there that could have been used to deliver chemical weapons. Anything on the ground was made short work of by the A-10 Warthogs with their 30-mm Gatling guns, capable of firing 3,000 armor-piercing rounds a minute, mounted in their noses. Further backup was provided by the Harriers and the F-16s.

Once the coalition air support had taken care of any defenses the airfields could put up, Special Forces drove straight in. With the airfields secure, Chinooks and C-130 Hercules began ferrying in ammunition, supplies, vehicles, and more men. When the Royal Marine's 45 Commando and the US 75th Airborne Rangers arrived, they took over control of the airfields, while the British and Australian SAS headed out into the desert.

From the second day of Operation Iraqi Freedom onward, the Special Forces used the two captured airfields as bases for long-range reconnaissance patrols. US Air Force Predator unmanned observation flew ahead, scouting for targets to be attacked. Special Forces then pushed eastward across the desert toward Baghdad backed by air support from RAF GR7 Harriers.

Half a squadron of Australian SAS then moved northward toward the Syrian border. Intelligence reports indicated that Iraqi Scuds moving across the border from Syria were setting up there. Meanwhile the F-16s and A-10s moved up to H-3 to be on hand to provide close air support as the SAS moved northward and eastward. The main highways from Baghdad to Jordan and Syria were being kept open by small groups of Iraqi commandos, leaving an escape route for

Saddam Hussein and his henchmen. The British and Australian SAS moved on them, dispersing them and undertaking further area denial operations.

According to American intelligence, the Iraqis were hiding their Scud missile launchers in Syria and were planning to run them over the border, fire them, then run them back into Syria before they could be hit by an air strike. A troop of six Australian SAS were sent out in two six-wheeled Land Rovers to put a stop to this by taking out the command, control, and communication headquarters of the Iraqi batteries, which operated out of five vehicles in a well-entrenched position and was guarded by 50 Iraqis, according to American intelligence.

As the SAS men approached, they came under heavy fire. However, the Aussies decided that, if they made a direct attack on board their vehicles, they could take the center of the Iraqi position. They came speeding out of cover, only to find their way blocked by two Iraqi vehicles manned by 20 Iraqis who were putting up a barrage of automatic fire. It was plain that they were an elite Iraqi unit, trained to take on the SAS.

"They definitely weren't conscript soldiers," said one SAS man. "They were very aggressive. They were very well trained. They moved toward us. We moved toward them."

The battle was on.

"They were operating in sport-utility vehicles with large machine guns mounted in the rear tray," said the troop commander, "and on observing our location, they began engaging us with heavy machine-gun fire, small-arms fire, and rocket-propelled grenades."

The SAS opened fire on them with their .50-caliber Browning machine guns, scattering the Iraqis.

"When you come under fire, you really don't think about it at all," said another patrol member. "You think about getting to the next vantage point so you can return fire. You really don't think about the rounds coming in at you. You're just making sure that you're doing your drills correctly and that you're backing up your mate in the next car."

The truth is he did rather more than that. Under heavy fire, he picked up a Javelin shoulder-mounted missile launcher and took out the first Iraqi vehicle.

"Both sides in this particular instance actually stopped shooting to watch this rocket cruise through the air and engage a moving vehicle at high speed, moving away from us, and I think that changed the battlefield," said the troop commander.

A second Javelin missile also found its target.

"It was a little bit daunting seeing so many enemy coming toward us," said a third man, "but we saw how effective our weapons systems were in neutralizing their vehicles, and you could actually physically see the shock on the enemy's faces when they did see their vehicles destroyed."

The battle was far from over.

"We were getting rounds splashing all around the vehicles and around the guys when they dismounted," said the squadron commander. "We were getting RPG exploding over our heads, at times, and behind us."

Under the covering fire of more .50-caliber rounds, the rest of the patrol moved forward. After seeing two of their vehicles destroyed, quite a few of the enemy started to surrender at this stage. But others were hiding in the grass, returning fire with rocket launchers and small arms.

"Several also attempted to set up an 82-mm mortar tube, and they were about to try and engage us with that," said an

SAS man. "We couldn't really engage the enemy around the mortar tube because there were some surrendering, so we engaged the mortar tube with a sniper rifle, and that was very effective. The round hit the tube and caused a mortar bomb that was in the tube to explode."

That finished off the mortar crew. The other Iraqis had moved in among some Bedouin tents. As there were civilians in there, the SAS had to stop firing because of the threat to the locals.

"They exploited that component of our professionalism," said the squadron commander. "It was a difficult time. We were also trying to affect the capture of about eight enemy who were surrendering with their arms in the air, but as soon as we had gotten within range they dropped their weapons and continued firing. It was a very difficult situation."

The SAS men had no choice but to fire back.

"As soon as they were in an aggressive pose, and a threat, they were then neutralized," said the squadron commander.

Those Iraqi soldiers who surrendered were disarmed and allowed to go free. They were surprised by this and even a little hesitant to walk away in case the SAS men were not really going to let them go. They may even have been worried about being shot in the back. Even though these men might walk over the hill, pick up another gun, and start shooting again, the SAS had no other choice except to kill them. They could not take prisoners along with them if they were going to complete their mission.

Six Aussies had killed 12 Iraqis out of a platoon of around 30. The rest surrendered. The mission was a complete success with no Australian loss of life.

This unit then moved on to take the Kubaysah cement factory, one of the biggest in the Middle East. They had been ordered to clear it of all Iraqi troops and check the site for hidden weapons. They did not want to damage the cement factory because it was part of the infrastructure of Iraq.

"If we wanted Iraq to get back on its feet quickly," said the squadron commander, "then we didn't want to destroy it."

However, it was guarded by scores of Iraqi soldiers who ignored the SAS demands to surrender. It was a difficult target to assault, and the Australians did not want to risk the lives of civilians inside by fighting their way in. So their commander came up with a novel solution: He called the US Air Force.

"We requested that an aircraft, an F14, come and do a low fly, breaking the sound barrier," said the squadron commander. "The effect of this was a sonic boom—a massive explosion. We actually thought he had detonated ammunition inside the facility. That wasn't the case. But it broke in several windows, and as a result people came running out with their arms up."

He had gotten the idea from one of his men who had been in the RAAF.

"I remembered before I joined the army, with the Australian Air Force, we broke the sound barrier by mistake and broke a lot of greenhouses in South Australia," he said.

The cement works fell without a single shot being fired and netted 40 prisoners of war.

On March 25, members of the US Army's 75th Ranger Regiment captured a third strategic airfield, H-1, in a night-time parachute assault. Their immediate objective was to take complete control of the two main roads that linked Baghdad to Jordan and Syria. They were also to search for further Scud sites and close the Syrian border to prevent more missiles being brought up from there.

Over the next two weeks, the Special Forces teams moved steadily toward the Euphrates Valley. However, apart from these airfields and their small bases, which were guarded by US Rangers and UK Marines, the Special Forces teams were not trying to occupy ground. Instead they aimed to keep the small Iraqi garrisons in the region off-guard. Travelers on the road from Baghdad to the Jordanian border reported few signs of Western troops apart from occasional vehicle checkpoints, suggesting they largely moved at night away from populated areas.

By the end of March, American and British Special Forces were closing in on Baghdad. The Australians, in a convoy of 15 vehicles, were some 80 kilometers behind, having stopped off with some US Special Forces to call in an air strike on Al-Rutbah Prison, which was now a smoking ruin.

US Special Forces were now linking up with the Marines, while all the oil installations in southern Iraqi and the gulf had fallen to the SEALs, the SBS, and GROM. But everything had not gone Special Forces' way. The British had an embarrassing moment on March 31 when Al Jazeera television showed a Special Forces Land Rover being paraded through the streets of the city, then a quad-bike and a collection of British weapons on display at an Iraqi military base. They included handheld rocket launchers, 40-mm grenades, machine guns, and specialized radio equipment, suggesting that they did not come from a conventional British Army unit. Iraqi television said the equipment had been captured after an attempted airborne assault. The location of the incident, far from the main UK operating area around Kuwait and Basra, immediately led to media speculation that the SAS was involved. British military spokesmen refused to comment.

In fact, the equipment belong to the SBS, which had been patrolling the area around Mosul in northwest Iraq when they had driven right passed an Iraqi patrol without a shot being fired. However, the Iraqis were a point reconnaissance unit for a much larger force armed with tanks. The SBS only realized this when they ran into the larger force face-to-face. Normally this would not have caused a problem. They would simply have made a run for it and headed for the emergency rendezvous point to be airlifted out. As it was, the Iraqis had blocked off all exit points on the road. Behind them was a steep hill cut with deep ravines.

An SOV Land Rover is well armed, but they did not have enough weaponry to take on the large force that now confronted them. As the Iraqis opened fire, the SBS men had no alternative but to abandon their Land Rover and make a dash for it. Once in the relative safety of the hills, they decided that it would better to split into smaller groups, which would give them a better chance of survival. Most of the men got clear away, called in a helicopter, and were airlifted out. But two men missed the ERV point and had to race the 65 miles to the Syrian border with half the Iraqi Army on their tail. After intense diplomatic negotiations, the two SBS men were eventually returned.

While Al-Jazeera said that the Iraqis had captured the Land Rover, Britain's Ministry of Defence dismissed this as propaganda. The Land Rover, they said, had been jettisoned from a Chinook when it had engine problems.

The US military was less than pleased though. One of the pieces of equipment the SBS had left behind was a Stinger surface-to-air missile, later used to bring down an F-16 Fighting Falcon. Nevertheless, the coalition commander, General

Tommy Franks, publicly praised UK Special Forces, saying, "They have accomplished some wonderful things out there."

While the Americans and British have traditionally kept quiet about the activities of their Special Forces, the Australians are more open.

"In all there were around eight of us operating in the western desert, but to the Iraqis it must have seemed like eight hundred," said one Aussie SAS man. "Our primary role was to stop weapons of mass destruction from being launched from the 1991 Scud Line in the western Iraqi desert, while our secondary role was to raise merry hell, 'Digger-style.' Basically we were an enormous itch that the Iraqis could not scratch, as we were everywhere and anywhere. One day we were in the desert, the next in a giant cement works."

The cement works they attacked—dubbed "The Temple of Doom" by the SAS—was at Kubaysah, 40 miles north of Highway 1 between Baghdad and Amman and 12 miles south of south of al-Asad Air Base, which the Australian SAS would also take. Along the way they had a number of running battles and captured more that 2,000 Iraqis, including Republican Guards and men from dedicated anti-Special Forces units. They largely tended the wounded, fed and watered the prisoners, then sent them home. During their 42 days in-country, the Australian SAS suffered no casualties.

Despite their best efforts, they found no Scuds, though they called in air strikes that dropped more than 45 tons of bombs in the first week alone.

"The fact that the squadron suffered no casualties did not surprise me, as we minimized the risks to our own people and to the Iraqis," said one SAS man. "Despite the lack of casualties and the string of victories, this was no picnic, as the

Iraqis were well organized and well equipped. It was one-on-one, and it was tough."

Due to the presence of Bedouins and local Iraqis, it was impossible to move around the flat western desert in daylight. They had to go in at night. The first challenge was to negotiate a system of trenches and earth berms without being detected by the network of Iraqi border posts. Having done that successively, they ran into an Iraqi military convoy about 20 miles beyond the border. The ensuing firefight ended with SAS medics tending the Iraqi wounded, whom they released since it would not have been possible to continue the mission encumbered with prisoners.

However, another SAS patrol that had crossed into Iraq by night spent 96 hours in the open desert without being spotted by anyone, including local Bedouin herdsmen. It was an achievement in itself not to be spotted in such flat terrain. After their experience in the First Gulf War, they concluded that the Iraqis must have figured the SAS would be there and tried to second-guess them. So they adopted a strategy they called "maneuver warfare" to put pressure on the enemy and force them to give away their position. As they were a small force, their aim was always to create a disproportionate effect by utilizing the element of surprise. Consequently, they made an effort to be completely unpredictable in their tactics. On the other hand, they had to deal with an unpredictable enemy. Sometimes they would raise their hands in surrender, then resume firing when the SAS got closer. One of the regiment's flags bears eloquent testimony to that: It has bullet holes and powder burns from being shot at close range.

"Adding to our operational experience we also had the weather to contend with, as temperatures often ranged from minus-five degrees to plus-forty-three degrees Celsius—and we thought Oz varied," said the SAS man. "All in all it was a magnificent effort and a ripper achievement."

On top of the extremes of temperature, they endured sandstorms that reduced visibility to 30 feet and blew for days on end. On another occasion it rained so heavily that the group's weapons systems were clogged with windblown mud. The atrocious weather conditions were also a problem for the helicopters used to keep the forward team supplied. They flew as much as 400 miles behind enemy lines at night, dodging Iraqi air defenses and refueling in the air along the way.

Contacts with the enemy occurred almost daily, partially because the Iraqis were seeking them out. The SAS assumed that the best form of defense was attack, so they constantly hit the Iraqis to keep the on the defensive.

On their second night inside Iraq, the SAS staged a well-planned attack on a well-defended radio relay station. Achieving total surprise, a phased assault cleared the facility in what became a one-sided firefight. Then an air strike was called in to destroy the tower. This effectively undermined Iraq's ballistic missile capability.

The Iraqis responded the following morning. They sent five or six armed vehicles, but the SAS simply outmaneuvered them. Fire from heavy weapons, Javelin rockets, M19 grenade launchers, heavy machine guns, and sniper rifles forced the Iraqis to seek shelter in a number of buildings, where air strikes finished them off.

Several days later, another SAS patrol was confronted by a force of 50 Iraqis on civilian trucks and 4x4s. They were armed with mortars, RPGs, and heavy machine guns. But the SAS held their own. Within the first few minutes, they knocked out one of the trucks, forcing the Iraqis to advance on foot and leaving them particularly vulnerable. However, the SAS suffered from repeated equipment failure. One SAS man had to employ all four weapons systems on his long-range desert patrol vehicle, one after another, as each one in turn jammed.

While some elements of the SAS were moving constantly from action to action, another team remained undetected in an observation post overlooking Highway 10. At one point down the highway, there was a crossroads and a truck stop that was defended by some 200 Iraqis. The SAS called in air strikes over a period of 48 hours, then moved in to clear the facility. Unfortunately, the enemy had withdrawn under cover of a sandstorm. But they could confirm that the target had been neutralized. This action put an end to any possibility that Iraq might launch ballistic missiles.

Coalition leaders were particularly pleased because no Scuds were fired at Israel—a development that could have massively complicated allied war plans. Indeed, no Scuds were found. The main opposition to the Special Forces came from Iraqi commando units that were attempting to keep the main roads to Jordan and Syria open to allow key members of the regime to potentially escape if Baghdad should fall.

After the first week, action in the western desert slowed. The SAS then changed strategy and began stopping people on the highway to prevent members of the regime from escaping over the border. They captured numerous Ba'ath Party members and paramilitary Fedayeen, carrying large amounts of cash as they tried to flee the country. They also stopped a convoy carrying looted communications equipment and gas masks, and they made friends with local sheiks who persuaded the enemy occupying the town of Ar Ramadi, 60 miles west of Baghdad, to surrender.

The Australian SAS were then tasked with taking al-Asad Air Base, which was held by a force of 100 or so armed looters. One small SAS team was hardly likely to triumph against such a force if they engaged them head-to-head, even though the SAS had Royal Australian Air Force F/A-18s circling above. So while the defenders fired heavy weapons at them, the SAS responded with sniper shots, fired not to kill but close enough to their mark to scare the enemy away.

"It was a warning shot," said the Australian squadron commander. "If they didn't leave, then potentially we had the right to engage them, and thankfully they took their course—the right course of action—and withdrew."

Once the air base was in coalition hands, they had to go through the buildings room-by-room, checking for any remaining enemy booby traps or mines. The air base was so large that the search took 36 hours. Once the air base was secured, the TIRR came in to check for weapons of mass destruction. Although they did not find any, they did find bunkers and abandoned buildings that were stuffed with arms and ammunition. The Al-Asad Air Base was one of Saddam's prize installations. The enemy had left 57 MiG jet fighters at the air base, along with near 8,000 tons of ordnance. After the search was over, engineers moved in to clear and mend the runway. The first fixed-wing aircraft to land there was a C-130 Hercules transport of Australia's 36 Squadron. The base was then handed over to the US 3rd Armored Cavalry Regiment.

Other Special Forces did not have nearly such an exciting time. One team complained that they found it positively boring to man an observation post on a quiet road. Their job was to watch, report, and target. However, there was nothing to target, as any munitions used would have been worth more that the vehicles they took out. The road was largely used by smugglers moving contraband. There was some military movement—troops, artillery, armor—but no Scuds, certainly nothing worth compromising their position by calling in an air strike.

As they were on the top of a high embankment, they were unlikely to be stumbled upon. The nearest they came to being discovered was when a caravan of camels came within 250 feet of their position, but the men with them were far too concerned with keeping the body of a Mercedes they were transporting on the back of a camel in position to notice the observation post above them.

As the war heated up, there was more military traffic, but still no Scuds or anything that would constitute a threat—certainly no weapons of mass destruction. But then they had no desire to get into a fight with ordinary Iraqi soldiers.

"I personally had no beef with the rank-and-file Iraqi Army, as they were just as much victims of Saddam's regime as anyone else," said one of them. "It was the Republican Guard and the Fedayeen who I despised, as they persecuted their own people."

The only time their lives were in danger was when US ground-attack aircraft flew overhead just as a convoy was making its way down the road. They lined up to attack, but broke off. This came as some relief, as the OP was close to the side of the road, and if the convoy was attacked, the Special Forces team also risked getting hit. They could have tried to call them off with their tactical beacons, but that would have risked giving their position away.

While the Green Berets were active in the west and the SEALs undertook operations in the south, Delta Force led 6,000 Peshmerga fighters into battle against Ansar al-Islam in the northeast. Between March 27 and March 30, they cleared the Beyara Valley. With an observation post established on high ground and a drone overhead, they could direct Tomahawk cruise missiles and laser-guided ordinance onto targets designated by Special Forces operatives on the ground.

CHAPTER 20

BATTLE OF DEBECKA PASS

THE MOST FAMOUS SPECIAL FORCES ACTION of the Second Gulf War was the Battle of Debecka Pass, which is sometimes referred to as the Alamo of the Iraq War. On April 6, 2003, 26 Green Berets were given the task of securing a key crossroads near the town of Debecka in northern Iraq between the cities of Irbil and Kirkuk. If they succeeded, they would cut off Highway 2, preventing the Iraqi Army from moving north into Kurdistan and allowing friendly forces to take the crucial Kirkuk oil fields.

The battle was fought by two 3rd Special Forces Group A-teams who went through their final battle training in the pinelands of Fort Bragg, North Carolina, and Fort Pickett, Virginia, from October through December 2002. The teams specialized in reconnaissance deep behind enemy lines. Their Ground Mobility Vehicles—souped-up Humvees equipped with Mark 19 automatic grenade launchers or .50-caliber heavy machine guns—took them a thousand miles in 10 days without resupply. At Fort Pickett, the teams practiced how they would defend themselves against Iraqi armor.

The GMVs did not have the firepower to resist an all-out attack by Soviet-built T-55 tanks. But they were to receive the Javelin, the Army's latest shoulder-held "fire and forget" antitank missile.

On March 8, 2003, the two teams flew from Pope Air Force Base to Romania, and on March 26 they infiltrated Iraq on an MC-130 Combat Talon, landing at As-Sulaymaniya, some 60 miles east of Kirkuk.

Their first few days were spent fighting the Ansar Al-Islam militant Islamic group near Halabja. On April 1 they moved to Irbil and on to a staging area where they linked with ODA 044, a 10th Group A-team who were working with the Kurdish Peshmerga militia, known to the Green Berets as "the Pesh" or "Peshies."

On April 4 they were given a new mission, code-named Northern Safari. Together with ODA 044 and their Pesh-merga allies, the 3rd were to seize the Debecka intersection and hold it until they were relieved by the 173rd Airborne. The crossroads sat just to the west of a ridgeline that formed the border that had divided Kurdish-held Iraq from the rest of the country. The plan of attack was simple. Some 200 Pesh-merga forces and a handful of ODA 044 troops would dash forward and seize the ridgeline, while ODAs 391 and 392 would support them with fire from their GMVs. There was just one problem. There was no intelligence on Iraqi forces in the area.

Thick haze shrouded the ridgeline and the valley beyond it, limiting visibility to less than two miles. However, the Green Berets quickly discovered that they were in for a fight. In the absence of aerial reconnaissance, they sought out hu-man intelligence. Farmers who grazed their livestock on the ridge told the Green Berets that there were Iraqi forces on the ridge and beyond, and their positions were defended by minefields and trenches.

On April 5, the 3rd sent two GMVs forward to reconnoiter the Iraqi positions on the ridge. From a position just behind a 12-foot berm east of the ridge, they saw Iraqi soldiers on the ridgeline standing on top of their bunkers. That night they called in a B-52 air strike.

In the morning, only 80 of the expected 200 Peshmerga showed up, driving straight down the road toward the 12-foot dirt berm. They were stopped by a minefield and began picking their way through it, piling plastic Valmira antitank and antipersonnel mines alongside the road.

The Green Berets decided to outflank the berm and drive straight up the ridgeline instead. Chief Warrant Officer Martin McKenna was eager to breach the berm anyway in case they had to make a hasty retreat. But there was no time. They heard gunfire erupting from the other side of the berm, and Captain Eric Wright, commander of ODA 391, ordered them forward to support the Peshmerga. But catching up with them was difficult. ODA 391 hit a trench too deep and wide for the GMVs to cross. The Green Berets had to dismount and demolish a sandbag fighting position and top-fill the trench.

The next obstacle was unexploded ordnance dropped by the B-52s the night before. Again the Green Berets had to dismount and go on foot to guide the GMVs through what was essentially a minefield 700 meters deep.

South of the road, 392 had advanced up to the berm when they heard the Peshmerga's recoilless rifle firing somewhere up ahead. They also found themselves in a minefield. As the driver of the lead GMV tried to navigate a concertina wire barrier, Warrant Officer Robert Parker, 392's assistant detachment commander, leaned out the door to look underneath.

He yelled for them to stop. The driver slammed on the brakes, and the GMV stopped with its wheels just 12 inches from the prongs of an antipersonnel mine.

By now, the fire had intensified, and ODA 392 had decided to reverse back down to the road on the flattened grass trail they had made on their way into the minefield.

The Peshmerga already had taken the ridge. When the Green Berets caught up with them, they saw Iraqi trenches and fighting positions dug for armored vehicles, along with two abandoned T-55 tanks. The two A-teams linked up with the Peshmerga and engaged the Iraqis in their bunkers. After a fierce firefight, they fought their way through to the crossroads, capturing about 20 Iraqi soldiers. One of them was a major, who revealed that an Iraqi armor unit had withdrawn to the south after the bombing, leaving him and his men behind.

There was no time to prepare defensive positions if they were attacked from the south. So the 391 team leader decided it was a good time to follow McKenna's advice and blast a path through the berm where it crossed the road. This would allow them to withdraw quickly if necessary. It would also clear the way for them to be resupplied.

The intersection did not offer the commanding view of the plains, so the Green Berets sent a team up to a small ridge known as Press Hill. From there, they saw Iraqi vehicles approaching from the south. While half of 391 was busy collecting land mines to help blow the berm, the rest of the men were in a gunfight with Iraqi infantry. They tried to engage the vehicles with a .50-caliber machine gun, but it proved ineffective against the fast-moving trucks. The A-Teams then moved forward to a position designated the "Alamo" some 900 meters from the intersection. Here they were dangerously exposed. As Iraqi air-defense cannon shells burst overhead and incoming mortar and artillery rounds were exploding all around, they watched transfixed as an armored column bore down on their position.

It was then that they turned to their new Javelins. The first weapon was in the hands of Staff Sergeant Jason Brown, who had only fired one once before. He sat cross-legged on a hillside. He did not think they stood a chance, but he knew that the Javelin missile system he held was his team's best hope for survival.

Although inexperienced, he thought that his best chance of hitting an armored target was to use the launcher's thermal sights to penetrate the haze. But it would take at least 45 seconds before the launcher's cooling system would let him do that. Using the day sights, he could have fired immediately.

As the seconds ticked away, he saw muzzle flashes. A few seconds later, the rounds exploded on his hillside around him. The tanks were less than a mile away, but still the Javelin would not arm.

Finally the sight cooled. Brown loosed off his, and his team's first Javelin fired in anger. The missile streaked across the open ground. It hit an Iraqi troop truck about 3,000 meters away that burst into flames. The occupants leapt out, and the Green Berets sped down the slope in their GMVs, shooting at the Iraqis as they fled.

But it was far from a one-way fight. The Special Forces men at the crossroads found themselves under mortar fire. USAF forward air controllers with the Green Berets identified two mortar tubes to the east near the town of Debecka, and four GMVs set off to destroy them.

At the crossroads, Staff Sergeant Bobby Farmer, ODA 391's junior engineer, was sitting on top of the GMV when he saw two white SUVs coming out of the haze to the west. They drove slowly down the road with their lights flashing toward the American positions. Special Forces Commander Frank Antenori, 391's senior NCO, told his men to hold their fire since the troops approaching might be trying to surrender.

Then, behind the gray metal form, Iraqi armored personnel carriers emerged from the mist. The American GMVs pulled off the road to the left and right to take up defensive positions. Worse was to come. As soon as the Iraqis in the APCs saw the Americans, the lead vehicle began pumping out smoke. Then through the smoke, a column of at least five T-55 tanks appeared. They were about a mile away and closing at about 40 miles an hour with their 100mm main guns firing round after round of high-explosive shells.

Farmer banged on the roof of his GMV, yelling "Tanks!" to alert his comrades.

When he heard this, Antenori jumped up on the roof of the vehicle to take a look. Master Sergeant Kenneth Thompson and Sergeant Jeff Adamec grabbed Javelin launchers and jumped from the GMVs. They, too, had to wait the nail-biting seconds for the sights to cool down.

Meanwhile, the team attacking the mortars got the message that tanks were coming from the south and disengaged.

The Javelins were taking longer than normal to cool down, so the Green Berets pulled back 900 meters to the Alamo ridgeline along with the Peshmerga in one overloaded old truck.

Alerted to what was happening, Staff Sergeant Brown grabbed another Javelin and jumped on the hood of a GMV, and the US Air Force forward air controllers put out an urgent call for close air support.

With the combined Special Forces and Peshmerga force back on the Alamo, Brown's Javelin was ready to fire. He squeezed the trigger. The missile shot out of the tube and slowed to almost a standstill. Then its booster kicked in. It arched upward, then came down like an arrow, scoring a direct hit on the moving personnel carrier. Iraqi soldiers piled out of the burning vehicle and ran for cover in a field of the tall wheat beside the road.

Sergeant Adamec and Staff Sergeant Eugene Zawojski, both armed with Javelins, joined Brown on the ridge. Together, they destroyed two trucks and two APCs within a couple of minutes. As Iraqis leapt from the burning vehicles, Sergeant Farmer, Sergeant First Class Scot Marlow, and Sergeant First Class Van Hines rained .50-caliber fire and Mark 19 40-mm grenades on them.

The T-55s had taken cover in defilade positions on the far side of the road, making it impossible for the Javelins to get a lock on their heat signatures. The Green Berets had already used up about half of their ammunition, but waves of Iraqis kept coming.

Then two US Navy F-14 Tomcats arrived to give close air support. They dropped 750-pound ordnance and Paveway II laser-guided smart bombs. The Iraqis responded with anti-aircraft fire, and airburst shells began to explode some 300 meters in front of the Green Berets' position. An Iraqi artillery piece firing 152-mm high-explosive shells then began to find its range. A smoke round nearly scored a direct hit. It was clear that the enemy artillery had accurately bracketed their position, so the Green Berets withdrew to Press Hill.

Despite this, some 12 Iraqi soldiers threw down their arms and attempted to surrender under a white flag. For a moment it seemed that other Iraqi soldiers might join them, but two white trucks pulled up. Six Arabs in white robes—the uniform of Ba'ath Party enforcers—jumped out and began shooting the surrendering soldiers. An Air Force controller called for an air strike on the white trucks, which were destroyed.

At 0720, Special Forces resupply vehicles arrived carrying ammunition and more Javelins. By then, they had only three missiles left. The Green Berets and the Peshmerga allies were in a position to hold their own while, for two hours, the enemy was bombed. Eventually Iraqi soldiers abandoned their vehicles and fled the battlefield on foot.

For the next two days Iraqi artillery and multiple rocket launchers continued to fire upon the Special Forces positions. However, the crossroads were secured, and the Green Berets crossed to Kirkuk to prevent the destruction of oil facilities by Iraqi forces.

CHAPTER 21

PACK OF CARDS

On May 1, 2003, President George W. Bush declared "mission accomplished" on the aircraft carrier USS *Abraham Lincoln*, but the fighting in Iraq was far from over, especially for the Special Forces. Delta Force and 22 SAS formed Task Force 20, while the Green Berets and the SBS formed Task Force 121. These units began searching the country for Iraq's "most wanted." These men were famously displayed on packs of playing cards showing pictures of the 55 most wanted men.

Even though Saddam Hussein—the ace of spades in the pack—had disappeared, his army had disbanded, and the country was in the hands of the coalition, allied troops were regularly hit by small-arms fire, RPGs, and roadside IEDs, or improvised explosive devices. Most of this was aimed at the American sectors in Baghdad and the Sunni-dominated north. Saddam Hussein, a Sunni Muslim, had favored the denomination in his administration. The Shiites in the south were less trouble, initially, as they were grateful for having been released from the choke hold Saddam Hussein had on them.

The situation was not improved by the notoriously trigger-happy attitude of Task Force 20. Named for March 20, 2003—the day the invasion of Iraq officially began—the force originally comprised a 40-man assault team backed by a private aviation unit from the 160th Special Operations Group. It was supported by a Special Forces intelligence unit called Gray Fox—formally the US Army Intelligence Support Activity, USAISA, commonly shortened to the ISA or just the Activity. It had its headquarters in Baghdad International Airport and was commanded by a US Air Force Brigadier General. Task Force 20 seconded men from the Green Berets, Delta Force, Air Force Pararescue, and commandos from the US Navy's elite DEVGRU. As the unit expanded, operators were also brought in from Australia's and Britain's SAS counterterrorism units, along with Poland's elite GROM, bringing its total manpower to 750. Its primary goal was to capture or kill high-value targets—HVTs—particularly former Ba'ath party members and leaders of the regime.

In several missions in Baghdad, Task Force 20 seems to have shot first and asked questions later. The most infamous occurred on July 27, 2003, when several members of the unit, dressed as a group of Westerners in civilian clothing, pulled up in an expensive customized 4x4 outside the exclusive Al Sa'ah restaurant in the affluent Mansur district of Baghdad and began to observe the comings and goings from the house of Prince Rahiah Mohammed al-Habib, a prominent tribal leader, two blocks away. After a while, they got out of the car and moved slowly toward the house, believing that Saddam Hussein's son Ali was inside.

At that moment, six US Army Humvees appeared, sealing off the surrounding roads. Then there was a loud explosion, and men dressed in black wearing gas masks and body armor stormed into Prince al-Habib's house. A crowd gathered around the perimeter. While the operation was unfolding, Prince al-Habib's neighbors, 16-year-old student Mohammed Imad Khazalalrubai and his brother, 13-year-old Zaid, were driving home after collecting their family's monthly rations of flour, rice, and cooking oil. They approached a hastily established American checkpoint. The boys were nudging their white Chevrolet Malibu through a crowd of onlookers when suddenly, according to witnesses, US soldiers in a Humvee 150 yards away opened up. They fired high-velocity rounds through the windshield of the boys' car. The two boys dived for cover. When the firing stopped, Zaid opened the car door and stuck his head out to shake off the shattered glass. At that point, Mohammed says, a single American bullet killed him.

"My brother's blood will not go for nothing," Mohammed screamed in anguish two days later, his wounds from the shooting still swathed in bandages. "I'll take revenge on those American sons of bitches."

With one careless action, Task Force 20 had turned an innocent student into a potential insurgent. But Zaid was not the only innocent casualty that day. A disabled man driving a Toyota Corolla carrying his wife and daughter took a wrong turn near another of the roadblocks. He was killed in a hail of bullets, and his wife and daughter were wounded. On a nearby highway, a man in a Mitsubishi Pajero slowed down to see what was going on and was hit by a ricochet. In all, five Iraqis lost their lives in the action, and Ali Hussein was not in the house, nor had he been there for months.

After the Baghdad raid, tribal leaders from around the country descended on the home of al-Habib, a prominent tribal prince whose house was the target of the raid.

"My people are asking 'What action should we take?'" said al-Habib. "I'm trying to calm them down. I'm telling them that the Americans are probably desperate. But I cannot control the feeling of my people at the moment."

Such action turned even the enemies of Saddam Hussein against the Americans.

"We have no relation whatsoever with the old regime. Most of us were imprisoned and humiliated in Saddam's time," said Abu Bilal al-Fallujah, whose cousin launched at least two attacks on American convoys before he was killed in an explosion at Fallujah's central mosque. "The problems started with the way the Americans ignored our ideas and customs. They humiliated us; they occupied our mosque. Of course, I will seek revenge if I am insulted."

Many could not even see the point of tracking down Saddam Hussein.

"Saddam being caught or killed isn't good for the Americans," says Marouf Sami Noori, brother-in-law of the then fugitive Taha Yassin Ramadan, Saddam's vice president, the 10 of diamonds, who was captured on August 19, 2003, and hanged the following March. "There are many people who would like to fight against the Americans, but if they fight now, they'll be considered Saddam's people. So the resistance will be stronger if Saddam is captured or killed."

The US apologized for the behavior of Task Force 20. The unit continued to carry out a number of operations in Tikrit, Saddam's home town, though they failed to find him. Meanwhile the country continued its descent into anarchy. The Jordanian Embassy was bombed on August 7, killing 19. At 1645 on August 19, 2003, a truck bomb went off outside the United Nations building in Baghdad, killing at least 17 people including the UN Secretary-General's Special Representative for Iraq, Sergio Vieira de Mello, who was organizing humanitarian aid for the Iraqi people. One hundred were estimated to have been injured in the blast. On August 30, more than 124 people were killed by a car-bomb attack on the Shiite holy city of Najaf. Attacks continued throughout the summer. On October 26, the Al-Rashid Hotel, where international administrators stayed, was hit by fire from a multibarreled rocket launcher while US Deputy Secretary of State for Defense Paul Wolfowitz was visiting. The following day, four suicide bombers targeted the headquarters of the International Committee of the Red Cross and Iraqi police stations across Baghdad, killing 40.

With security now a major problem, the US requested further assistance from the SAS and SBS to help guard the "Green Zone," the heavily defended palaces, offices, and hotels where the administrators and other foreign workers now sought refuge. A British lieutenant colonel was sent to the American headquarters to command the British Special Forces in Baghdad. Around 120 Special Forces men from the SAS, SBS, and 14th Intelligence Company, largely formed of ex-SBS men, fell under his command. These British Special Forces men were integrated into the intelligence unit Gray Fox, also known as the Activity, the Group, or the Collective. Alongside colleagues from Delta Force and the US Navy SEALs, they collected intelligence that was collated and processed by the CIA, the NSA (National Security Agency), and the DIS (Defense Intelligence Service). Raw intelligence was not hard to come by. Some 3,000 men— usually former members of Delta Force, SAS, SBS, German GSG-9, or some other Special Forces outfit—were offering their services as security experts around Baghdad. With so many former colleagues working hand-in-hand with Iraqis, it was not hard to find out what was going on. Gray Fox depended on such information.

On July 22, 2003, Task Force 20 scored its first major success. An Iraqi businessman informed the headquarters of the 101st Airborne Division that Saddam Hussein's two sons, Qusay and Uday, were hiding out in his house in the prosperous al-Falah suburb of Mosul, some 200 miles north of Baghdad. They had both been prominent in their father's administration and were in the deck of cards. Qusay was the ace of hearts, Uday the ace of clubs. Both had $15 million bounties on their heads.

Neither of Saddam's sons was popular. Qusay Hussein had been a senior officer with the Republican Guard who had crushed the Shiite uprising after the First Gulf War. He had masterminded the draining of the southern marshes to punish the Marsh Arabs who lived there and had sided with the coalition. As Saddam Hussein's heir-apparent, he was in charge of security and known for his brutality. He was accused of ordering the summary execution of thousands of political prisoners to make room in the jails for more inmates.

Uday had even more enemies. As head of the Olympic Committee, he had tortured athletes who failed him. The country's soccer players were jailed after failing to qualify for the World Cup in 1994 and were forced to kick a concrete ball around. He famously abducted any woman who took his fancy and raped her, sometimes murdering his victim afterward. Any husband, boyfriend, or family member who got in his way would also be dispatched. Even Saddam Hussein did not trust him. As Saddam's first-born, he was to have succeeded his father, but he was dropped as heir-apparent after he killed Saddam's most trusted advisor. The man had introduced Saddam to the woman who would become his second wife. For Uday, this was an insult to his mother, and he publicly murdered the man with an electric carving knife.

Afterward, Saddam had Uday jailed briefly. When he was released, an attempt was made to assassinate Uday. So the Hussein brothers did not have many friends. It was probably the reward set at $15 million a piece that led to their betrayal.

The information was passed via the division's Special Forces' liaison officer to Task Force 20. At the time there was a 12-man SAS team working in Mosul. They had the advantage over American units in undercover operations as they trained in the Gulf and tended to speak Arabic and other local languages. Their smaller teams were less conspicuous than the large units US Special Forces brought in, and they made more of an effort to blend in.

The SAS men went to reconnoiter the target, a two-story building. According to the reports they had received, there were just four men holed up there. Besides Qusay and Uday, there were a bodyguard and Qusay's 14-year-old son, Mustafa. He was not in the deck of cards, and there was no reason he should die.

The SAS reckoned that they could storm the house using the close-quarter battle tactics they had practiced so often at their "killing house" in Herefordshire, where they had learned the assault tactics that worked so well in breaking the Iranian Embassy siege in London in 1980.

First a four-man detachment was sent in on close-target reconnaissance. They were to double-check that the house was indeed occupied. It was a common practice in Iraq for false intelligence to be fed to the Special Forces in an attempt to lure them into a trap. They were also to ascertain what defenses the house had and what sort of a fight the Hussein brothers might put up.

The CRT team reported back that there were four individuals in the house and no sign of heavy weapons. There were two entrances to the house, and they reckoned that 12 SAS men were more than enough to storm the house using explosive entry equipment and kill or capture the men inside. The SAS planned to go in that night, before the Hussein brothers got any wind that they had been betrayed.

However, the SAS were not free agents. The 101st Airborne was in charge of Mosul, and the US authorities did not believe that the SAS could storm the house without taking heavy casualties. Lots of dead coalition soldiers, they thought, would send the wrong message to the Iraqi people, who were being told that the insurgency was almost over. Lieutenant General Ricardo Sanchez, who had taken over from General Franks as commander of coalition ground forces in Iraq, authorized an altogether larger operation, and the SAS were sidelined.

Shortly before 1000 the following morning, the 101st Airborne cordoned off the area. Then a team from the Delta Force approached the front door and knocked. When they received no reply, a megaphone was used to issue a demand: Whoever was inside the house must come out. There was no response, so 10 minutes later, troops began to enter the house, even though it was broad daylight and the occupants had warned the defenders they were coming. The assault force was immediately fired on by the occupants, who had barricaded themselves into a fortified part of the first floor of the building. Four American soldiers were wounded, and the assault team was forced to withdraw.

As any potential element of surprise had been thrown away, stealth was no longer an option. They called in more men in the form of a quick-reaction force and called up heavy weaponry. Meanwhile, sporadic gunfire continued from the house. At 1045, the American forces began to "prep the objective." They began firing on the part of the building where the four targets were holed up with Mark-19 automatic 40-mm grenade launchers, Humvee-mounted .50-caliber machine guns, and AT4 84-mm antiarmor rockets. At 1122, more ground forces moved in, including an antitank platoon. Half-an-hour later, an OH-58D Kiowa attack helicopter joined the assault, pounding the position with 2.75-inch rockets, 7.62-mm miniguns, and .50-caliber machine guns. By then the antitank platoon was in position, and a psy-ops team moved in.

At 1155, the US commander decided to make a second attempt to enter the house. Troops went in and secured the ground floor. But again they came under fire from the first floor, and the commander decided to withdraw. An hour later, 10 larger Humvee-mounted TOW missiles were fired into house. Apache helicopters and A-10 Warthogs were standing by, but the US commander decided not to use them because of the risk of collateral damage.

At 1320, troops entered the building for the third time, believing the people in the building to have been killed in the missile attack. They faced no fire as they move upstairs, but when they reached the second floor they were fired on again. They returned fire, killing the remaining individual, who was believed to have been Qusay Hussein's 14-year-old son. Once the building was secured, the four bodies were taken away for identification. DNA analysis confirmed that Qusay and Uday were among them.

The SAS were appalled. The siege had lasted six hours. One Iraqi bystander was killed and five wounded. The SAS believed that they could have done the job in a fraction of the time and saved lives and injuries. To add insult to injury, the

SAS team was then taken on as a quick-reaction force for the 101st Airborne.

Following the debacle at Mosul, the situation in Iraq continued to deteriorate. Most civilian agencies pulled out, and Task Force 20 was disbanded. The remaining British, Australian, and Polish Special Forces men would join the SBS, Delta Force, and DEVGRU men who now made up Task Force 121.

On October 31, they were tipped off that a number of Hussein loyalists—Ba'athist, Fedayeen, Republican Guard, and Saddam's security services, many of them in the pack of cards—were holed up in another compound in Mosul. It was thought that they had been joined by al-Qaeda fighters who had infiltrated across the border from Saudi Arabia, Jordan, and Syria. They were armed not just with AK-47s but also with grenades, mortars, RPGs, and shoulder-launched SAM missiles. Things were getting out of hand in Mosul. That morning the US headquarters at the airport had been hit by Katyushi rockets from a Soviet-made multibarreled rocket launcher. An American vehicle had been hit by a roadside bomb in the Qasr al-Mutran district of the city, and an Iraqi police station had been peppered with rounds in a drive-by shooting.

US helicopters were sent up to overfly the city. Armed men were seen going in and out of the compound, some carrying RPGs. That afternoon, mortars were seen being loaded onto a pickup truck parked outside. This activity was confirmed by local informants as well as Special Forces close reconnaissance. Something had to be done. The US commander on the ground decided to attack the compound that night.

The assault team would be made up of men from Delta Force, SAS, and SBS. As before, the area would be cordoned off by a large force from the 101st Airborne and Iraqi police.

Again there would be massive firepower on hand—OH-58D Kiowa attack helicopters and Humvees armed with TOW missiles, M-19 grenade launchers, and .50-caliber Brownings. The assault force would be flown into position on board MH-53 Pave Low helicopters, then driven forward in heavily armed Humvees that would drop them 500 meters from their objective. The six four-man teams would then approach the compound from various directions, backed up by fire support teams armed with 40-mm grenade launchers. The moment they heard shooting, they were to fire grenades into the compound before the Special Forces teams went in. They were also to target the Toyota pickup outside, which was laden with ground-to-air missiles and 82-mm mortars.

Around 2200, it was clear that the men inside the compound were about to make a move, and the order was given to go in. Task Force 121 attacked from four different directions. The main gates were hit by a series of rifle grenades and strafed with machine-gun fire. Startled guards returned fire. The Special Forces men began pouring over the walls. SAS and SBS teams blew open the front gates and went in with their Diemacos blazing. In a heavy exchange of fire, three SAS men were wounded and one SBS man, Corporal Ian "Planky" Plank, was killed—the first British Special Forces man to be lost in the Second Gulf War. He had served with the SBS in Sierra Leone, the Balkans, and Afghanistan. Nevertheless, the compound was taken at the further cost of 10 Iraqi dead. A large number of foreign fighters were captured.

Meanwhile, the search for members of Saddam Hussein's toppled regime was still on. On April 16, 2003, Task Force 121 captured Saddam's half-brother, Watban Hassan al-Tikriti, the five of spades and the 37th on the most wanted list. They caught him on the road from Mosul to Syria, trying to flee the country. As Minister of the Interior, he used to torture and murder political prisoners. He was also wanted in connection with the disappearance of 180,000 Kurds in the 1980s and the vicious repression following the Iraqi defeat in the First Gulf War. He also arrested dozens of Baghdad market vendors for alleged profiteering in foodstuffs, then had them hanged from lampposts after trials that lasted less than a day. Watban Hassan al-Tikriti was handed over to the Iraqi Interim Government in 2004 and went on trial in 2008. On March 11, 2009, he was hanged.

CHAPTER 22

RESCUE OF JESSICA LYNCH

THE SECOND GULF WAR was at its height when a US supply convoy took a wrong turn into the city of Nasiriyah, where the US Marines were involved in a major action to secure a vital bridge over the Euphrates River. Eleven soldiers were killed, and six soldiers, including 19-year-old Private Jessica Lynch, were captured.

Private Lynch, from Palestine, West Virginia, was with 507th Maintenance Company, and the convoy was led by Captain Troy King, a supply officer with no training as a combat officer. The convoy was hit with small-arms fire, RPGs, mortars, and shells from Iraqi tanks. The story circulated that Jessica had kept on firing until she ran out of ammunition, then she had resisted capture, was shot in the leg, was stabbed, and had then been beaten and raped. She later told Congress that her M16 had jammed, along with all the other weapons assigned to her unit. She had not been shot but was knocked unconscious when the Humvee she was in swerved off the road and crashed, breaking her arm and thigh and dislocating her ankle. She also denied being raped and, it seems, was well treated by her captors, who took Jessica and the Humvee's driver, Private Lori Piestewa, to the Saddam hospital, a civilian hospital in Nasiriyah. Piestewa had a serious head wound and died, making her the first Native American woman to be killed in combat on foreign soil.

Doctor Harith Al-Houssona said that he shielded Jessica from the Fedayeen, who had moved into the hospital at the outbreak of war. He found no injuries on her other than those consistent with a road traffic accident. However, 32-year-old lawyer Mohammed Odeh al Rehaief noticed that the security at the hospital had been tightened. His wife worked there as a nurse, he said.

As he passed by a first-floor emergency ward, he said he looked through a window and saw an Iraqi paramilitary man give Lynch two open-handed slaps to the face. Jessica denies she was mistreated.

"I saw them hit the female soldier, and my heart stopped," said Mohammed. "I knew then I must help her be saved. I decided to go to the Americans and tell them the story."

He walked six miles to a checkpoint manned by Marines. Mohammed, who had learned some English while studying in Basra Law College, told a young Marine that he had important information about a woman soldier. The Marine took him to see his superior officer. With to the help of Mohammed's wife, he was able to explain the rough layout of the hospital, including the vital fact that a helicopter could land on its flat roof.

Mohammed also saw the bodies of other Americans who were being buried on the hospital grounds, but Jessica was the only one he saw alive. He agreed to go back to the hospital and find out more about the security there and Jessica's exact location. With the help of a doctor at the hospital who was a friend, he drew maps that helped in the rescue. Mohammed and his family were later granted refugee status and moved to the US.

He estimated that there were some 40 Fedayeen there. In fact, they pulled out the day before the Special Forces arrived. Dr. Al-Houssona claimed that he tried to return Private Lynch in an ambulance, but when he approached a US checkpoint, the troops opened fire, forcing them to flee back to the hospital.

Plans were already underway to rescue Jessica. A combined force of Green Berets, US Navy SEALs, US Army Rangers, Pararescue jumpers, and others from Task Force 121 was formed. On the night of April 1, 2003, the US Marines staged a diversionary attack, while the special-operations force went in. The Pararescue jumpers parachuted onto the hospital, while a larger security force came in by road.

"It was like a Hollywood film," said Dr. Anmar Uday. "They cried, 'Go, go, go!' with guns and blanks without bullets, blanks and the sound of explosions. They made a show for the American attack on the hospital—action movies like Sylvester Stallone or Jackie Chan."

All the time with the camera rolling. The rescuers took no chances, restraining doctors and handcuffing a patient to a bed frame. One team member approached Jessica's bed. She was scared and had the sheet over her head. When she lowered it, he said, "Jessica Lynch, we're United States soldiers and we're here to take you home."

She replied, famously, "I'm an American soldier, too."

A Ranger doctor then checked her over. She grabbed his hand and held on to it.

"Please don't let anyone leave me," she said.

"It was clear she knew where she was and didn't want to be left in the hands of the enemy," said the doctor. It was also clear that she was in some pain, and she was stretchered out to a waiting helicopter and flown to safety.

There were allegations that the US forces knew that the Fedayeen had fled and the rescue had been staged for the cameras. However, General Vincent Brooks, US spokesman in Doha, said, "Some brave souls put their lives on the line to make this happen, loyal to a creed that they know that they'll never leave a fallen comrade."

CHAPTER 23

CAPTURE OF SADDAM HUSSEIN

THE IRAQI DICTATOR SADDAM HUSSEIN was captured on December 13, 2003, hiding in a spider hole in the ground at a farmhouse in ad-Dawr, 12 miles south of his hometown of Tikrit. Ostensibly, he was arrested by the 1st Combat Team of the US 4th Infantry Division. However, along with the 600 infantrymen involved in the operation, a team from Task Force 121 was on hand. Delta Force were flown to the farm by helicopters from the 160th SOAR. In the picture shown in the press of a bearded Saddam being man-handled from his hiding place, the man hauling him out is a 34-year-old Iraqi-American named Samir, an interpreter from Special Forces.

Information on Saddam's whereabouts came from distant relatives and members of the PUK, the Kurdish independence party that the CIA and Special Forces had been grooming. They deduced that Saddam was in the area of Tikrit. This was where he had hidden out after his attempted coup in 1959 had failed. Then in a Special Forces raid in Baghdad on December 12, one of Saddam's "enablers" was captured. He was dubbed "the Fatman" or "the Source." He revealed that Saddam was hiding in an underground facility at a farmhouse at ad-Dawr, just three miles from his birthplace, Owja, and not far from a place where $1 million worth of jewelry belonging to Saddam's wife had been found.

By 1050 on December 13, coalition intelligence had narrowed down his hiding place to two possible locations in ad-Dawr, which were code-named Wolverine 1 and Wolverine 2. Operation Red Dawn was then put into operation. Only the top commanders knew that the target was the ace of spades himself, Saddam Hussein al-Tikriti, also known as HVT (high value target) Number 1. For everyone else involved, it was just a regular HVT operation.

At 1800, as darkness fell, some 600 men moved into place by helicopter and truck. Among them were Special Forces operatives from Task Force 121. In command of the main force was Colonel Jim Hickey of the 4th Infantry Division, supported by Apache helicopter gunships, artillery, light armor, and Humvees. The Special Forces contingent on hand was under the personal command of General Ricardo Sanchez, at that time Corps commander in Iraq. His orders were clear: "Kill or capture HVT Number 1."

At 2000, the power was cut. Troops donned their night-vision goggles, and Task Force 121 was seen going in. The darkness was occasionally slashed by red beams of laser-aiming light. In the background, the hum of OH-58 Little Bird and other Special Operations aircraft could be heard as they waited for extraction, reinforcement, or attack.

At 2010, the perimeter around ad-Dawr was sealed, and Task Force 121 began a "sweep and clear operation." One arrest was made at Wolverine 1, but there was no sign of Saddam. Wolverine 2 was empty. When the initial sweep yielded nothing, Special Ops sealed off a smaller area, about one square mile around the two farmhouses. Then began a more thorough search. Inside the second perimeter was a small mud hut in a palm grove, which belonged to an orange picker. This was of special interest because an orange-and-white Toyota Corolla taxi was parked outside. There had been rumors that Saddam Hussein had masqueraded as a taxi driver so he could move around.

As the special-operations force approached, one man tried to make his escape. A second was detained in the hut. One was the owner of the property; the other, his brother, was Saddam's cook. Inside was a single room with two beds and an open kitchen. A refrigerator contained a can of Happy Brand tuna, a package of hot dogs, a box of Belgian chocolates, a can of lemonade, and a tube of ointment. There was a poster on the wall showing Noah's Ark, and there were packages of new clothes. More telling, there were two AK-47s leaning against the wall, and when a green footlocker was opened, it was found to contain $750,000 in US $100 bills. But still no Saddam.

Special Operations were about to move on when one of the detainees became agitated. He said that Saddam was hiding elsewhere and promised to lead his captors to him. Plainly Saddam was close by. Then, through his night-vision goggles, one of the Special Forces men noticed that the ground looked odd. The earth and stones were spread out evenly as if someone were trying to conceal something. It was around 2030.

Under a rug, they found an entranceway covered with bricks and dirt. Removing them revealed a Styrofoam insert that acted as a hatch cover. One of the Special Forces operatives pulled the pin on a grenade and cautiously removed the Styrofoam while the rest of the team trained their guns on the hole beneath. Under the Styrofoam was a shaft some six to eight feet deep. By the light of their flashlights, they could see the haggard figure of a man cowering in a corner.

"I am Saddam Hussein," he said. "I am the president of Iraq, and I am willing to negotiate."

He looked more like a tramp that a feared dictator.

The Task Force 121 commando then said calmly, "President Bush sends his regards."

They pulled him out of the hole and took a 9mm pistol from his belt.

"He was caught like a rat in a trap," said US military spokesman Major General Ray Odierno. "He was disorientated as he came up, then he was just very much bewildered. Then he was taken away. He didn't say hardly anything at all. There was no resistance of any sort. They got him out of there very quickly once we figured out who it was. The soldiers were extremely happy and extremely excited, but very professional."

General Odierno described Saddam Hussein's hole as just large enough for a man to lie down in. It had a pipe and a fan for ventilation. Nearby on the Tigris River were two small boats that were used to bring in supplies, and a battered taxi that served as his presidential limousine. The circumstances of Saddam Hussein's capture stood in stark contrast to the opulent lifestyle he had enjoyed while in power, said General Odierno. "It is very interesting that in fact you could just about see some of these palace complexes from there. And I think it's rather ironic that he was in a hole in the ground across the river from these great palaces that he built where he robbed all the money from the Iraqi people."

No communication equipment was found in the hut or farmhouse, so it was not thought that he was directing insurgent attacks on the coalition from his lair. Saddam was whisked off in a helicopter for a medical examination and interrogation. A DNA sample was taken from the inside of his mouth to be used to confirm his identity.

Saddam Hussein was held in custody at the US base Camp Cropper with 11 other senior Ba'athist leaders. They were handed over legally—though not physically—to the interim Iraqi government to stand trial for crimes against humanity and other offenses.

"He talked of fighting to the end and of death for Iraq," said one Baghdad shopkeeper. "His wife said he slept with a bomb strapped to his chest so that he would not be taken alive. But he did not fire a single shot."

In the end, the Iraqi Special Tribunal convicted Saddam Hussein of crimes committed against residents of Dujail following a failed assassination attempt in 1982. These included the murder of 148 people, the illegal arrest of 399 others, and the torture of women and children. Throughout, Saddam and his lawyers contested the court's authority to try him and maintained that he was still president of Iraq.

On November 5, 2006, Saddam Hussein was sentenced to death by hanging, along with his codefendants—his half brother, Barzan-Ibrahim, and Awad Hamed al-Bandar, head of Iraq's Revolutionary Court in 1982. Both the verdict and the sentence were appealed, but they were upheld by Iraq's Supreme Court of Appeals, and on December 30, 2006, Saddam Hussein was hanged.

CHAPTER 24

HOSTAGE RESCUE IRAQ

AFTER THE INVASION OF IRAQ WAS OVER, insurgents began kidnapping foreigners, and rescuing hostages became part of the remit of Special Forces. They were to use the intelligence networks they had built up chasing Saddam Hussein and other high-value targets to counter the threat from kidnappers.

On June 1, 2004, Polish businessman Jerzy Kos, the director of a construction company, was abducted by armed insurgents, along with employee Radoslaw Kadri and two female Iraqis. Kadri escaped, and the two women were released shortly after their capture. Kos was taken to a house in Ramadi, west of Baghdad, where he was held with three Italian security guards: Maurizio Agliana, Umberto Cupertino, and Salvatore Stefio. A fourth Italian, 36-year-old Fabrizio Quattrocchi, was killed by the kidnappers.

Kos thought they were going to kill him too. They beat him over the head with a gun. But then the physical abuse stopped, and he realized that they "wanted to do some business." Even so, he described the conditions he suffered in captivity as "extreme," and the food he was fed was so bad that it gave him diarrhea.

The Italians also said that they were not treated very well. They had to sleep on the floor, and for three days they were locked in a bathroom just six feet by six feet. A kidnapper tried to strip Stefio of his wedding ring. Stefio refused to hand it over, saying he would rather die.

"Then I'll take you outside," said the insurgent.

"No, don't shoot me outside," said Stefio. "Shoot me in front of the other men."

After interviewing Kadri and the two women taken with Kos, Polish intelligence was able to identify the group responsible for the kidnapping. The hideout was then identified by an Iraqi in the pay of US intelligence.

After a week of captivity, Kos said he heard a helicopter. It came down outside the house, its rotors kicking up a dust storm. Then a number of highly trained men—variously identified as US Navy SEAL and Delta Force operatives—leaped out. The iron door of the house was blown in, knocking the hostages to the ground.

"There was lots of dust and you couldn't see through it," said Kos. "When I opened my eyes, I saw American soldiers. They said, 'Don't worry, we are Americans.' They held our hands, and we ran to the helicopter—I will remember that for the rest of my life. It was fast and unexpected. They did it perfectly."

Umberto Cupertino remembered that an American soldier cut the bonds on his wrist and said in English, "You're mine," before leading him to a helicopter.

The hostages were then returned to their home countries. They were lucky. Things did not always work out so well. On September 16, 2004, US citizen Eugene Armstrong, a contractor for the construction firm Gulf Supplies Commercial Services of the United Arab Emirates, was kidnapped. Six days later he was beheaded. The execution was thought to have been done personally by Abu Musab al-Zarqawi, al-Qaeda's top man in Iraq. It was filmed, and the footage was posted on the Internet. The masked terrorists, who were holding other hostages, demanded that the coalition release all women prisoners in the Iraqi jails of Abu Ghraib and Umm Qasr within 48 hours. The US military pointed out that no women were being held in those prisons. Only two women were in American custody at the time. They were "Dr. Germ" and "Mrs. Anthrax," accused of working on Saddam Hussein's biological weapons program, and they were being held in a prison for high-profile detainees. The following day, the kidnappers beheaded another American, Jack Hensley, an engineer from Cobb County, Georgia. Two weeks later, they killed their third hostage, British engineer Kenneth Bigley, after the UK's Secret Intelligence Service, commonly known as MI6, attempted to rescue him.

Two weeks after that, another Briton, humanitarian aid worker Margaret Hassan, who had worked in Iraq for many years, was also killed. In May 2005, three men were arrested for the kidnapping. One of them, Mustafa Salman al-Jubouri, was sentenced to life imprisonment for aiding and abetting her kidnappers. The other two were acquitted. In 2008, US forces arrested Ali Lutfi Jassar al-Rawi after he told the British Embassy he would reveal where Hassan's body was—for $1 million. He was also sentenced to life imprisonment for involvement in Hassan's abduction and murder. However, in 2010, he escaped.

On November 26, 2005, US peace activist Tom Fox, Briton Norman Kember, and Canadians James Loney and Harmeet Singh Sooden, all volunteers from the Christian Peacemaker Team, were kidnapped in the street in Baghdad.

Gunmen pulled their driver and translator from their vehicle and abducted them. Four days later, al-Jazeera, the Qatar-based cable TV channel, received a tape showing the hostages. With it was a communiqué from a previously unknown terrorist group calling themselves the Swords of Righteousness Brigade, who demanded that the coalition release all their prisoners. Like the hostages murdered before them, Fox and Kember were dressed in orange jumpsuits similar to those worn by detainees at Guantanamo Bay. Unusually, Moazzem Begg, a British Muslim recently released from Guantanamo Bay, and Abu Qutada, named as Osama bin Laden's ambassador in Europe, who was in detention in Britain, called for their release.

The kidnappers took no notice and continued releasing videos, renewing their demands. Then on March 7, 2006, the State Department grew concerned when the latest video showed Professor Kember and the two Canadians, but not Tom Fox. Three days later, his body was found by a railroad line in a suburb of Baghdad. It seems that the kidnappers had taken him because he was an American and had been a Marine before he became a Quaker and a peace activist. He had been tortured and handcuffed before being shot. Fears grew that once again the hostages were going to be killed one by one.

From the videos, US intelligence deduced that the Swords of Righteousness Brigade was an offshoot of the Army of Islam, or possibly a cover name for it. For some months, the NSA had been recording all cell phone traffic in Iraq. Checking all calls from cell phones taken from the members of the Army of Islam that had been arrested, it was possible to build up a picture of where the hostage-takers were holed up. The hostage rescue was put in the hands of

Task Force Knight. This comprised B Squadron of the SAS and Canadian Special Forces. Together they set up Operation Lightwater. Soon SAS men were kicking in doors and arresting the kidnappers' associates. During these raids, assault teams would seize cell phones and computers and undertake "tactical questioning": The SAS found that interrogating a suspect on the spot while they were still suffering the shock of capture often produced results.

Some 50 raids were made during Operation Lightwater—44 by the SAS, the rest by US Special Forces. Only four of these turned out to be "dry holes" where no useful intelligence was gleaned.

Scotland Yard also sent in trained negotiators. The Canadians flew in their kidnap experts, and FBI agents and MI6 officers in Baghdad tried to make contact with intermediaries who could put them in direct touch with the kidnappers. Meanwhile, undercover SAS men wearing beards and dressed as Iraqis met religious leaders and tribal elders to piece together scraps of information about the hostage-taking Swords of Righteousness Brigade. Satellite photographs, telephone intercepts, and reams of other information were examined in minute detail. Intelligence officers followed up dozens of tip-offs from paid informants, community leaders, and Iraqi police.

The SAS had already narrowed down the likely location of the kidnappers' base to the scruffy suburbs of western Baghdad around al-Hurriyah, a stronghold of mainly Sunni insurgents and criminal gangs responsible for dozens of abductions of Iraqis. The detainees disclosed the precise address, describing the location and making sketches of the house and the nearby roads.

For weeks, the SAS had been practicing strategies for taking kidnappers by surprise. They used mock-ups of the types of properties where they thought the hostages were held, even though they were unsure if it was in a basement or in a house where children lived. Meanwhile, US intelligence had been keeping a young Iraqi who had been under surveillance. In the early hours of March 23, 2006, the SAS made a night raid, code-named Operation Ney 3, on the house where he was staying in Mishada, some 20 miles northwest of central Baghdad. The mission was led by a veteran sergeant major who had survived being shot in Iraq two years earlier. Having burst into the building, the assault team found two men they had been looking for. Interrogated forcefully on the spot, one of them admitted knowing where Professor Kember and the two Canadians were. Now Task Force Knight had to act fast. Their main concern was that the hostage-takers might realize that one of their gang had been captured, kill the three Westerners, and flee.

Around 0300 on March 23, 2006, the SAS squadron commander in charge of the rescue force summoned his team to their base inside the heavily fortified green zone. The force consisted mainly of SAS troopers, backed by about 50 soldiers from the 1st Battalion, the Parachute Regiment, and Royal Marines—all members of the Special Forces Support Group now code-named Task Force Maroon. The Australian SAS, Canadian Joint Task Force 2, Delta Force, and DEVGRU were also involved.

To attract the minimum attention, the rescue forces approached the area in a convoy of cars disguised as local taxis and pickup trucks. Predator unmanned aerial vehicles, which can monitor movements on the ground from 20,000 feet, were deployed, while helicopter gunships circled high above with reconnaissance cameras, ready to swoop in if required. First the SFSG troops set up a cordon several streets away from the target so that innocent civilians did not blunder into an operation that might end in a shoot-out.

To ensure that minimum force was used and give the hostages the maximum chance of survival, the SAS commander had phoned the kidnappers and informed them of the situation. Special Forces were on their way, and if the terrorists disappeared leaving their hostages unharmed, they would not come after them.

The 25-man assault group, led by the SAS, burst into the two-story building, using classic hostage-rescue techniques and storming every room simultaneously to ensure no one escaped. They found the three hostages sitting on the floor of a first-story room, bound but unguarded. There was no sign of their kidnappers. No shots were fired during the operation. In case the kidnappers were lurking nearby, the hostages were rushed out of the building and bundled into the back of an army Land Rover. Less than two minutes after the rescue force had entered the building, the three Westerners were on their way to freedom.

They were driven to the Green Zone, where they were handed over to waiting officials. Meanwhile the rest of Task Force Maroon moved in to search the hideout, looking for clues as to the identity of the kidnappers and evidence indicating where other Western hostages might be held. Major-General Rick Lynch, a spokesman for the coalition forces, revealed they suspected that the peace activists had been taken by "a kidnapping cell" that was behind other abductions in Baghdad. However, Professor Kember, who had always maintained that he did not want to be rescued by military force, was loath to express his gratitude.

Two weeks after the hostages were freed, Lieutenant General Stanley A. McChrystal, then head of the Joint Special Operations Command, visited the SAS's headquarters in Herefordshire, England. He asked for Task Force Knight to work in the future with the full US target set in Iraq.

CHAPTER 25

OPERATION REDWING

ON THE EVENING OF JUNE 27, 2005, Lieutenant Michael P. Murphy and his four-man SEAL team fast-roped down from a Chinook helicopter onto a grassy ridge near the Pakistani border with Afghanistan. The mission—code-named Operation Redwing—was to kill or capture Ahmad Shah, whom US intelligence believed was close to Osama bin Laden. As Taliban leader in Kunar Province, his attacks were taking a heavy toll on the Marines in eastern Afghanistan. With Petty Officers Matthew G. Axleson, Danny P. Dietz, and Marcus Luttrell, Murphy was to stay in position for 24 to 72 hours and report any sighting of Ahmad Shah or his men. If they spotted them, he was to call in the main force.

The SEAL team was a highly trained and highly motivated force. Born and brought up in New York, Murphy had joined the US Navy SEALs in 2002 after graduating from college. He had been stationed in Pearl Harbor, Hawaii, and in Jordan before being assigned to Special Operations Central Command in Florida. Then he had been deployed to Qatar in the Persian Gulf in support of Operation Iraqi Freedom. After that, he had been sent to Afghanistan, where he served with Alpha Platoon of SEAL Delivery Vehicle Team One.

Graduating with a degree in political science from California State University, Chico, Axelson had joined the US Navy in 2000, becoming a sonar technician. He then underwent his Basic Underwater Demolition/SEAL training and was sent to Afghanistan in April 2005. Dietz had enlisted in the Navy in 1999 and earned his SEAL trident in 2001. In April 2005, he had deployed to Afghanistan with his Special Reconnaissance team to support Naval Special Warfare Squadron Ten. Luttrell had joined the Navy in 1999 and deployed to Afghanistan as a SEAL in 2005. His twin brother was also a SEAL, and they each had half a trident tattooed on their chests.

Luttrell was clear about the aim of operations in Afghanistan. They were, he said, "payback time for the World Trade Center," and his goal was to kill every SOB he could find—twice as many as they had killed. To remind him what the war was all about, he kept the picture of one of the World Trade Center victims cut from a magazine in his pocket. He did not even know the victim's name.

The pre-mission intelligence reports said there were anywhere from 80 to 200 Taliban fighters in the area. They had little idea of the terrain they would be facing, whether it was going to be rock beds or trees or a mixture. But, as Luttrell said, "It's our job to do the mission, no matter what."

From the landing zone, the four SEALs moved swiftly through the night. Reaching a wooded slope, they happened upon an Afghan man wearing a turban. Then another goatherd and a teenage boy turned up. Luttrell gave the boy a candy bar, while the SEALs discussed whether the Afghans should live or die. Plainly they could not hold them prisoner. But if they let them go, they might alert the Taliban.

According to Luttrell, Axelson voted to kill them. They were on active duty behind enemy lines, sent there on a vital task by their senior commanders. He thought they had the right to do everything they could to fulfill their mission and save their own lives. The military decision is obvious.

"To turn them loose would be wrong," he said.

Murphy voted to let the Afghans go. He was adamant that he was not going to kill innocent people.

Dietz abstained.

"I don't really give a shit what we do," he said. "You want me to kill 'em, I'll kill 'em. Just give me the word. I only work here."

Murphy warned his men that if they did kill the Afghans, they would have to report the deaths. The liberal media would attack them, and the Taliban would publicize the killings. As a result, they would almost certainly be charged with murder.

Luttrell was left with the deciding vote. In other branches of the service, it would seem strange that a commissioned officer should put such decision to the vote, but Luttrell said it was part of SEAL culture.

"Most people don't understand how the SEAL teams are made up," he said. "It's not straight-up 'You will do this my way.' I guess it could be if you had some guy like that. But the teams are designed differently. That's why the officers go through the same training as we do and we're together the whole time."

The SEAL mind-set, he said, was, "Two heads are better than one, three are better than two. So if you're stuck in a situation like that, would you want to make the decision that killed all of us? That's why we talked about it ... A good officer listens to his men."

Luttrell also voted against killing the goatherds. The Afghans seemed like ordinary people to him, and he decided that he did not want to be a murderer.

The SEALs had been deployed in Afghanistan for three months and, between them, had been on more than 10 missions.

"We had never been compromised before," Luttrell said. "That was a reputation that we were proud of, that we had never been walked on. But we got walked on this time."

Afterward, he was tormented by the fact that he may have made the wrong decision because the men they spared betrayed them.

"It was the stupidest, most Southern-fried, lame-brained decision I ever made in my life," he said. "I must have been out of my mind. I had actually cast a vote which I knew could sign our death warrant. I'd turned into a f—ing liberal, a half-assed, no-logic nitwit, all heart, no brain, and the judgment of a jackrabbit."

Nevertheless, he later admitted that he would have done the same thing again.

Two hours after they had let the goatherds go, 140 Taliban turned up. Attacked from three sides, the SEALs tried to retreat down the mountainside to flat ground, hoping to find a village where they could hold out until help arrived.

Dietz, the communications expert, risked his life by staying on the high ground with the radio, trying to call for help. As the others fell back, he was shot two or three times but kept on putting out the distress call. The microphone was then blown out of his hand. Retreating down the mountain, Dietz was hit another couple of times. He was still firing when a sixth bullet caught him in the head and he died in Luttrell's arms.

Murphy had been shot in the stomach early in the fight but kept leading his men until he was shot a second time in the chest. He then he exposed himself to enemy fire to make a last-ditch satellite phone call. Contacting headquarters in Bagram, 80 miles away, he pleaded for a quick-reaction force to be sent.

"My guys are dying," he said.

Then he was shot in the back. He slumped forward, somehow continuing the conversation. Luttrell heard him say, "Roger that, sir. Thank you." He was still firing at the Taliban when he died.

Axelson was wounded first in the chest and then in the head. By then he was separated from Luttrell and fought on alone. He expended two more magazines before finally succumbing to his wounds.

Luttrell was hit by the blast from an RPG that ripped his pants off and hurled him down a ravine, cracking three of his vertebrae. His nose was broken, his face shredded. He had a broken wrist, and he was riddled with shrapnel. When rescue helicopters arrived, he could barely see them through the blood in his eyes. He tried to contact them with his radio, but his throat was so clogged with dirt that he could not speak.

"If you're out there, show yourself," the pilot said.

Though Luttrell could not respond, his channel was open so the pilot knew he was there.

"Show yourself," said the pilot again. "We cannot stay much longer."

The HH-60 Pave Hawk helicopters were running short of fuel, and now that the sun was rising, they would make an easy target for an RPG or small-arms fire. As the Pave Hawks turned for home, one of the pilots said to himself, "That man is going to die."

But the US military does not give up that easily. A few hours later, an MH-47 Chinook carrying 16 rescuers appeared over the gulch where Luttrell was laying. As it approached, a Taliban fired an RPG, bringing the helicopter down. There were eight SEALs and eight aviators from 160 SOAR on board. None of them survived. More of Luttrell's comrades were dead, and his chance of being rescued had been snatched from him.

"It was deathly quiet," he said.

His own life was still in danger. The hills were full of Taliban. Leaving a bloody trail, he dragged himself away.

As the sun came up, it began to get fiercely hot. Luttrell grew thirsty. He licked the sweat off his arms. He even drank his own urine. But eventually he dragged himself to a pool of water. He drank deep. When he lifted his head, he saw an Afghan and reached for his rifle.

"American," said the man, giving Luttrell the thumbs up.

"You Taliban?" asked Luttrell.

The villager indicated that he wasn't. Then two more men arrived carrying AK-47s. They, too, were friendly. The three of them carried Luttrell to the nearby village of Sabray-Minah, where the first villager, who was named Mohammed Gulab, fed him warm goat's milk, washed him, and gave him new clothes.

But after an hour, the Taliban turned up and demanded that the villagers hand over Luttrell. Gulab refused, even turning down bribes. It seemed that, according to local tribal law, once they had carried the wounded man to the village, they were obliged to look after him. Even the Taliban seemed to accept this. Nevertheless, they kept the village surrounded, so Gulab brought in uncles and cousins, all brandishing firearms, to defend Luttrell.

"They protected me like a child," said Luttrell. "They treated me like I was their eldest son."

The local children gathered around and tried to teach him words in Pashto and to say "There is no god by Allah" in Arabic. Luttrell quietly prayed to Jesus to get him out of there.

He occasionally heard helicopters overhead looking for him. In one of them was his unlikely rescuer, 39-year-old Air Force reservist Major Jeff Peterson, a man who had been airsick during training and considered himself anything but a hero. When the Chinooks were down, Peterson was sent out to look for survivors. Peterson flew an HH-60 for the 305th Rescue Squadron, whose motto is, "Anytime, anywhere." So far in Afghanistan, he had made just two Red Cross runs, and he now had just three days to go before he was posted home. On his first trip over the area, Peterson drew a blank.

By July 1, the Taliban's threats were intensifying. Gulab sent his father, a village elder, to the Marine outpost five miles down the valley to seek help. He carried a note from Luttrell that said, "This man gave me shelter and food, and must be helped."

The following day, Staff Sergeant Chris Piercecchi, an Air Force Pararescue jumper, flew the old man to Bagram, where he handed over the note and described Luttrell's tattoo. One of the largest search-and-rescue operations since the Vietnam War was mounted. First Army Rangers and Special Forces were sent in to tie down the Taliban. Then a helicopter would be sent in to rescue Luttrell.

At first the mission planners thought of sending a Chinook, but then it was decided that the smaller HH-60 Pave Hawk could make the approach more easily. Peterson, who had never been in combat, was selected. His copilot, 41-year-old First Lieutenant David Gonzales, irritated the rest of the party by clicking his rosary beads. Also on board were a doctor, Master Sergeant Josh Appel, and a 57-year-old door-gunner who had served in Vietnam and was now partially deaf.

Climbing into the mountains, Peterson found the heli-copter was too heavy to fly in the thin air at 7,000 feet and had to dump 500 pounds of fuel, which fell on an unfor-tunate village. Five minutes before they arrived at Sabray-Minah, A-10 attack aircraft and AC-130 gunships, guided by the ground troops below, began attacking the Taliban who surrounded the village. As Peterson approached the landing zone, the warning came over the radio: "Known enemy 100 meters south of your position."

The landing zone was a ledge on a terraced cliff. The HH-60's rotor threw up clouds of dust. Then the helicopter drifted toward the cliff. Those on board braced for a crash, but Peterson put her down safely. Gulab helped Luttrell to-ward the chopper.

As the two men in Afghan robes approached, Appel trained the laser dot of his M4 on them. Piercecchi then per-formed the identity check.

"What's your dog's name?"

"Emma," said Luttrell.

"Favorite superhero?"

"Spiderman."

"Welcome home," said Piercecchi, offering his hand.

Gulab flew with them back to base, but he refused the offer of money or Luttrell's watch. The two men hugged and parted, never to see each other again. Six days later search teams located the bodies of Murphy and Dietz. For another four days, search teams held out the hope that Axelson might be found alive, but they were eventually forced to give up.

Lieutenant Murphy was awarded the Medal of Honor posthumously; Dietz and Axelson received the Navy Cross. After convalescing, Luttrell was sent to Iraq, though he needed drugs to ease the pain from his injuries. He also avoided sleep, as he often dreamed of the other dead SEALs. Winner of the Navy Cross and the Purple Heart, he returned home in 2007 to write the book *Lone Survivor: The Eyewitness Account of Operation Redwing and the Lost Heroes of SEAL Team 10.*

TASK FORCE 88

ONCE THE MAJORITY OF SADDAM HUSSEIN'S regime had been rounded up, the SAS Squadron remaining in Iraq was assigned to the joint US–UK group special-operations unit, previously known as Task Force 145. This was the Combined Joint Special Operations Task Force, headed by the commander of Delta Force. Renamed Task Force 88, it was composed of the cream of Western Special Forces. Several elements were brought to it. There was Task Force Orange, the electronic intelligence gatherers. Task Force Green was the 1st Special Forces Operational Detachment—that is, Delta Force. The designation "Green" comes from its association with the Army. Task Force Blue comprised US Navy SEALs from the DEVGRU, formerly SEAL Team 6. The "Blue" comes from its association with the Navy. Then there was the British Task Force Black, made up of an SAS saber squadron operating initially in southern Iraq. The "Black" came from color of the uniforms they wore in their counterrevolutionary warfare role. Some SBS operators were thought to be attached to Task Force Black, as were members of the British Special Reconnaissance Regiment, formed in April 2005 to perform covert surveillance work. Task Force Black was supported by a company of the Joint Special Forces Support Group—or SFSG, also known as Task Force Red.

The Joint Special Forces Support Group was another relatively new British special-operations unit. Formed around a core component of members of the 1st Battalion, Parachute Regiment—1 Para—with additional troops from the Royal Marines and the RAF Regiment, the SFSG provided infantry and specialized support to SAS and SBS special operations. It acted as a quick-reaction force for the SAS and SBS, sealing off and guarding an area of operation. It also took part in large-scale assaults alongside SAS and SBS forces, carrying out secondary assaults and diversionary raids. And it acted as a blocking force against counterattacks; provided chemical, biological, radiological, and nuclear detection and protection; and supported domestic antiterrorist operations.

Elements of the 160th Special Operations Aviation Regiment (SOAR), the US 24th Special Tactics Squadron, and the UK's 7 and 47 RAF Squadrons provided specialized air support for Task Force 88. The CIA's Special Activities Division provided intelligence support, while secure communications and eavesdropping capabilities were provided by 18 UK Special Forces Signals and their US equivalents in Task Force Orange.

The primary role of Task Force 88 was to hunt down senior members of al-Qaeda operating in Iraq. Elements have also been employed against al-Qaeda forces in Afghanistan. One of their great successes was the killing of Abu Musab al-Zarqawi on June 7, 2006. Al-Qaeda's top man in Iraq, al-Zarqawi was a Jordanian who built his reputation on the Internet, posting clips of himself beheading foreign captives. He was believed to have masterminded the bombing of the UN headquarters in Baghdad in August 2003 and was thought to have personally beheaded the British hostage Ken

Bigley in October 2004. Avoiding capture for years, he eventually topped coalition forces' most-wanted list in Iraq with a reward of $25 million posted for his capture—the same as was being offered for Osama bin Laden.

As part of Task Force 88, the SAS and Delta Force had become very close. Billeted together at Mission Support Station Fernandez—named for Master Sergeant George Fernandez of Delta Force, who had been killed in northern Iraq—they knocked a hole in the dividing wall so they could spend more time with their neighbors. The only cause for friction was the raucous barbecues the SAS had on Thursday nights where the British drank copious quantities of beer, a thing denied to the Americans. They were also going out on operations together in the "triangle of death" between Yusufiyah, Mahmudiyah, and Latifiyah, southwest of Baghdad.

If things were not bad enough in that area already, some US soldiers from the 1st Battalion of the 502nd Infantry got drunk on the local moonshine, left their checkpoint, and raped and murdered a 15-year-old girl named Abeer Qasim Hamza. To cover up their crime, they also murdered her parents and her seven-year-old sister. This provoked a series of revenge attacks.

JSOC had planned a raid on the al-Qaeda cell in Yusufiyah to capture the man they were calling the "Admin Emir" of Abu Ghraib, whose cell phone had been traced to a house on the outskirts.

Helicopters hit the landing zone at 0200, and four assault teams went in. Yusufiyah was riven with sectarian rivalry between Sunnis and Shiites. This meant that there were booby traps and press pads all over the area, so the Special Forces had to move very carefully. When they reached the house, it was quiet. There was an open door at the back of the build-

ing, and they decided to go
But as they rushed in, ther
had been guarding the c(
with their wounded, taki
southeast of the house.
attended to the casual'

The inhabitants of
firing on the berm. One (
began lobbing grenades. At this p
in the AC-130 Spectre circling above, o.
an F-16, but the team leader decided that they
to capture the Admin Emir rather than kill him, and the
renewed the assault. They attacked under covering fire, lobbing grenades. Two more men were injured by gunfire and
grenade fragments. Back at MSS Fernandez and the base at
Balad, the Special Forces commanders were watching the action on what they called "Kill TV." From the camera in the
command aircraft flying above, they could see a terrorist in a
suicide vest carrying an assault rifle as he fled from the house.
Airborne snipers engaged him, and he took cover under a
parked car. He was killed in a hail of bullets.

As the assault team stormed back into the building, they
killed the gunman guarding the corridor, then began searching the house. In one room, they found women and children.
One woman had been killed in the fighting; three others and
a child had been wounded.

Once the rooms had been cleared, the assault force headed
for the roof. As the lead man reached the top of the stairs, he
was confronted by another man in a suicide vest, who detonated it. The soldier was blown backward down the stairs.

Five insurgents were now dead. Another five were arrested.
The assault team then did a quick search of the house, find-

videos and an M4 5.56-mm assault rifle, a
by the coalition. This was a dangerous process,
e dead insurgents was clutching a grenade with
lled.

A and JSOC experts examined the material taken from
arget house. On the videos they found up-to-date images
al-Zarqawi. There were also pictures of him in a room with
the M4 they had taken from the target house, indicating that
he might have been close by on the night of the raid.

This prompted more raids into the area. On May 14, Delta Force B Squadron targeted a building amid a number of rural dwellings close to a waterway. The landing zone was a road that ran between a line of electricity pylons and a row of trees. As soon as they landed, the Delta Force men began to take fire from a house nearby. Firing small arms and mortars, al-Qaeda soon gained the upper hand. The insurgents, one wearing a suicide vest, jumped into a truck and launched an assault on Delta Force, but a hail of bullets detonated the vest.

Helicopters circled above, peppering the scene with fire from their miniguns. The terrorists responded with heavy machine-gun fire. Two AH-6 Little Birds made a run at the insurgents. One was downed by a surface-to-air missile and the crew was killed. Even so, Delta Force managed to arrest four suspects and treat three injured women. But when they tried to medevac them out at dusk, the helicopter came under fire. Delta Force had no option but to call in air strikes.

Eventually, interrogators managed to win the confidence of one of the men detained at Yusufiyah, who revealed that he knew Sheikh Rahman, al-Zarqawi's religious advisor. Using cell phone data, JSOC managed to locate him. On June 7, 2006, Sheikh Rahman was spotted getting into a small blue car. A short way into the journey, he switched off his phone.

But that did not matter, as a drone high above had the car on camera, and the command team back at Balad were watching it on Kill TV. General McChrystal was in the audience. Around 1815, the car reached a remote farmhouse in date palm groves in Hibhib, a village outside Baquba, 30 miles northeast of Baghdad. When Sheikh Rahman got out of the car, he was greeted by a stout man dressed in black—the man they had seen in the captured videos.

They called in an air strike. An F-16C circling above dropped a 500-pound GBU-12 laser-guided bomb. A second 500-pound GPS-guided GBU-38 bomb followed it. Two men, two women, and a small girl were killed in the air strike. Al-Zarqawi was still alive when they found him in the rubble. He tried to get off the stretcher and had to be restrained but died soon afterward. His body was flown back to Balad for identification. General McChrystal viewed the corpse. His men then examined the body closely, looking for telltale green tattoos and old war wounds that confirmed the dead man was al-Zarqawi. Intelligence gathered at the house in Hibhib led to raids on 17 places in Baghdad that night.

The death of al-Zarqawi did not end the insurgency in Iraq, and the threat from suicide bombers continued. However, the special-operations force had developed tactics to deal with them, which they perfected in another combined operation in July 2005. Operation Marlborough employed Special Forces to neutralize an al-Qaeda suicide bomb squad in Baghdad before they could reach their targets in the city.

Intelligence supplied by double agents run by MI6 had identified a house in Baghdad as a base for suicide bombers. It was believed that three insurgents, each with homemade explosives strapped to their chests, were planning to hit targets in the city, most likely cafés, markets, or other public establishments. The SAS considered storming the building, but it was decided this was too risky. If any of the insurgents detonated a bomb inside, its blast would be amplified within the structure, killing civilians in adjoining buildings. So it was decided to engage the insurgents as they left.

Just before the dawn rush hour in the Iraqi capital on July 31, a 16-man SAS troop set up around the house at a range of around 300 yards. The main element of the troop was four sniper teams, each with a shooter and a spotter. The snipers were armed with L115A sniper rifles chambered in .338 Lapua known as an AWM. The rest of the troop provided security for the sniper teams and ensured that all possible escape routes from the house were covered. Rangers from Task Force Red, the Special Forces Support Group quick-reaction force, were situated nearby in case things went wrong, and bomb-disposal experts were on hand nearby.

High above the city, a US predator spy drone kept the house under video surveillance, beaming its imagery back to the Task Force Black headquarters. Listening devices had also been hidden inside the house and were being monitored by Arabic-speaking translators.

In the rising heat of a July morning, the team lay hidden around the safe house. An Arabic-speaking intelligence officer, monitoring the voices inside, warned, "Targets preparing to exit." The snipers readied themselves.

It was just past 0800 when the insurgents stepped outside onto the street. Clad in explosive vests, the bombers had represented an immediate threat to all around them; it meant that the SAS had legal authority to open fire.

Once they were all in clear sight, the command was given over the radio to engage. As there were civilians close by, it was essential to shoot all three bombers simultaneously to prevent any of them from detonating their explosives. If one went down first, the other two might have a chance to set their bombs off. On the word of command, three SAS snipers opened fire together; the fourth was held in reserve to act as a backup. The sniper rifles were barely heard as the bombers jerked and hit the ground. Each insurgent was hit in the head and killed instantly. The .338 Lapua Magnum round is deadly, and although at a range of 300 yards it sounds like an air gun, it can crack an engine block from that distance. On a human target at close range, it was utterly devastating. None of the explosives was detonated, and many lives were saved.

CHAPTER 27

DECAPITATING THE TALIBAN AND AL-QAEDA

IN MARCH 2006, TASK FORCE 145, the specialist al-Qaeda hunter-killer team, made a cross-border raid to hit an al-Qaeda training camp in Danda Saidgai in the Taliban-controlled tribal area of North Waziristan in Pakistan. The camp was run by the Black Guard, the elite Praetorian Guard for Osama bin Laden. The camp commandant was Imam Asad, who was also a senior commander in the Chechen wing of al-Qaeda and an associate of Shamil Basayev, the Chechen al-Qaeda leader killed by Russian security forces in July 2006. US intelligence believed that either bin Laden or his chief lieutenant, Ayman al-Zawahiri, was at the camp along with hundreds of foreign fighters at the time of the raid.

Using a coordinated ground force and air attack, Task Force 145 killed Asad and 45 al-Qaeda recruits, including more than a dozen of the Black Guard. At least five missiles struck home at around 0330 local time. The Pakistani authorities claimed that the explosions were a "work accident" when the terrorist bomb factory blew up.

The raid took place just before President Bush's visit to Pakistan. Al-Qaeda responded with an attack on the US consulate in Karachi, where a suicide car bomb killed a US diplomat.

Earlier there had been an attack on the home of Maulana Noor Mohammad, the influential cleric who negotiated the Waziristan Accord, under which Pakistan ceded control of the region to the Taliban and al-Qaeda. Two of his religious schools had been hit. Task Force 145 also attacked a Taliban madrassa and training camp in the town of Chingai in the Bajaur region after the signing of the Bajaur Accord, again ceding power to the Taliban in the region. Eighty Taliban were killed. Al-Zawahiri, who frequented the facility, emerged unscathed. However, Maulana Noor Mohammad was killed by an explosion at the Wana mosque in South Waziristan in August 2010. At the same time, suspected US missiles fired from unmanned aircraft hit a house in Miran Shah in North Waziristan, killing nine militants.

Another high-profile raid took place on Madagascar. In January 2007, US commandos attacked the home of Osama bin Laden's brother-in-law, Mohammed Jamal Khalifa, and killed him. Arrested in Saudi Arabia after 9/11, he had been released without charge. While he then publicly distanced himself from bin Laden and al-Qaeda, he was thought to retain an influential position as a financier and facilitator. According to US intelligence officials, special operations waited for Khalifa to leave the safety of Saudi Arabia and targeted him when he was most vulnerable. Khalifa's computer and other documents were stolen to make the raid look like a robbery, though it was reported that the house had been attacked by 25 to 30 armed men.

When President George W. Bush visited Britain in June 2008, he asked once again for help from British Special Forces in a final attempt to capture Osama bin Laden before Bush left the White House. The SBS were sent to join Delta Force again in operations in the frontier region of northern Pakistan. After securing the permission of the Pakistani government, they began making regular cross-border sorties, operating on intelligence provided by the US Security Coordination Detachment and its UK counterpart, the Special Reconnaissance Regiment.

These operations often involved the use of Predator and Reaper unmanned aerial vehicles fitted with Hellfire missiles that could be used to take out specific terrorist targets. America rarely acknowledged the use of Predator and Reaper drones but admitted that a strike was made on a suspected al-Qaeda safe house in the Pakistani province of North Waziristan earlier in June. Villagers said the house was empty. Sources believed that bin Laden was in the Bajaur tribal zone in northwest Pakistan. By then he had evaded capture for nearly seven years. A Pentagon source said Special Forces were rolling up al-Qaeda's network in Pakistan in the hope of pushing bin Laden back toward the Afghan border, where the coalition forces, bombers and guided missiles were lying in wait. "They are prepping for a major battle," he said.

Another US commando raid into Pakistan took place in September 2008, when US special-operations forces made a helicopter assault on three houses in the village of Musa Nikow in South Waziristan. Pakistani authorities claimed that civilians, including women and children, were killed during the raid, but no senior al-Qaeda or Taliban leader was reported killed or captured.

In October 2008, helicopter-borne US commandos assaulted a compound in the town of Sukkariya in eastern Syria, just five miles from the border with Iraq. They killed Abu Ghadiya and several members of his staff. A close associate of Abu Musab al-Zarqawi, Ghadiya funneled suicide bombers, foreign fighters, weapons, and cash from Syria into Iraq. Two years earlier, he had been sentenced to death in absentia by a court in Jordan after being found guilty of planning chemical attacks in the kingdom.

In Afghanistan, US Special Forces and the SBS joined the Canadian-led Operation Medusa to drive the Taliban from the strategically important Panjwayi district of Kandahar province in September 2006. They acted as the vanguard of a large-scale attack by conventional forces and the Special Forces Support Group.

But in May 2007, the SBS led the raid on Taliban military leader Mullah Dadullah. In the war on terror, he was a highly valued prize, and a sophisticated operation was put into place to find him. Two months earlier, a controversial prisoner exchange had taken place. An Italian reporter named Daniele Mastrogiacomo, along with his two Afghani assistants, had been taken hostage by the Taliban. In a much-criticized move, the Kabul authorities agreed to Dadullah's demands that they release two senior Taliban commanders held in custody in exchange for the safe return of the journalist and aides.

Although the authorities seemed to be giving in to terrorist demands, it was in fact a classic military deception. It turned out that the top-secret US electronic surveillance unit Task Force Orange was able to tag the two Taliban commanders, perhaps with trackers inside their bodies. Satellite phone conversations between the released Taliban commanders and Dadullah were also monitored and traced.

By May, Task Force Orange had pinpointed Dadullah's location. He was holed up at Bahram Chah in the south of Helmand province, close to the border with Pakistan. Some 50 SBS commandos from C Squadron were given the mission to storm Dadullah's stronghold. First a reconnaissance party approached the area in a Supacat 6x6 all-terrain vehicle. The team quickly determined that an air strike on Dadullah's mud-walled compound would not guarantee that he was taken out, so it was decided that C Squadron would go in and finish the job.

The rest of C Squadron, along with a party of Afghani soldiers, loaded into two RAF Chinooks, but as they were inserted into the area, they came under fire from the Taliban defenders. Once on the ground, the SBS made a classic infantry attack on the compound, "pepper-potting" toward the objective. One group went firm and provided covering fire as another group pressed forward, before going firm themselves. The Taliban defenders numbered only 20 but put up a fanatical defense with rifles, machine guns and RPGs. After a four-hour battle, the SBS were able to clear the compound, suffering only four wounded. Dadullah was killed in the attack. He had been shot twice in the torso and once in the head in a typical "double-tap" favored by Special Forces operators.

The Taliban evened the score when an SBS commando was cut down in a hail of bullets in July 2007 in the remote province of Nimruz, which borders Iran. He was flown to a field hospital, where he died of his wounds. However, it is said that as many as 30 AQT fighters were cut down in the assault, which was backed by attack helicopters and jets. The target—"a significant Taliban commander"—was also said to be among the dead.

In September 2007, two Italian soldiers, possibly intelligence operatives, went missing in Afghanistan. They were believed to have been captured by Taliban militia. An operation to free them was put into motion when intelligence pinpointed the location of the hostages, close to Farah, in western Afghanistan.

A force of SBS commandos from C Squadron were loaded onto four Lynx Mk7 helicopters. SBS snipers armed with .50-caliber rifles covered the assault teams as they swooped down on the militia, which was moving the hostages in a convoy of 4x4 vehicles. As the snipers disabled the vehicles by shooting through their engine blocks, other SBS men were inserted onto the ground to engage any kidnappers not already taken out by the airborne snipers. Nine AQT fighters were killed. The two Italian hostages were recovered, although they were injured in the operation.

Then in February 2008, the SBS reportedly took out a senior Taliban figure, Mullah Abdul Matin, in a shootout at Gereshk, Helmand province. Matin, his lieutenant, Mullah Karim Agha, and a bodyguard were traveling across the desert on motorcycles when the SBS were dropped into his path by helicopter after a tip-off on his whereabouts. Matin opened fire with an AK-47 but was cut down in a hail of bullets, along with his two accomplices. Troops recovered night vision goggles, grenades, and a detonator.

Matin, a deputy of Taliban chief Mullah Omar, had been one of the coalition's top targets for several months. He had organized several suicide bomb attacks on British convoys, killing two British servicemen and wounding a dozen in the previous 18 months. His men had also murdered dozens of Afghan civilians.

According to a senior officer in the region, "Mullah Matin's been a priority target for some time. He commanded fighters and reported directly to the highest Taliban levels of command. He's responsible for the kidnapping of local nationals, had links with the narcotics trade, and had provided security to the traffickers."

Three months later, a special-operations team took part in a mission to recover sensitive electronics gear from a Reaper unmanned spy drone that had crashed in Afghanistan. Then a Harrier jump-jet was scrambled to blow up the $80-million Reaper with a 1,000-pound laser-guided bomb. A senior military source said, "There was no way we could take even the slightest risk of the Taliban getting hold of any parts."

CHAPTER 28

RESCUE FROM SOMALI PIRATES

SINCE THE HIJACKING OF THE OIL SUPERTANKER *Sirius Star* off the coast of Somalia in 2008, piracy in the region has become an increasing problem. But the hijackers got more than they bargained for when they took the MV *Maersk Alabama* 280 miles off the Somali port of Eyl on April 8, 2009. It was the first time pirates had seized a vessel sailing under the American flag since the early 19th century.

The Danish-owned *Maersk Alabama*, carrying food aid for Somalia and Uganda, was sailing for Mombassa, Kenya, with a crew of 20 Americans when four pirates attacked the ship from the *Win Far 161*, a Taiwanese fishing vessel they had hijacked two days earlier. The crew of the *Maersk Alabama* fired flares at them. They tried swinging the rudder to swamp the pirate skiff, to no avail. When the pirates boarded, the crew locked themselves in the engine room. Chief Engineer Mike Perry held off the pirate chief with a knife and took him prisoner. The other three pirates grabbed Captain Richard Phillips but found they could not control the ships, as Chief Perry had closed down all the systems.

After 12 hours, an attempt at a prisoner exchange was made, but when the crew released the pirate chief, the pirates made off with Captain Phillips in one of the ship's covered lifeboats with nine days' rations.

The following day, the *New York Daily News* reported that Special Operations Command at McDill Air Force Base in Tampa, Florida, were planning a rescue. "US military commanders have already prepared battle plans for ending the scourge of piracy on the high seas off Somalia if President Obama pulls the trigger," sources told the newspaper.

The former US special envoy to Somalia said that Special Forces had drawn up detailed plans to attack piracy groups where they lived on land. They were just awaiting the green light.

"Our special operations people have been itching to clean them up," he said. "So far, no one had let them."

In January, the US Navy had set up an antipiracy command called Task Force 151. This comprised Marines and Navy SEALs trained in boarding and seizing hijacked ships. Delta Force and the SEALs were already operating out of secret bases in Djibouti, Ethiopia, Somalia, and Manda Bay, Kenya. It was said that if they were allowed to hit the pirates' shore bases, US special operations teams could take care of the pirates in 72 hours.

The destroyer USS *Bainbridge* was already on its way to the scene of the hijacking. But when she arrived, she kept her distance. Meanwhile a P-3 Orion surveillance plane flew overhead to assess the scene. A two-way radio was dropped to establish contact. But the pirates threw it overboard when Captain Phillips tried to escape by jumping into the sea the next day. After that, he was tied up and beaten.

While the amphibious assault ship USS *Boxer* and USS *Halyburton*, a guided-missile frigate, raced to the scene, the pirates also mustered their forces. Four other foreign vessels captured by pirates, carrying a total of 54 hostages of various nationalities, arrived, making any assault on the lifeboat more problematic. They also moored close to shore so they could easily escape by land if attacked.

Further negotiations were conducted by satellite phone under the direction of an FBI hostage negotiator. When these failed, the pirates opened fire on the *Halyburton*. As it was only small-arms fire, and no one on board the *Halyburton* was injured, she did not return fire. However, President Obama reaffirmed the Navy's standing orders to take action if the hostage's life was in imminent danger. What the pirates did not know was that there was a team of US Navy snipers from SEAL Team 6—DEVGRU—on board. They had made a perilous parachute jump into the sea on the afternoon of April 10, when the *Halyburton* was on its way. They later transferred to the *Bainbridge*.

Nevertheless, negotiations continued. As sea conditions deteriorated, the *Bainbridge* offered to tow the lifeboat into calmer waters, while the pirate chief Abduwali Abdukhadir Muse came on board to discuss the ransom. From the deck of the *Bainbridge*, the SEAL commander could see one of the pirates pointing an AK-47 at Phillips's back. Then Vice-Admiral William Gortney saw the heads of all three pirates popped out of the top of the covered lifeboat and gave the order to fire.

Fortunately, Captain Philips moved to one side of the lifeboat to relieve himself, giving the sharpshooters on the *Bainbridge*'s fantail a clean shot. They opened fire simultaneously, using Mark 11 Mod 0 (SR-25) sniper rifles, killing the three hijackers. Gortney later said the SEALs made "phenomenal shots" at targets 100 feet away on a choppy sea.

"They were shooting a moving target from a moving platform, and you need a lot of patience too," said ex-SEAL Jamey Cummings. "On something like this they probably had to go for head shots... And they had to do it simultaneously."

The SEALs then boarded the lifeboat and found Captain Phillips tied up and tethered, but uninjured.

Abduwali Abdukhadir Muse was arrested. He was then taken to New York where he was charged with 10 offenses, including piracy. He pleaded guilty and, though only between ages 17 and 19, faces life imprisonment.

President Obama said, "I share the country's admiration for the bravery of Captain Phillips and his selfless concern for his crew. His courage is a model for all Americans."

He said he was also "very proud of the efforts of the US military and many other departments and agencies who worked tirelessly to secure Captain Phillips's safe recovery."

Freed after five days, Phillips deflected all the praise.

"I'm just the byline. The real heroes are the Navy, the SEALs, those who have brought me home," he said. He later published a book titled *A Captain's Duty: Somali Pirates, Navy SEALs, and Dangerous Days at Sea.*

The Maersk Line, owners of the *Maersk Alabama*, donated the bullet-marked fiberglass lifeboat to the UDT-SEAL Museum at Fort Pierce, Florida.

CHAPTER 29

OPERATION CELESTIAL BALANCE

US SPECIAL FORCES WERE NOT CONTENT with targeting pirates on the coast of Somalia. On September 14, 2009, they staged a daring raid to take out Saleh Ali Shale Nabhan, a senior al-Qaeda leader in East Africa. He trained terrorists in Somalia and was al-Qaeda's liaison with al-Shabaab, a guerrilla army of young militant Muslims. He was also wanted for his involvement in the bombing of the US embassies in Kenya and Tanzania in 1998. And he was one of the named suspects in the bombing of the Israeli-owned Paradise Hotel and an Israeli airplane in Mombassa, Kenya, in 2008.

It seems that the CIA's Special Activities Division had been tracking Nabhan for some time. They noted that he traveled regularly between the al-Shabaab–controlled ports of Kismayo and Merko. He traveled in a car with five other foreign fighters, accompanied by another car carrying three al-Shabaab escorts. Nabhan had been a target since the Battle of Ras Kamboni, when he and other members of al-Qaeda joined the Islamic Courts Union and attacked the town of Ras Kamboni, which had once served as a terrorist training camp on the Kenyan border. On that occasion, the US had launched air strikes using AC-130 gunships.

This time it was decided not to use Tomahawk cruise missiles or other aerial assets in case of collateral damage. Instead, Special Operations teams would take him out on a stretch of road away from the civilian population. US Special Forces and DEVGRU SEALs set off on AH-6 Little Bird helicopters from a US Navy vessel stationed off the Somali coast.

At least six helicopters were used in the raid. They attacked the two-vehicle convoy when they stopped for their breakfast near the small town of Baraawe. Two of the Little Birds strafed the cars, killing Nabhan and three of his associates. A helicopter landed, dropping off a SEAL team who picked up Nabhan's body and carried it back to the ship to confirm his identity. Two wounded militants were also taken. Unconfirmed reports indicate that Sheikh Hussein Ali Fidow, a senior Shabaab leader, was also killed in the raid.

This followed a daring rescue by the French Special Forces, GIGN, after the hijacking of the 850-ton luxury yacht *Le Ponant* off the coast of Somalia in December 2007. Once the ransom had been paid and the hostages released, French surveillance aircraft patrolling 10 kilometers offshore monitored the movements of the pirates. They could identify some of them moving into the village of Garacad.

"We could not intervene immediately to avoid causing injuries to civilians," said Admiral Main Gillier, a commander of the Marine commandos who had parachuted into the sea of French Navy ships offshore. Then they saw a large 4x4 leaving the village. "That's when we launched the ambush."

As the 4x4 headed out into the desert, four helicopters—one Aérospatiale Gazelle, one Eurocopter Panther and two Aérospatiale Alouettes—took off from the frigate *Jean*

Bart and the training ship *Jeanne d'Arc* with Marine commandos and GIGN men on board. A French Navy sniper in the Gazelle put a 12.7-mm ball from his MacMillan Tac-50 sniper rifle into the engine of the 4x4, bringing the vehicle to a halt.

"The pirates did not understand what was happening," said Admiral Gillier. "They did not see the helicopter."

The GIGN and French Marine commandos on other helicopters closed in. The six occupants of the 4x4 were reluctant to surrender, even though they were outnumbered. Warning shots were fired. Three GIGN men landed from a helicopter. One or two bursts of automatic fire were loosed off into the air. This was enough to intimidate the pirates. They realized that they were not going to be able to escape and surrendered. The French Marines and gendarmes quickly had them down on the ground. Their hands were tied behind their backs. Then they were bundled into the helicopters and flown back to the *Jean Bart*.

"No one was killed during the operation," said Admiral Gillier. However, one of the men in the front of the 4x4 was slightly injured in the calf. It seems he was hit by a ricochet from the engine.

"It was an intervention, not a pulverization," said French Army Chief of Staff General Jean-Louis Georgelin. "We made shots and intimidated them, forcing them to abandon their vehicle. There was no direct fire on the pirates."

Local officials claimed that three people were killed in the raid and eight more were wounded, but President Sarkozy denied this. The district commissioner of the Garacad region, Abdiaziz Olu-Yusuf Mohamed, said that three French helicopters landed and tried to intercept the pirates after they came ashore.

"Local residents came out to see the helicopters on the ground," he said. "The helicopters took off and fired rockets on the vehicles and the residents there, killing five local people."

Witness Mohamed Ibrahim said, "I could see clouds of smoke as six helicopters were bombing the pirates. The pirates were also firing antiaircraft machine guns in reaction. I cannot tell the exact casualties."

Naval captain Christophe Prazuck, the spokesman for the French military chiefs of staff, countered this by reiterating the French version of the incident.

"There were four helicopters involved," he said. "A sniper shot out the motor of the pirates' four-wheel-drive vehicle. A second helicopter then landed nearby, allowing the six pirates to be arrested under covering fire from two other helicopters. We are absolutely sure that there were no collateral victims."

Troops also recovered some of the ransom money paid by the owners of the yacht for the release of the crew. The six captured pirates, all aged between 25 and 40, were then flown to Paris, where they faced trial for piracy.

"It is the first time that an act of piracy in this area has been resolved so quickly...and it is also the first time that some of the pirates have been apprehended," said Admiral Edouard Guillard.

The Transitional Federal Government in Mogadishu called for other nations to join the battle against pirates off Somalia.

Said a spokesman, Abdi Gobdon Haj, "If each government conducts operations like the French, I think we will see no more pirates in Somali waters."

CHAPTER 30

HAITI EARTHQUAKE

DESPITE THEIR TOUGH-GUY IMAGE, Special Forces also have a humanitarian role. In the late 1970s, the Green Berets were used in a program called SPARTAN, which stands for Special Proficiency at Rugged Training and Nation-building. Under the program, the 5th and 7th Special Forces Groups worked with Native American tribes in Florida, Arizona, and Montana, building hospitals and roads. And they provided free medical treatment to the impoverished citizens of Hoke and Anson counties in North Carolina. And when President Ronald Reagan took office in 1981, Special Forces teams were once again deployed to dozens of countries around the globe. Missions varied from training local armies and running counterinsurgency programs to providing humanitarian aid such as medical care to remote villages in the Third World.

More recently, the Air Force Special Operations Command from Hurlbert Field, Florida, were sent to Haiti after an earthquake devastated the island in January 2010. They were to provide medical support, airfield management, and weather observation in the devastated country.

"We arrived the first evening with three US aircraft. Within 28 minutes we established command and control, airfield management, and were able to land aircraft that night," said Colonel "Buck" Elton, Joint Special Operations Task Force commander.

It was a monumental task. On an ordinary day, three aircraft took off and landed at Port-au-Prince airport. Following the earthquake, they handling more than 100 planes a day carrying humanitarian aid. There were only two fuel trucks and tow bars at the airfield, and at one point there were 44 airplanes on the ground.

Pararescue men from the Air Force Special Operations command also dug survivors out of devastated buildings. It took them 28 hours to extricate a 25-year-old Haitian woman from the rubble at the university. In their first few days, they rescued seven people buried under collapsed buildings.

The Air Force Special Operations Command were no strangers to Haiti. In 1994, they spearheaded Operation Uphold Democracy to restore order in Haiti following the collapse of the democratic government there. United States Special Operations Command (USSOCOM) sent patrol craft carrying US Navy SEALs and Canadian Special Forces to police the waters around the island, boarding ships to maintain sanctions and search for embargoed goods. Special Forces were also sent in to secure the countryside, using the aircraft carrier USS *America* as a mobile launch platform. While the 10th Mountain Division held the capital, Port-au-Prince, and Cap Haitien, the 3rd Special Forces Group was sent out to take over the rest of the country. They were deployed by the Air Force Special Operations Command, which had been assigned to a combat role under General Cedras.

Delta Force and Poland's GROM served as bodyguards for visiting UN officials and diplomats, while the 193rd Special Operations Wing flew EC-130 Command Solos overhead, broadcasting radio and television to the people. The psy-ops team transmitted 900 hours of broadcasts sent over three FM bands before the task force landed. Propaganda messages were mixed with programs of Haitian music and local news. To make sure the message was getting across, 10,000 radio sets were sent to Haiti. During that time, former President Jimmy Carter persuaded the military junta under General Raoul Cedras to stand down and leave the country. As a result, there was little opposition to the US landings, which were achieved without bloodshed. The psy-ops campaign also deterred large numbers of Haitians from taking to leaky craft and making for Florida.

President Jean-Bertand Aristide, who had been elected with 67 percent of the popular vote, was allowed to tape broadcasts. However, the psy-ops team at Fort Bragg employed Haitian linguists to vet his speeches. Previously, he had made references to torturing political opponents and the hideous practice of "necklacing"—putting a car tire filled with gasoline around a victim's neck and setting fire to it. In a speech in 1992, he reportedly said, "A faker who pretends to be one of our supporters, just grab him; make sure he gets what he deserves…the burning tire. What a beautiful tool! What a beautiful instrument! It's fashionable. It smells good. Wherever you go, you want to smell it."

The psy-ops group also dropped some seven million leaflets over Haiti displaying the words "democracy," "prosperity," "education," "opportunity," and "law," and showing people moving into the sunlight. Others depicted a radio and gave broadcast frequencies or showed a picture of President Aristide in front of a Haitian flag with text in Creole saying, "The sun of democracy, the light of justice, the warmth of reconciliation with the return of President Aristide."

Readers were told that the US Army had arrived to re-establish democracy. People were told to stay calm, remain indoors, and keep away from windows. They would not block the streets and would leave the US Army to do their work.

Four-man tactical psy-ops teams, sometimes split into two two-man teams, accompanied Special Forces in remote operations with loudspeakers and taped messages demanding immediate surrender. They were also deployed to discourage vigilantes from taking retribution against supporters of the Cedras regime. When an angry mob of 2,000 Haitians surrounded the military headquarters in Gonaives, a mobile loudspeaker team played Garth Brooks to lure the crowd out of town. However, in Cap Haitian police station, a firefight broke out between the US Marines and the Haitian army, resulting in the death of 10 Haitian soldiers. Meanwhile in Fort Liberté, Special Forces and Rangers apprehended 17 suspected "attachés," the US term for pro-regime vigilantes in a barracks, and seized 50 to 60 semiautomatic assault weapons. The guns turned out to be in poor condition but still could have posed a threat.

In one small town, Sergeant Sam Makanani single-handedly captured one hated member of the Haitian Army and was soon celebrated in song. At Jacmel, Special Forces commander Major Tony Schwaim looked on as a crowd disarmed a member of the Haitian army who was guarding the local airfield. A Special Forces NCO then dived into the crowd to seize the weapon and return it to the Haitian soldiers. Besides securing the country, it was also important to maintain order. However, when another Haitian soldier shot and wounded a Special Forces operative in Les Cayes, Major Schwaim ordered the disarming of all Haitian soldiers, and Brigadier

General Richard Potter sent in two companies of Rangers on board MH-47 Chinooks to seize their weapons.

There were frequent disagreements between Special Forces and regular US soldiers, who were ordered to keep their body armor on while the Special Forces routinely dispensed with helmets and Kevlar due to the heat. However, According to the *New York Times*, "The more ambiguous threat is better addressed by the Special Forces, not the infantry, which has had little to do in Haiti since October except guard itself. They [Special Forces] do everything from repairing wells and delivering babies to arresting notorious thugs and rescuing victims of mob violence."

Aerial loudspeaker teams on UH-60 Black Hawks also flew 67 missions in support of ground operations. Tactical psy-ops teams were later used to help round up members of the Haitian Army and political activists wanted for questioning. During raids on houses where wanted men were thought to be hiding, a simple surrender message was followed by a countdown. In 80 percent of cases, the suspect surrendered immediately. In the other cases, no resistance was offered when the assault team went in. More leaflets showed Haitians how to conduct themselves when they were being arrested, and not a single shot was fired during the entire operation.

Special Forces quickly became attuned to Haitian cultural concerns. They handcuffed detainees in front of their bodies, rather than behind, as that was associated with slavery and was considered particularly humiliating. One Special Forces medic took a voodoo priest with him on his rounds. They also had to deal with reports of zombies, werewolves, and ghosts.

The psy-ops teams also gave away T-shirts, signs, posters, street banners, bumpers stickers, buttons, and even soccer balls carrying slogans and images such as doves of peace, clasped hands, and the flags of the United States and Haiti, showing kinship between the American and Haitian people.

The EC-130J Commando Solos took to the air again in January 2010 to broadcast to the earthquake survivors on AM and FM radio, and VHF and UHF television. No propaganda was required this time, only vital information advising victims where to get food, water, shelter, and medical assistance.

CHAPTER 31

KILLING OF OSAMA BIN LADEN

For 10 years, the CIA and other intelligence agencies had been searching for Osama bin Laden, the international terrorist who masterminded the devastating jetliner attacks in New York City and greater Washington, D.C., on September 11, 2001, killing nearly 3,000 innocent victims. In August 2010, they got lucky. One of bin Laden's trusted aides had received a phone call. He had no idea he was being monitored and that the simple act of picking up his phone would lead US intelligence to the location of his boss, the world's most wanted terrorist.

Though evil, Osama bin Laden was clever and careful. He insisted that no computers or phones were to be used anywhere near him so he could not be tracked by the NSA. All messages between him and al-Qaeda, his worldwide terrorist organization, were carried by hand or by mouth by a small number of trusted couriers. Not even senior al-Qaeda commanders knew where bin Laden was, and the CIA were convinced that the only way to find him was by tracking these couriers.

In March 2003, al-Qaeda's third-in-command and operations leader Khaled Sheikh Mohammed was captured in Pakistan. Before being taken to Guantanamo Bay, he was interrogated and gave up the aliases of several of bin Laden's couriers. One of these names was Abu Ahmed al-Kuwaiti, aka Arshad Khan. At first the CIA did not realize the significance of al-Kuwaiti, but he became of particular interest after the capture and interrogation of Abu Faraj al-Libi, who succeeded Khaled Sheikh Mohammed as operations leader of al-Qaeda. Al-Libi told his interrogators that he had received word of his promotion by bin Laden through al-Kuwaiti. The CIA believed that if they could track down the courier al-Kuwaiti, he would lead them straight to bin Laden.

The CIA now had a solid lead, but the trail soon ran cold. Al-Kuwaiti had numerous aliases, and it took years of intelligence work just to find out his real name. Even then, they did not know where he was. Then in August 2010, the NSA was monitoring a cell phone when al-Kuwaiti called—and he was making the call from just outside the Waziristan Haveli compound. Now they could pinpoint his location and track him, and he soon led them straight there.

US intelligence had been aware of the compound's existence for years, but they had never suspected that it was bin Laden's hideout. They had always supposed that wherever bin Laden was holed up, it would be extremely well guarded—but there were no guards at Waziristan Haveli. However, in light of this new lead, they began to monitor the compound more closely. They noticed there were no telephone lines coming from the compound, and that hardly anyone ever went in or came out. They even burned all their trash rather than take it outside.

The CIA soon realized that bin Laden was hiding in plain sight. But there was no way to be sure. They continued to watch the place for eight months. Then in February 2011, they reported to President Barack Obama that the compound contained a "high-value target, very possibly Osama bin Laden," and although they were not 100 percent certain, it was thought this would be the best-ever chance to get the terror chief. The president gave the order to go in, and the planning of Operation Neptune Spear began.

On Sunday May 1, 2011, as the local time approached midnight, four helicopters flew out of Bagram Air Base in southeastern Afghanistan and headed over the border into Pakistan. They were heading for the city of Abbottabad, 70 miles north of the Pakistani capital, Islamabad, on what was going to be the greatest Special Forces raid since World War II. Their mission was to eliminate terror-king Osama bin Laden, code-named Geronimo. He had eluded capture for almost 10 years since 9/11. Now he had been found living in a small fortified compound barely half a mile from the gates of the Pakistani Military Academy, Pakistan's equivalent of West Point.

The two UH-60 Sikorsky Black Hawks and two Boeing CH-47 Chinooks flew low over the mountains of the Hindu Kush to avoid being detected by radar. The Black Hawks carrying the assault force had their rotors and stabilizers modified to reduce their radar profile and increase their stealth capability. No one had told the Pakistanis they were coming, so Special Forces had to be sure they would not be detected to avoid a confrontation with what was, after all, a friendly nation.

The four helicopters carried 79 Special Forces commandos and one sniffer dog. Months before, they had been selected for an extremely important mission and began holding dry runs on both American coasts at training facilities made up to resemble the compound. Then, with just weeks to go, they were told, "We think we found Osama bin Laden—your job is to kill him." The commandos raised the roof with their cheers. Operation Neptune Spear was underway. It was payback time.

Aboard the Black Hawks were 24 members of the elite SEAL Team 6. Also known as DEVGRU, this highly classified Navy SEAL team did not officially exist. However, in less than 24 hours, it would make headlines worldwide. For two weeks, SEAL Team 6 had been training on a full-size replica of the Waziristan Haveli compound where bin Laden was hiding, which had been built inside Camp Alpha at Bagram in Afghanistan. Now in the back of the Black Hawks they sat in silence, preparing themselves to face the real thing. As their target came into view, they checked their equipment. Each man was equipped with night-vision goggles, M4 rifles with laser sights, and handguns.

The height of the walls of the triangular compound ranged from 10 to 18 feet. Inside, there were two buildings—a three-story house and a single-story guesthouse just to the south. The team from the first Black Hawk would land in the yard to the west of the main building and attack the guesthouse. The second team would fast-rope down onto the roof of the main building and take out bin Laden, who lived on the third floor. That was the plan, at least. But as the first Black Hawk helicopter was coming in to land, the second stalled during the approach and grazed the compound wall. It broke a rotor and was forced to crash-land in the yard, rolling onto its side. Nevertheless, all 24 SEALs scrambled out of their helicopters uninjured and continued their mission undaunted.

As the first team approached the door of the guesthouse, Arshad Khan, bin Laden's courier, fired on them with an AK-47. The SEALs returned fire and, after a brief exchange, Khan was shot dead. His wife was killed in the crossfire as the SEALs entered and cleared the building. This would be the only resistance the SEALs faced on their mission.

The second team now had to attack the main building from the ground. They surrounded it and blew out the windows and doors. As they entered the building, they came face-to-face with Tariq Khan, Arshad's brother. Khan had his hands behind his back. Did he have a weapon? Was he about to detonate an IED? The SEALs did what they had been trained for; Khan was killed with a single shot. Later he was be found to be unarmed, but there was a firearm concealed close by.

The SEALs moved swiftly through the first floor, clearing each room before heading for the stairs. On their way up to the second floor, a young man charged toward them. He was quickly eliminated. This turned out to be Khaled bin Laden, Osama bin Laden's 22-year-old son. The SEALs cleared each room on the second floor before moving up to the top floor.

As they reached the top-floor landing, the SEALs caught the first glimpse of their quarry. Bin Laden was standing in the doorway to his quarters. As bullets struck the doorway, he ran back into the room. In such a scenario, retreat was considered a hostile action; he could have had any number of weapons or explosive devices in his quarters. As the SEALs charged into the room, they were confronted with one of bin Laden's wives, who tried to get between the SEALs and their objective. It was not a good place to be. She was quickly put down with a shot to the leg. Then two more shots were fired. The first shot hit bin Laden in the chest; the second shot hit him in the head. It was a "double tap," which all Special Forces use to take out an enemy. There was no doubt that bin Laden was dead. The action, so far, had lasted just seven minutes.

The SEALs immediately radioed in: "Geronimo EKIA," the acronym for "enemy killed in action."

The SEALs did not pause for a moment. They continued their sweep of the third floor, room by room, until they could be sure the buildings and the compound were secure. The occupants were rounded up. There were a number of women and children in the main building. Most belonged to the family of Tariq Khan, but there was also bin Laden's 12-year-old daughter, Safia, who had been injured by flying debris. They were assembled in the courtyard with their hands tied and left for the Pakistanis to deal with.

The SEALs then searched the buildings for weapons stashes and intelligence material. They recovered a wealth of electronic equipment, including DVDs, SIM cards, and computer hard drives, as well as two handguns and three AK-47 assault rifles. Bin Laden's body was then prepared for transportation. The entire raid had lasted nearly 40 minutes.

The SEALs made their way back to the helicopters to find that the crash-landed Black Hawk was badly damaged and unable to fly. The decision was made to destroy the aircraft to ensure that none of the classified equipment aboard, especially the modified stealth systems, would fall into the wrong hands. The SEALs packed the downed craft with explosives and blew it up. Then they called in one of the supporting Chinooks to pick bin Laden's body and the remaining SEALs. The body was taken to USS *Carl Vinson*, an aircraft carrier stationed in the North Arabian Sea off the south coast of Pakistan.

Once aboard the ship, bin Laden's identity was confirmed by a DNA test. Samples were taken from the corpse

and compared
bers, notably t
the previous y
was made, the
one in 11.8 qu

Bin Lader
white sheet in
put in a weigh
and bin Lader
death, in keep
dead within or

As the SE
the Situation

The tense silence in the S
moment. Then President O
"We got him," he sai
As the SEALs w
body made its wa
began prepara
world.
At a
flash

watching the raid unfold via cameras attached to each Navy SEAL's helmet. The President was joined by Vice President Joe Biden, Secretary of State Hillary Clinton, Secretary of Defense Robert Gates, CIA Director Leon Panetta, and other military and intelligence top brass.

"Once those teams went into the compound, I can tell you that there was a time period of almost 20 or 25 minutes where we really didn't know just exactly what going on," Panetta said. "We had some observation of the approach there, but we did not have direct flow of information as to the actual conduct of the operation itself as they were going through the compound."

So those assembled in the Situation Room had sat in tense silence, transfixed on the confusing visual imagery displayed on the screens in front of them. Vice President Biden gripped tightly on a chain of rosary beads. Things could have gone badly wrong, as they had in Operation Eagle Claw, which essentially ended Jimmy Carter's presidency. But then, to their relief, they received radio confirmation from the SEAL team leader: "Geronimo EKIA."

...uation Room remained for a ...ama broke the silence.

...d.

...apped up the mission and bin Laden's ...y to the USS *Carl Vinson*, the White House ...tions to release the news of his death to the

...round 10:30 p.m. eastern daylight time, a TV news-...announced that the president was about to address the ...tion. Newspapers across the world were told to hold the front page. At 11:30 p.m., almost 57 million people across America tuned in to see the president deliver a speech from the White House.

"Good evening," he said. "Tonight I can report to the American people and to the world that the United States has conducted an operation that killed Osama bin Laden, the leader of al-Qaeda and a terrorist who's responsible for the murder of thousands of innocent men, women, and children...

"Over the last 10 years, thanks to the tireless and heroic work of our military and our counterterrorism professionals, we've made great strides in that effort. We've disrupted terrorist attacks and strengthened our homeland defense. In Afghanistan, we removed the Taliban government, which had given bin Laden and al-Qaeda safe haven and support. And around the globe, we worked with our friends and allies to capture or kill scores of al-Qaeda terrorists, including several who were a part of the 9/11 plot.

"Yet Osama bin Laden avoided capture and escaped across the Afghan border into Pakistan. Meanwhile, al-Qaeda continued to operate from along that border and operate through its affiliates across the world.

"And so shortly after taking office, I directed Leon Panetta, the director of the CIA, to make the killing or capture of bin Laden the top priority of our war against al-Qaeda, even as we continued our broader efforts to disrupt, dismantle, and defeat his network.

"Then, last August, after years of painstaking work by our intelligence community, I was briefed on a possible lead to bin Laden. It was far from certain, and it took many months to run this thread to ground. I met repeatedly with my national security team as we developed more information about the possibility that we had located bin Laden hiding within a compound deep inside of Pakistan. And finally, last week, I determined that we had enough intelligence to take action, and authorized an operation to get Osama bin Laden and bring him to justice.

"Today, at my direction, the United States launched a targeted operation against that compound in Abbottabad, Pakistan. A small team carried out the operation with extraordinary courage and capability. No Americans were harmed. They took care to avoid civilian casualties. After a firefight, they killed Osama bin Laden and took custody of his body...

"Tonight we give thanks to the countless intelligence and counterterrorism professionals who've worked tirelessly to achieve this outcome. The American people do not see their work, nor know their names. But tonight they feel the satisfaction of their work and the result of their pursuit of justice...

"Thank you. May God bless you. And may God bless the United States of America."

Within minutes of the announcement, massive crowds began to gather outside the White House to celebrate. In New York City, thousands took to streets near Ground Zero and Times Square. They brought flags and placards, and hollered

"USA! USA!" long into the night. No doubt there were also celebrations at Virginia Beach, home of SEAL Team 6, as there were in Mogadishu, where Somalis blame bin Laden for bringing terror to their country.

Osama bin Laden had been a wanted man before 9/11. But the pursuit of him after that event lasted nine years, seven months, and 19 days, making it the world's longest and most expensive manhunt ever. Osama bin Laden now was dead. The men who had performed the heroic deed were part of a military group that does not officially exist. They will be honored in private, and it is unlikely that we will ever know their names. All that is known is they were from Red squadron of SEAL Team 6.

"The Blue team is more reserved, cold, unemotional," said former Red squadron member 38-year-old Mike Grommet (not his real name, which was withheld for security reasons). "The Gold guys are more laid-back. And Silver are new, so I never worked with them. But the Red squadron? They're the farm animals. They can't wait to shoot the target in the face."

According to Grommet, the men who took out bin Laden will remain silent. Members of Red squadron would not take a book deal for $10 million, or even $20 million. They would rather cut someone's head off.

"All they want is to keep doing their jobs and get back into action," he said.

While the man who pulled the trigger remains anonymous, Grommet is sure that his name is "common knowledge around the bars at Virginia Beach." It is thought unlikely that he will have to pay for a drink again.

GLOSSARY

AQT Al-Qaeda–Taliban

British Ministry of Defence The UK's equivalent to the US Department of Defense

British Special Forces Consists of the Special Air Service (SAS), Special Boat Service (SBS), Special Reconnaissance Regiment (SRR), Special Forces Support Group (SFSG), and 18 (UKSF) Signals Regiment.

Carabinieri Italian national police force

CQB Close-quarters battle

CQC Close-quarters combat

CRW Counter-revolutionary warfare

Darby's Rangers US equivalent of British Royal Marine Commandos in World War II; forerunner of the US Army Rangers

DIA Defense Intelligence Agency

Delta Force The more common term for the United State's 1st Special Forces Operational Detachment–Delta (SFOD-D)

DEVGRU Elite US Navy unit

EOD Explosive ordinance disposal

FBI Federal Bureau of Investigation

Force 777 Egyptian counterterrorist unit

GIGN Groupe d'Intervention de la Gendarmerie
Nationale; French equivalent of Delta Force

Green Berets A member of the US Army Special
Forces; derived from the green beret that is part of the
organization's uniform

GROM Grupa Reagowania Operacyjno Manewrowego;
Polish Operational Maneuver Reconnaissance Group

GSG-9 Grenz Schutz Gruppe 9; German special ops

IED Improvised explosive devices

Iranian Revolutionary Guard Group founded in 1979
to protect the Islamic revolution in Iran

ISA Shortened acronym for the US Army Intelligence
Support Activity (USAISA), a supersecret Pentagon
group also known as simply the Activity

Japanese Red Army Far-left terrorist group that
undertook hijackings and bombings in the 1970s and
1980s; also known as the Red Army Faction

KSK Kommando Spezialkräfte German Special Forces
Command

M15 UK's Security Service

M16 UK's Secret Intelligence Service

Military Assistance Command, Vietnam
(MACV) The US command structure in Southeast
Asia during the Vietnam war

Mossad Israeli secret intelligence service

PLO Palestine Liberation Organization, larger group that
includes the Palestine Liberation Front

PDF Panama Defense Forces

Popular Front for the Liberation of
Palestine Palestinian Marxist national liberation
movement; a terrorist group founded in 1967

RAF Royal Air Force

Republican Guard (Iraq) A branch of the Iraqi military that reported directly to Saddam Hussein

SAS (Britain) Special Air Services

Sayeret Matkal Israeli Special Forces, or General Staff Reconnaissance Unit

SBS Special Boat Service; British Marine equivalent of the SAS

SOAR Special Operations Aviation Regiment

SOW Special Operations Wing

Special Air Service Regiment Australia's air force

Special Branch UK's antiterrorist police force

SWAT Special Weapons Assault Team

SWCC Special Warfare Combatant-craft Crewmen

Swords of Righteousness Brigade Terrorist group responsible for kidnappings in postinvasion Iraq

T-39 Navy executive jet

TACP Tactical air control party

Taliban Extremist Islamic group in Afghanistan

TFR Terrain-following radar

TIRR The Incident Response Regiment

UDT Underwater Demolition Team

USAF US Air Force

USAISA The US Army Intelligence Support Activity, a supersecret Pentagon group that is also known as just the ISA or the Activity

USAR US Army Reserve

USASOC US Army Special Operations Command

USN US Navy

USSOCOM United States Special Operations Command

Other Ulysses Press Books

Kill Shot: The 15 Deadliest Snipers of All Time
Charles Stronge, $16.95

Of all the stories to come from the front lines of battle, none are more adrenaline-fired than the ones about deadly covert sharpshooters. *Kill Shot* includes riveting accounts of the 15 most feared and honored snipers in history.

Save Your Ass: An Illustrated Handbook for Surviving a Natural Disaster, Terrorist Attack, Pandemic or Catastrophic Collapse
Alexander Stilwell, $15.95

From Hurricane Katrina and terrorist bombings to swine flu's outbreak and frozen financial markets, the false security provided by modern civilization has now been exposed. With over 300 illustrations and handy pullout lists, *Save Your Ass* is the definitive crisis survival guide for today's dangerous world.

The U.S. Army Survival Manual: Department of the Army Field Manual 21-76
Headquarters, Department of the Army, $11.95

U.S. soldiers are trained for battle against any enemy, but war sometimes leaves them in a fight for their lives against the harsh forces of nature as well. *The U.S. Army Survival Manual* is the one weapon they rely on to get out of the most treacherous situations.

To order any of our titles directly call 800-377-2542 or 510-601-8301; fax 510-601-8307; e-mail ulysses@ulyssespress.com; or write to Ulysses Press, P.O. Box 3440, Berkeley, CA 94703. All retail orders are shipped free of charge. California residents must include sales tax. Allow two to three weeks for delivery.

ABOUT THE AUTHOR

Nigel Cawthorne is known for his best-selling Sex Lives series, including *Sex Lives of the Kings and Queens of England* and *Sex Lives of the Roman Emperors*; the books are available in 23 languages. He is also the author of *Serial Killers and Mass Murderers* (Ulysses Press), *Strange Laws of Old England*, *Curious Cures of Old England*, and more than 60 other books.